MODERN CHINA

MODERN CHINA

THE MIRAGE OF MODERNITY

IAN MABBETT

ST. MARTIN'S PRESS
New York

© 1985 I.W. Mabbett
All rights reserved. For Information, write:
St. Martin's Press, Inc., 175 Fifth Avenue, New York, NY 10010
Printed in Great Britain
First published in the United States of America in 1985

Library of Congress Cataloging in Publication Data

Mabbett, Ian.
  Modern China.

  Includes Index.
  1. China: – History – 1949-   . I. Title.
DS777.55.M2216   1985   951.05   85-2114
ISBN 0-312-53786-7

CONTENTS

PREFACE

This book is an essay on modern China which seeks to suggest ways of thinking about the country that draw on its history. Changes which have occurred in the past can throw light upon changes occurring in the present. The essay is written from the point of view of an historian of traditional Asia, not that of a political scientist, or an economist, or a traveller. It ranges, however, over a great deal of territory, and at many points it owes much to the advice and comments of others, whose help is gratefully acknowledged here. Notoriously, everything to do with the interpretation of what goes on in China is contentious; those who have helped can clearly be held in no degree responsible for any part of what is written in these pages.

Mr. R.J. Beveridge inspired the work as a whole and made detailed comments; many valuable suggestions came from Dr. M.R. Godley, and Professor W. Brugger offered useful criticisms at a number of points. Dr. B.E. Kennedy, a recent traveller in China, and the late Mr. P. Clarke discussed with the author the social and physical environment that can be observed by the outside visitor, and Dr. L. Li commented on various historical aspects. The chapters on education and manpower benefited considerably from the advice of Professor M. Berkowitz, Mr. J.A. Fyfield and Dr. R.F. Price.

Parts of Chapters 11, 12 and 13 are based upon work done at the Institute of Southeast Asian Studies in Singapore, which issued in the publication of the Institute's Occasional Paper No. 26, *Displaced Intellectuals in Modern China*. Parts of Chapter 13 are based upon an article entitled 'Education, Youth and Social Change in Twentieth Century China' that appeared in the *Journal of International Education and Development*, vol. 1, no. 1 (1976), pp. 59-78. This phase of the work was supported by a study leave grant from Monash University.

During successive drafts of the work, a great deal of patient typing has been done by Mrs. B. Brudenell, Mrs. V. Edens, Mrs. C. McKee and Mrs. J. Prince.

PART ONE

INTRODUCTION

1 THE UNKNOWN LAND

> The inhabited part of our earth is bounded on the east by the Unknown Land which lies along the region occupied by the easternmost races of Asia Minor, the SINAE and the natives of Serice.
>
> Claudius Ptolemy

It is remarkable how mighty is the chasm that divides the China seen by the outside world today from the China known and described by foreigners before 1949.

The Old China Hands thought they understood the land, but their wisdom seems to be a casualty of history. The rise to dominance of Mao Zedong (Tse-tung) and his new men baffled their predictions, made flotsam of their science. Since the 1950s, our knowledge has been derived from the assiduous culling of party-controlled newspapers and broadcasts and from (at least until recently) short supervised visits. It is only in the last few years that the country has even begun to acquire a little of the openness to informal travel and social contact by outsiders normal in most other parts of the world. This is thin soil for the growth of knowledge.

So much of what must be said about modern China is speculation that it is very much as if the country had suddenly come into being full-grown, without a context and without a history through which we could seek to understand the present. Commentators very rarely seek to use history as an avenue of understanding. Too many scholars have, by and large, planted across 1949 a fence that divides the territory of historians from the territory of political scientists. For most of the period, there has been no unfiltered cultural traffic to round out the science of scholars with direct knowledge of a rich, full-textured society. Perforce, therefore, Chinese society has come to seem very remote, and very political. The purpose of this essay is to offer, in a few impressionistic strokes, a sketch of modern China that shows it to be shaped at least as much by the customs and culture of the past as by the decisions of rulers. In it, politics are not sovereign but epiphenomenal.

This sketch will seek to suggest that for understanding China today we need to supplement the wisdom of political sciences with that of history. The political scientist seeks to manifest the inner logic of institutions by isolating them from their surroundings and deducing how they would work if left to themselves. He builds 'models'; when these represent closed 'systems' they can often predict indefinite cyclic series of events. They are wind-up-and-watch models. The historian's rigour, on the other hand, is addressed to the interpretation of documents, not of the working of institutions, and, despite a common belief to the contrary, it is not his *métier* to offer broad theoretical explanations. In compensation, he is not disposed by his technique to depend upon the abstract logic of closed systems for his explanations of events. The working-out of the logic of systems is in real life constantly upset by the adventitious interference of social forces, international events, weather, cultural contacts and all manner of things that cannot be programmed into the cyclic predictions of one model. It is precisely to such random intrusions upon the closed circles of the political order, from sources unpredictable from within it, that we must refer if we are to supplement political knowledge with a more general understanding.

The intention here is not in any way to deny the importance of politics but to suggest that there is more to China than what party leaders and officials do and say. Today's conventional images of the country (never mind whether of the left or right, friendly or unfriendly) are flat, politicocentric, two-dimensional — they are shadows cast by governors. In the 1950s, the paucity and partiality of the evidence bearing on real life in China encouraged the myth that a monolithic 'communism' determined everything of its own will. After the breach with the Soviet Union, the identity of the first cause of all that happened had to be redefined: it was the Chinese Communist Party. In the 1960s, the 'Great Proletarian Cultural Revolution' showed the inadequacy of this assumption too. Scholars and observers studied with increasing finesse the interplay of faction, personality, conviction and interest group in Chinese life: there was no monolith. But politics and political decisions still seemed to determine everything. Official Chinese sources, partial first-hand reports by sympathetic visitors, the absence of much other useful evidence and the fact that political scientists dominated China scholarship all combined to maintain the currency of an essentially politicocentric vision of the country.

By and large, this vision still persists. In the 1970s, students of China began to attend to the roots of modern politics in pre-Communist and non-Communist culture, but there is a long way to go. As Lloyd Eastman wrote in 1974, in his study of the Party's Nationalist predecessors earlier in the century, 'the study of Chinese Political Culture is still at an exceedingly primitive level'.[1]

This book is offered, modestly enough, as a preliminary sketch, not a workshop manual. It seeks to hint at the light and shade of a more solid rounded image especially by the perspective that it offers, selecting a few aspects of China in turn and working from the bottom up. The whole, by its articulation, is designed to achieve a sketch (however elliptical) of a civilization in its integrity rather than of the shadows it throws.

In some ways, China is today as remote, to most of the outside world, as when contacts with the West began. These contacts were indirect, and Western knowledge of the Middle Kingdom was a pungent brew of fantasy coloured by the legends of trading intermediaries. The more remote a land, the greater the challenge to our objectivity. China, the China of soil and people, has over the centuries exercised a fascination for Westerners that makes it hard for them to respond to it with calmness of judgement. For, where knowledge is wanting, imagination is always ready to leap to its aid. Kinglake, surely among the most acute of travellers, saw this well: 'The superior veneration so often excited by objects that are distant and unknown, shows — not perhaps the wrong-headedness of a man, but rather the transcendent power of his imagination'.[2]

To be sure, Kinglake was not writing about China. He was writing about pilgrims to the Holy Land in the 1830s:

> Crowds of disciples were rushing about in all directions — some laughing and talking, some begging, but most going round in a regular and methodical way to kiss the sancitified spots, and speak the appointed syllables, and lay down the accustomed coin.[3]

Imagination, of course, can produce dragons and ogres as well as utopias. Sir John Mandeville's account of eastern lands shows how richly a few thin shreds of fact can be sauced with prodigies, so that what is said about one land might just as well be said of another.

> In that contree ben folk that han but o foot & thei gon so blyme that it is mervaylle. And the foot is so large that it schadeweth all the body azen the sonne whanne thei wole lye & reste hem. In Ethiope when the children ben zonge & lytill thei ben all zalowe and whan that thei wexen of age that zalowness turneth to ben all blak.[4]

This is not about China, any more than the extracts from Kinglake; but it bears pondering. (Why should Mao exhort his countrymen to walk upon two legs if they had not previously been accustomed to walk upon one?)

Perhaps some Western observers have in the past over-idealized modern China, and some have made unnecessary nightmares of the Communist demon. Either way, the error springs from ignorance. But what of the other China, the one that was so confidently described in a long series of relations by missionaries, businessmen and cosmopolitans in many previous generations? (We can go back to AD 1600 if we start with the Jesuit pioneer missionary Matteo Ricci (1552-1610), who reached Peking around then. In 1598 he first visited the capital. In 1601 he took up residence.)

Certainly there is in their accounts much that is distasteful to modern canons of scholarship. Many of those who were professionally concerned to make moral judgements did so, ponderously.

Female infanticide in some parts openly confessed, and divested of all disgrace and penalties everwhere; the dreadful prevalence of all the vices charged by the Apostle Paul upon the ancient heathen world; the alarming extent of the use of opium (furnished, too, under the patronage, and supplied in purity by the power and skill of Great Britain from India), destroying the production and natural resources of the people; the universal practice of lying and dishonest dealings; the unblushing lewdness of old and young; harsh cruelty toward prisoners by officers, and tyranny over slaves by masters — all form a full unchecked torrent of human depravity, and prove the existence of a kind and degree of moral degradation of which an excessive statement can scarcely be made, or an adequate conception hardly be formed.[5]

Such glib resource to original sin as a category of historical explanation, such facile readiness to condemn, stands as a barrier between such authors' experience and our reception of it, even when they tell us (as they often do) things about Chinese society that are informative:

On the most trivial occasions, they almost without exception are in the habit of imprecating upon those who have excited their anger the most direful vengeance, or expressing their feelings in the most filthy language. [Mao did, incidentally. The official English-language translations of news reports sometimes bowdlerize them.] Their common language, when offended or insulted, is usually of the most

vile description, abounding with indelicate and obscene allusions. They seem to strive with themselves, as though a wager were at stake, who shall excel in the use of filthy, loathsome and vindictive terms . . .
The Chinese here have a saying that their 'mouths are exceedingly filthy', and no one who has acquired their dialect can have the least doubt of its truth. They have another saying that the 'heart of woman is superlatively poisonous', meaning that the language uttered by females, when cursing others, is more virulent and filthy than that used by men. It is not easy for a foreigner to perceive the truth of this saying when both sexes seem to have arrived at the highest attainable facility in heaping up the vilest language and the most awful curses upon those with whom they happen to be at variance.[6] [It has been rare for politicians to express public disapproval of individuals in measured terms, leaving the door open for debate with mutual respect. To be disapproved of at all is more commonly to be damned to hell.]

Of course it is not fair to the labours of so many, often dedicated, authors to represent generations of them by the more narrow-minded. But the point here is not that China before 1949 was described for Westerners by narrow-minded people. The point here is simply that such narrow-mindedness as there is encourages us to believe, wrongly, that whatever has been said about China in the past is irrelevant to the understanding of China in the present. We are prone to accept the teaching that a 'new society', if it has not already been created, is just now at last in the process of being created. We slip into the assumption that everything in China is dominated by what politicians of a completely new breed do. The myths of a monolithic 'world communism' and of a monolithic Chinese Communist Party have successively been discredited, but the circumstances of our knowledge of the country make it hard to rid ourselves of the feeling that everything that happens in it is to be accounted for, ultimately, by political decisions.
It therefore comes naturally to dismiss the images crafted by Old China Hands. What, we are tempted to ask, did they know about the real people? Those foreigners who did not have chips on their shoulders were superficial visitors, perpetually quarantined by the cultural gulf that divided them from their hosts. The Chinese they knew were the servants to whom they gave orders in their houses and the functionaries with whom they dealt in their offices and clubs. In between, what they saw of the nation was embodied chiefly in the bobbing heads of their

rickshaw coolies. What went on in those heads, and in millions of similar heads, was to decide the course of history; yet to foreigners it had to remain utterly unscrutable.

But let us remember that what went on in the heads of rickshaw coolies was just as inscrutable to Chinese reformist intellectuals, who romanticized them, as to the foreigners. It was the atomism of Chinese society ('a sheet of loose sand'), not the myopia of outside observers, that baffled insight with screens of ignorance.

Further, there is one respect in which the authors of the old picture had an inestimable advantage over their successors. The Chinese they knew personally may have been few and unrepresentative, but at least they were actual people. The Chinese who have more recently been constructed from a bricollage of official reports, interpreted interviews and managed tours are, at their worst, abstractions. There is more rigour in present-day scholarship, but when the raw material is so precarious the danger is ever-present that the rigour may be misplaced.

Our quest for the identity of the Unknown Land is therefore difficult enough. Let us begin at the beginning, with its name. But which name? The Chinese name for China, as is well known, is the 'Middle Kingdom', Zhong Guo (Chung kuo) — not one country among others, but the heart of civilization itself. The outside world has, historically, used other names by indirect and misunderstood traditions. Foreigners have known of the country often only through the traffic of non-Chinese dynasties of conquest within it (hence *Cathay*) or as the semi-mythical source of silk (hence the Greek *Seres*) or porcelain of high quality (*China*).

Chatay is a grete contree & a fair, noble & rich & full of Marchauntes; thider gon Marchaundes all zeres for to sechen spices & all manere of marchandises more comounly than in any other partye.[7]

The old romantic 'Cathay' is derived from the name of the Khitans, a people who invaded and ruled part of northern China in Song (Sung) dynasty times. The Russian for 'China' preserves this name. But most Western languages use cognates of 'China'.

Hobson-Jobson, which must be the most fascinating thesaurus of semantic gems in common use, has a long entry under 'China'.[8] It refers first to the (in fact implausible) theory of Baron F. von Richthofen that the name is derived from *Jih-nan*, an old name of Tongking in modern northern Vietnam, then to the theory of Terrien de la Couperie that the origin must be sought in the name of the state of

Tsen, in the modern southern Chinese province of Yunnan, which once in ancient times controlled trade routes linking China with the outside world. These theories were guesses, as indeed was asserted by Giles, whose opinion is given at the end. This opinion was that 'China' comes from Qin (Ch'in), the dynasty which originally ruled in a part of western China and was the first to unify the Chinese under one empire late in the third century BC. This view has since come to be widely accepted.

Hobson-Jobson gives a series of quotations charting the history of western words for China. Two of them, which remind us of the long-standing role of China in the international trade network, will bear quoting. The first is from the *Periplus Maris Erythraei* late in the first century AD:

Behind this country (*Chryse*) the sea comes to a termination some-where in THIN, and in the interior of that country, quite to the north, there is a very great city called THINAE, from which raw silk and silk thread and silk stuffs are brought overland through Bactria to Barygaza, as they are on the other hand by the Ganges River to Limyrice. It is not easy, however, to get to this THIN, and few and far between are those who come from it.

The second is from the geographer Cosmas in the sixth century AD:

The country of silk, I may mention, is the remotest of all the Indies, lying towards the left when you enter the Indian Sea, but a vast distance further off than the Persian Gulf or that island which the Indians call Selediba, and the Greeks Taprobane [Ceylon. 'Selediba', incidentally, is equivalent to 'Serendip', whence by favour of Horace Walpole we have the happy word 'Serendipity'.] TZINITZA (else-where TZINISTA) is the name of the country . . . And the Indian philosophers called Brachmans tell you that if you were to stretch a straight cord from Tzinitza through Persia to the Roman territory, you would just divide the world in halves.

From ancient times, people in the West know of China vaguely and imperfectly through indirect trade contacts with particular emporia. In early days, it was silk, carried overland by the long arduous Silk Road, that introduced China to the notice of Westerners. Much later, it was porcelain. The *Shorter OED*, indeed, emphasizes the part played by Persian middlemen in giving currency to the word 'China' in the

English language, for the Persian *chini* meant Chinese porcelain, and used to be pronounced that way. 'Women, like Cheney, should be kept with care.'[9] Hence the term 'Chinamaniac', an enthusiast for China, which is durable and distinctive, has always been admired among the *cognoscenti*, and on no account must be abused or roughly handled. Long before the Muslim traders brought the wares of the Orient to the tables of Western patricians, Indians were using the Sanskrit *cīna* for China, ultimately derived, it is widely presumed, from the Qin dynasty.

It is appropriate enough to use the Qin dynasty as a handle on the identity of China, for it was these rulers of a kingdom deep in the interior who, in 221 BC, first unified the country in something like its present geographical shape, under a single imperial order. As a dynasty, they lasted only until 206 BC, but they paved the road that history was to follow. The first emperor, Qin Shi Huang Di (Ch'in Shih Huang Ti), attempted to burn the books of the Confucians and other scholars, turning in preference to the austere 'Legalism' expressed by the thinkers Li Si (Li Shu), Shang Yang and Han Feizi (Fei-Tzu).

The famous 'Anti-Confucius' campaign of the 1970s can be seen as part of the interplay between two ancient traditions in China, represented by Confucianism and Legalism. By the 'Gang of Four', Qin Shi Huang Di was held up as a man who, for all his terrifying ruthlessness, was progressive in his day. (And progressiveness actually justified terror.) This Legalism had an influence upon Chinese political culture nearly as great as the teachings of the historical Confucius, whose name was attached to the subsequent amalgam. Legalism insisted that the state should be an impersonal machine, capable of running itself according to fixed laws. These laws, not the whim of often incompetent individuals, should narrowly channel the options of government. Before the laws, all are equal. In thus setting up an ideal of impersonal state loyalty as a baffle to corruption, personal charisma and narrow group interest, Legalism is much closer to modern Western political principles than is often recognized. But its authoritarianism, its totalitarianism, and its anti-intellectual glorification of agriculture and war and condemnation of art and culture are *sui generis*. Above all, it is a gospel for the man of war.

Institutionally, Legalism perished with the Qin, and Confucianism was lavishly patronised by the following dynasty, the Han, which lasted four centuries and gave its name to the ethnic Chinese. But the trend of thought represented by Legalism, the military ethos, persisted as an influence upon orthodoxy and as an alternative ideology always avail-

able when circumstances called for it. We shall see later on the importance of the interplay between these two traditions, an interplay which
is vital to the dynamics of Chinese culture in modern times.

Notes

1. Lloyd E. Eastman, *The Abortive Revolution: China under Nationalist
Rule, 1927-1937*, Harvard University Press, Cambridge, Mass., 1974, p. 287.
2. Alexander William Kinglake, *Eothen*, Dent, London, 1908/1962 (Everyman's edn), p. 120.
3. Ibid., p. 121.
4. P. Hamelius (ed.), *Mandeville's Travels*, Oxford University Press, Oxford (for
the Early English Text Society), 1919/1960, p. 104.
5. S. Wells Williams, *The Middle Kingdom*, Charles Scribner's Sons, New York,
1883, vol. 1, p. 836.
6. J. Doolittle, *Social Life of the Chinese*, Harper, New York, 1865, vol. 2,
p. 273.
7. P. Hamelius (ed.), *Mandeville's Travels*, p. 140.
8. H. Yule, A.C. Burnell and W. Crooke (eds), *Hobson-Jobson*, John Murray/
Munshiram Manoharlal, London 1903/ Delhi 1979, s.v. China.
9. *The Shorter Oxford English Dictionary*, s.v. China.

2 THE FACE OF CHINA

Our celestial empire possesses all things in greatest abundance.

The Emperor Qianlong

Over 90 per cent of Chinese of today do not look back to the founding Qin dynasty to provide themselves with a formal identification, at least in name. They call themselves men of Han (*Han-ren*). This is the name of the following dynasty (206 BC–AD 220) which presided over the first long period of imperial unity, restored Confucius to favour (though Confucianism did not then attain its later form and status), began the long process of consolidating the territory of the empire (the southern half of which was at first only thinly garrisoned by Chinese-speakingpeople), and patronised the arts, letters and sciences.

Within the frontiers of China, about 6 per cent of the population are not ethnic or Han Chinese, but ethnic groups of very varied cultures, though some are related to the Han. These minorities may be more numerous in proportion to their corresponding majorities than, say, the Red Indians of North America or the Aborigines of Australia, but, considering the patchwork of peoples that China was at the very beginning of history, it is remarkable how ethnically dominant the Han are today, and therefore how homogeneous China has become. The Han Chinese, from a common stock, are by and large of a single physical type, though those from the North are often larger-framed.

Today the national minorities mostly dwell in the vast inland frontier-zones of China that are unsuitable for agriculture, which, measured by numbers of people employed, is the biggest sector of the Han economy, and in the hilly parts of the south. Small in proportion to the total population, they occupy territories consisting of about 60 per cent of the land area of China, nearly all of which is around the perimeter of the country and of very great strategic importance.

Tibetans, for one, number perhaps three million; there are rather more elsewhere in China than in Tibet itself; chiefly in Qinghai (Tsinghai), where lamaism has long been strong, in Yunnan, and in Sichuan (Szechwan). Then there are at least a million and a half Mongols in the Inner Mongolian Autonomous Region, descendants of the peoples who in the thirteenth century built a vast Eurasian empire that threatened Europe and supplied China with one of her foreign dynasties of conquest, the Mongol or Yuan (1279-1368). Nowadays they are peaceful herdsmen increasingly encroached upon by Han

Chinese settlement and increasingly facing the likelihood of assimilation to Chinese culture. Many of their fellows dwell across the frontier in the Mongolian People's Republic, which occupies territory over which China makes historical claims but whose independence, such as it is, stems from Russian sponsorship. Mongols in China have what is described as an autonomous region, Inner Mongolia, a type of administrative division in which, constitutionally, minority peoples keep their identity, but where in practice, through 'democratic centralism', it is abridged. With the example of their Russian-sponsored brethren before them, they have divided loyalties. The Inner Mongolian Autonomous Region was established under the present regime in 1954, occupying a vast area; in 1969 it was reduced to about a third of this size; in 1979 there was yet a further reduction.

Various Moslem peoples of Turkic racial affinity, more than four million, constitute a great part of the population of xinjiang (Sinkiang), a province in the west consisting largely of desert. They include Kirghiz, Uzbekis and Uighurs, and live in parts of Qinghai and Gansu as well. The province of Gansu is historically China's back door giving upon the bleak interior of Eurasia; here the agriculture of what used to be called China Proper shades into the desert economy of the sparse nomadic peoples of Central Asia; here archaeology reveals dimly something of the cultures and migrations from which Chinese prehistory was to turn into history; throughout history fresh currents were fed into China by Buddhist and Muslim pilgrims, traders and warriors.

Another group of peoples is of Tungusic stock, most notably the two and a half million Manchu inhabitants of Manchuria; these are descended from the same origins as the northern conquerors who supplied the last of the dynasties of imperial China, the Manchu or Qing (Ch'ing, 1644-1912). The Manchu dynasty attempted to keep its Manchu subjects apart from the Han Chinese as a privileged elite, and to keep Manchuria (the provinces of Liaoning, Jihin and Heilongjiang, now known as the North-East) as a separate homeland. But they failed. In social reality the Manchus, highly sinicized from the beginning, were never a totally distinct group. For the revolutionaries at the turn of the century it was natural to identify their opponents as foreigners, but Manchu assimilation to the Chinese had gone far. As for Manchuria, it was difficult indeed to prevent the tight-packed hard-pressed northern Chinese from migrating there and extending the domain of Chinese agriculture. In the present century, Manchuria became a hearth of modern industry. This was the doing initially of the Japanese, who occupied Manchuria in the 1930s and 1940s and created the country of Manchukuo under a puppet government. Unlike most of China, the land had not yet been greatly over-populated.

In the south of China, in Guangxı (Kwanghsi), Guizhou (Kweichow) and Yunnan, the Han are recent comers, and in the hills still dwell many scattered groups and some substantial populations that retain a distinct personality. They are the remnants of those who were once a majority in the south, and whose cultures injected into Han Chinese stock much more than is now obvious. The several million Zhuang (Chuang) are the most numerous of all the minorities, and smaller numbers of Thai, Dujia (Tu-chia), Miao, Yao, Buyi (Pu-yi), Hani, Lahu, Lisu and others are related to peoples in Thailand and Laos, notably the Zhuang and the Thais themselves.

All these minority peoples have often been under cultural and political pressure, for, despite the constitutional provisions of the 1950s, the Han Chinese are an overwhelming majority and have often threatened to swamp the smaller groups.

It is remarkable indeed that so many people should be, in race and culture, so alike. Superficially at least, China appears to be very much more homogeneous than, for example, India.

Many features of culture are specific, not only to China, but to the larger region of Far Eastern civilization which for the most part used to look to China for inspiratinn. Right until modern times, many territories where the Son of Heaven in his imperial capital seldom or never extended the direct administration of his mandarin officers have none the less been territories where Confucian ethics and Chinese language became the badges of superiority. The Vietnamese, though under direct Chinese rule for a millennium, were independent for an equal length of time. But, however fierce against China in their politics, they were until very recently earnest disciples of China in their institutions, arts and letters. The Japanese do not have a past as part of the empire, but in a formative state of their history they eagerly absorbed Chinese Buddhism, Chinese political ideas (suitably adapted), Chinese cosmology and Chinese writing.

Far Eastern culture is distinctive in many fields, including contingent and everyday matters that are easily overlooked. Take diet habits for example. A line can be drawn through South-East Asia that, fairly neatly, separates milk-lovers from milk-haters. The sanctity of the cow to the Indians may have, though it is not generally realized, a solid foundation in utility: a cow competes with men for food less than one might think, because it often survives by scavenging, and its milk, squeezed out remorselessly, may be important at the margin of survival.

Its dung is valuable as fuel whereas the Chinese seek out every available molecule of manure for fertilizer, using as fuel twigs, leaves and oil. In China the cattle compete with men for food in all areas that are not utterly unsuitable for agriculture and it is pigs and poultry that are left to scavenge. Good fresh milk (except, in some areas, goats' milk) is therefore difficult or impossible to find, and for many Chinese, southerners particularly, it is indigestible.

Again, in the southern part of Asia, etiquette demands that men eat with their right hands; Chinese deftly handle chopstcks. An American investigator in the 1930s wrote approvingly: 'Many educated Chinese no longer put their chopsticks into a common bowl.'[1] The trend has not continued. Nowadays, many Westerners, of any degree of education, enjoy eating Chinese food and like to eat it in the Chinese way. Houses, in China, are built on the ground, sometimes in it, but not above it on piles (except where certain south-western minorities have their home), even where this would make good sense. The Chinese, like their cultural pupils in Korea, Japan and until recently Vietnam, write in ideographic characters utterly unlike the alphabetic systems worked out in other parts of the world. The Chinese, men and often women, wear trousers.

This last custom is generally thought to be derived from the nomadic, horse-riding invaders of the past, for whom of course trousers were convenient. This may well be correct, but how surprising that the custom has stuck among an agricultural people which has so little use for the horse. Certainly, trousered Chinese women find it convenient for working in the fields; but for centuries, many Chinese women, including many in peasant families, were crippled by having their feet bound so that field labour was virtually impossible for them. Meanwhile, the Indians, who had a great deal of use for horses, wore *dhotis* and relaxed in *lungis*, while their womenfolk wore sarees or shalwar and khamize.

The Chinese that one sees today do not bind, and have not bound, the feet of their women, though there are still very old ladies unlucky enough to have been born into a world that prized tiny feet (only to die in a world that no longer has so much respect for mothers-in-law or for the old in general), ladies who as little girls cried themselves to sleep each night with the pain of it. The Chinese today still commonly wear trousers, but many women would like to wear Western-style skirts and in recent years have increasingly begun to do so. The clothing of all looks much alike, though there are differences in quality of cloth between those high and low in rank, and between town and country. Where and when weather permits, people wear light cotton shirts, and young girls wear patterned blouses. In the cold north one sees bulky coats padded with cotton, fur collars and hats. Earlier in the century, Western fashions were in vogue, and young or liberated women wore gowns or skirts slit up the sides that became a familiar sight in the bigger cities but a source of shocked surprise in the villages.

Chinese do not march in regimented squads wherever they go. The crowds in the cities hurry, stroll, loiter or stand in ones and twos and small groups. Newspapers and posters set up for public display attract small crowds of readers; at various periods in the recent past wall-newspapers or 'big character posters', *dazi bao* (*ta-tzu pao*), hand-painted posters made by individuals to express their ostensible, perhaps genuine, political views, have been a focus of attention in all public places. As straws in the political wind they attract avid attention from the literate public. News is carried also by radio, with public loud-speakers. Television is still a rarity, though sets may be seen in the canteens or recreation rooms of at least some factories and offices, and many urban families are now saving for their own sets. But all the news, like the television, is monochrome: there can be only one version of it, for it is a civil service activity, managed from above.

Western ideas of love may be bourgeois, but young men and women in China still walk in pairs; in parks and by river banks, though much more discreetly than in the West, they even hold hands. This varies greatly with the political climate. In the past and in remote country districts, such displays would offend many Chinese. In the 1940s, a boy and girl holding hands in a Yunnan street could attract pungent disapprobation in the form of a bucket of dung poured over their heads. The same austere climate of opinion prevailed much later, in the Cultural Revolution.

Children play games. Traditionally, shuttlecock and kite-flying have been popular children's pastimes. Infants used not to be encouraged to engage in energetic and possibly dangerous activities like climbing trees or swimming. After all, medical services have commonly been an impossibly remote luxury, and to endanger one's own body was an unfilial act, but there was always plenty of scope for harmless diversion, particularly in the countryside. Older people play table-tennis (often a ping-pong table is the chief piece of furniture in an austere common-room); organized callisthenics and traditional Chinese shadow-boxing are very respectable. Mah-jong, a game which well-off women used to play a great deal to fritter away the time, is not. Bridge or poker, as has recently been instanced, is politically dangerous, though with the rise of Deng Xiaoping it has recently returned to favour.

Traffic everywhere is mostly pedestrian, or at least animal-drawn. Private cars are virtually unknown. Such few cars as are to be seen belong to government or semi-government bodies, or the army, and they are used to transport officials on business, or foreign visitors. Taxis exist, and may be ordered through official channels, but do not cruise for hire in the streets. To travel by car is to be above the commonplace, and in some circumstances it might be thought corrupting. There was a rural official whose practice was to arrive from local party headquarters on bare feet when he made his visits, but it turned out that he took a car most of the way, hopping out to complete each trip in the proper proletarian style.

Lorries are important to economic betterment, but they are still few. They are made in many places, but especially in a few major industrial cities such as Changchun (the most important), Shanghai (a major centre of China's industry; anything made there has prestige throughout the country), Tianjin (Tientsin) and Wuhan. The first Chinese lorries were produced in 1957; in 1971 a production of about 75,000 was claimed. (Claims like these often need interpreting. It is entirely possible, for example, that many of the lorries said to be manufactured in quite remote country towns were in fact reconditioned vehicles.) In the towns, military lorries and tourist buses are ubiquitous. The rule of the road is *sauve qui peut*, and though motor traffic is thin the sound of horns is not. There is a 'rustic' attitude to traffic.

Transport mostly still depends on carts drawn by buffaloes or oxen (sometimes mules or horses in parts of the north), on pack animals, on wheelbarrows designed with all the weight over the wheel — such vehicles used to serve as taxis — on canals and rivers, and on men and women themselves; the shoulder pole balanced by baskets hanging from either end is still very common. Railways are vital to the modern economy, and much has been done to extend rail connections from the eastern seaboard, where they first developed in the service of early Westernization, to the interior; but the main routes still lack feeders that might integrate them with their hinterlands. Railways have yet to become as important a part of the Chinese way of life as long since happened in India. Roads are mostly dirt or gravel; in the past they were normally not even wide enough for carts, for men went on foot and goods went on poles across shoulders. (Yet some of these paths were surprisingly well paved and lighted, with roofed bridges, shady trees, resthouses, and carefully-cut steps in the mountain slopes.) A network of sealed roads, however, does now link most big cities, and sometimes extends into unexpectedly remote places — leading to centres of political pilgrimage such as Shaoshan.

In the countryside, ducks and geese are ubiquitous, chickens are kept in coops, and shallow fishponds are on every side, where children paddle. Pigs, as important to the farmers in their own ways as grain, are often kept in sties, especially in winter; piglets are often to be seen inside the houses. Some years ago there was a campaign to keep pigs in sties in the interests of hygiene and efficiency. Apart from this, and the herds of goats in some parts, animal life is not conspicuous. Pet animals are not kept; the few dogs that are to be seen mostly work for their living, often herding goats. And dog sausage is one of the delicacies that may be bought for a few *fen* at the numerous periodic fairs in the countryside where private trade flourishes.

Poverty makes for thrift, and thrift leaves little room for too much sentiment. Every living animal is an animal that lives on food that men, women and children could themselves eat, or turn into something edible, or wear, or keep warm with; and its survival is the issue of a nice economic calculation. Oxen and buffaloes are used for draft, and, surprisingly little, for ploughing. Children cut branches for them grudgingly. Pierre Gourou observed that civilization in East Asia is essentially vegetable.[2] Its origin lies in sheer numbers of people in relation to cultivable land. Metal utensils or machines of any sort are therefore difficult to come by, and even timber is scarce.

The origins of the problem are debatable (low level technology, Confucianism, over-population?), but where the choice is between a material imported at huge expense by an inadequate transport system from a distant place and a cheap but inefficient locally grown product, it is usually the second that wins on grounds of hard economic sense. Ploughs may have practically no metal on them but for a tiny share. Cotton, not wool, is preferred for clothing, with layers of cotton wadding inserted against the cruel northern winter. (Wool means using precious land for pasturage.) Soles of locally crafted shoes may be of esparto grass, not of leather; traditionally constructed southern houses are held together by bamboo and rattan ties, and timber, where it is used, may be joined without nails.

Until recently, waterproof containers were made of coated basketwork. Bamboo proved incredibly versatile. Pierre Gourou lists its uses: yokes, poles, scaffoldings, pipes, conduits, blinds, boats, tables, chairs, shelves, boxes, sieves, brooms, brushes, combs, ladders, yardsticks, bows, arrows, umbrella ribs, gates, barriers, posts, stakes, mats, hats, baskets, lanterns, torches, fans, chopsticks, birdcages, musical pipes, sandals, bellows pipes, containers for cooking rice on a fire, shoots to eat as vegetables, and leaves for forage.[3]

Housing, in the countryside, is usually traditional. (Communal barracks are a myth; the cost of their construction would have been prohibitive.) Houses are small and of locally available fabric. In the south, tiled roofs are needed against the abundant rain. Walls are quite often of brick (a survey in the 1930s, for what it is worth nowadays, revealed that about 23 per cent of houses in the south were of brick, 17 per cent in the north).[4] The structure is often supported by a timber framework even where walls are of brick. Alternative fabrics are woven bamboo or corn stalks. Floors are brick in luxury dwellings, most often tamped earth, with the structural posts set on stone slabs. Windows are traditionally small; this discourages thieves who might otherwise crawl in, and stems also from a belief that large openings bring bad luck, allowing wealth to escape. These may be two aspects of the same thing. Glass is now fairly normal in many areas, but it is a modern luxury: in the past, and in less favoured areas today, windows have been unglazed. Glass windows may be unopenable; often oiled paper serves the same purpose; sea-shells used to be made into windowpanes in wealthy homes in the South-East.

In the north, houses need to be more solid against the cold; they have low eaves; sometimes they have flat roofs. Walls are commonly of adobe or mud-brick, sometimes on a masonry foundation, and protected against the wet by the eaves. One of the disastrous effects of flooding is that it causes the walls of mud houses to collapse, with the loss of whatever grain may be stored indoors. Sometimes stores are kept on a flat roof; sometimes a supply of grain is buried, exactly as was done in the pits now revealed by archaeology by the Chinese of 4,000 years ago.

Farmers' houses have few rooms; in the past, it was common to combine farm with domestic purposes, with tools and animals in the bedroom or kitchen. The northern house needs to economise on space if it is to stay warm in winter, and, whether because of this or because the north is poorer, the same 1930s survey found that northern houses had only 80 square feet per person, while in the south they had a hundred. Heating is by a brick stove or *kang* (*k'ang*), an efficient form of central heating, for the same fuel that cooks the family's dinner supplies warmth to a brick bench, about the size of a double bed, on which the family sleeps.

In the loess soil area of the north and north-west, notably in Shaanxi (Shensi) (where the Communist Party had its chief base area during much of the Japanese war), whole villages of people live in caves that are cut into the cliff face (some into the sides of pits in level ground). They are not damp; they are snug as could be desired; and they last for longer than their makers are likely to have use for them. Their doorways lead directly into the main living areas. On either side of these open out bedrooms, which may or may not have their own windows to the fresh air.

Ventilation is obviously not good in these dwellings. Neither is it very efficient in more conventional houses, their small windows covered with paper or with wood bars in winter. Nor are the Chinese particularly self-indulgent with their domestic heating. South of Shanghai it is scarcely considered necessary, though by less spartan standards the winters in many parts seem distinctly cold. Another disadvantage, from the point of view of a Westerner accustomed to night-life, is the opacity of the black Chinese night that falls over the poorer and remoter villages. Puny oil-lamps use precious fuel. In the imperial past would-be officials had to study whenever they could for the examinations, and had held up to them the ideal of the scholar who studied by the light of glow-worms and the stars if necessary. In a village, it might practically be the case. It is one of the things that had to be endured by the millions of city youths sent down, since the Cultural Revolution, to live indefinitely unless they could bribe the local party secretary, or find some other reason for returning, in far-distant villages. For them, brought up to the relatively cosmopolitan expectations of city life, any venturing abroad after dusk, and purposes could be few, was a Stygian penance. Now, however, with the more relaxed political atmosphere, such people have largely returned to the cities. Controls are very strict, though, and it is almost impossible to move to Peking.

Certainly, modern facilities are constantly spreading, though in the absence of reliable figures we must guess as best we may what facility has spread to what proportion of the population. Electricity has indeed been brought to many villages where one might not expect it. There are many wells. Hygiene has almost certainly improved in most places. There are more pigsties than there used to be. Village dwellings used to have their privies at their entrances where it was hoped that casual passers-by would contribute to the family stock of fertiliser. Privies are now usually communal, some are kept clean, and they benefit the communal fields. Running water is supplied to many villages, at least in the vicinity of the cities. Always the most prosperous, villages near cities supply vegetables to the towns, and the possibilities for private trade are far better than in remoter areas. Bicycles, radios and wrist-watches, the chief indices of private prosperity, are spreading, if slowly.

The visitor to a farmhouse sees, typically, a small dwelling with a central living room, in which the cooking is done, and one or two bedrooms. Appointments are few. There will be a table, one or two chairs, not many utensils, various posters or photographs. Housing of a more modern type is quite common in cities. Around the outskirts there are often outcroppings of utilitarian flats, usually three and not more than five storeys high. In Shanghai there are fifteen-storey blocks. A typical flat is small, but probably has a couple of bedrooms, running water, its own toilet. The visitor sees a few pieces of furniture, plastic-topped tables, a radio, the inevitable vacuum flask, pot and teacups; there are more likely to be family group or portrait photographs than in the village houses.

Every city has its own character, its own architecture. Peking is still a Chinese city in a way that the one-time treaty ports, centres of Westernization, or Nanjing (Nanking), the Kuomintang capital (1928-49) are not. Along the lanes (*hutong*) low houses lurk behind grey walls of brick or stone; the greyness is drab and ubiquitous, but the people who have moved out from the older part of the city to the suburban flats still hanker after its familiar homeliness. In Nanking and Shanghai there is plenty of Western-style architecture. In the south, colour and white-wash liven the city while the summer whites of the people in the streets are a relief from the blue so generally worn.

Out in the countryside, especially in the dust-blown north, another colour that obtrudes upon the eye is *huang*. This is always translated as yellow, but the term trespasses upon brown, a dirty, muddy sort of brown favoured by nature when she limns the Chinese country. The Yellow River, China's Sorrow, is the Huang He (Huang Ho), muddy-yellowish with the rich load of silt that it carries down from the north-western uplands. The silt content is about 11 per cent and very good for the fields, though in the past it has often reached them only at the expense of appalling floods. In the beginning of the 1930s (as often throughout China's history) there were devastating floods that destroyed villages in huge numbers. In the following years the harvests were good. Geologically speaking, the Yellow River is still very young; it has several times changed its course and much depends on the efficiency of flood-control measures.

In winter, Siberia and central Asia become the centre of a massive high-pressure zone, from which northerly or north-westerly winds, dry and cold, flow out to the Pacific across northern China. They bring with them blankets of dust, which hazes the air and stings the throat, adding to the already adequate discomfort of a cold season in Peking. This wind-borne dust from across the Gobi desert has much to do with the origin of civilization in China. In the course of thousands of years it built up in the northern and north-western parts of China, through which the Yellow River cuts its way, to encrust the earth with a thick layer of loess, a friable type of soil whose special virtues are thought to have made easier the passage to agriculture of prehistoric societies. Here, men did not have to content themselves with horticulture in forest glades or wait until iron technology gave them the means to cut their fields out of the vegetation. The soil, with its exceptional porosity and capillarity, brings minerals to the surface, and so long as it receives enough water it is very fertile.

It is a strange sort of soil. The sides of a trench cut in it do not quickly crumble, and it lends itself to the excavation of the troglodyte dwellings which so well serve the needs of people in parts of Shaanxi. This has long been a poor, remote area, for, whatever the area may have done in prehistoric times for the agricultural revolution, passing millennia have taken their toll. Today, one sees agriculture pushed wherever it will go; terraces climb up the mountainside, transforming the rough shapes of nature into tidy artifice. But nature is not a meek servant. The battle for livelihood is harsh. It is an austere environment; men emerge from holes in the cliff-face, their villages rows of caves connected by steep paths, and everything the colour of the soil except where trees, often recently planted against erosion, grow on the slopes.

A little less remote in Shaanxi are the flat lands where Xian (Sian, 'Western Peace'), the provincial capital, lies. Here for centuries was Changan (Ch'ang-an), great capital of mighty empires until the Tang (T'ang) dynasty (618-907), through much of the early period when the wealth and population of China still lay chiefly in the north. Now Shaanxi is on the outskirts of Chinese civilization. It was here at Xian, in 1936, that Chiang Kai-shek was kidnapped when he went in a bid to persuade the reluctant Manchurian army stationed there to fight the Communists in addition to the Japanese. Today, a drab rural scene with fields of maize, wheat, millet and cotton stretches away flatly to the distant mountains. Few trees grow.

For contrast take the watery environment of Jiangsu (Kiangsu), far to the east. Here, when Chinese culture spread, it began to shade into the softer tinctures of its southern environment, where fertile lowlands are seamed with rivers and canals from which rice is irrigated. Around Suzhou (Soochow), sky is reflected in the canals that bisect lush green fields. Barges pass, in a languid rhythm; two men control each: one sculling at the stern, one parading the barge's length as he punts. But it is not the Cherwell at Oxford. From all these landscapes elements from bucolic Europe are missing. There are few trees, no woodland strolling-places, no meadows where cattle ruminate. It is a different sort of environment, a different ecology. Here it is agriculture that is sovereign; animals and trees are allowed only to serve the purpose of utility in the interstices. But within the bounds of this law there is unending variety. Consider Hunan, further south and inland, the province where Mao Zedong (Mao Tse-tung) grew up and from which so many of the older generation of Communist politicians came. Hunan, 'South of the Lakes', is in the centre of the moist rice-growing region; to the north of it, and separating it from Hubei (Hupeh), 'North of the Lakes', flows the Yangzi (Yangtze) with great lakes on either side. Here, villages nestle picturesquely against rolling hills. Rows of tea-bushes on the hills make long perspectives; fluffy cotton grows, its leaves a coppery green when the plant is mature. Ducks paddle in ponds where lotuses bloom.

These verdant southern lands were only very gradually peopled by the Han Chinese through the progress of the first millennium of our era; it was not until the Song (Sung) dynasty (960-1279) that the see-saw of population tilted decisively. Yet it was here that the chief source of agricultural prosperity lay, once the Chinese had learned in the north the techniques of water control and social organization.

Take next Guangxi: here likewise rice is sown twice a year. Around Guilin (Kweilin) the landscape is tamed, harmonious, yet almost eerily enchanting. For the vertical hills familiar from Chinese scroll-paintings are not artistic fantasies, they are real; and here they thrust themselves up disconcertingly amid flat fields. (Similar limestone outcrops may be seen in Malaysia as well.) Villages are washed by the tide of agriculture hard against their flanks. Great clumps of bamboo, 30 or 40 feet high, grow by the banks of streams where the ruggedly independent fisherfolk make their living, and boatloads of tourists exhaust their camera film.

A final contrast now: the flat delta land around Canton in Guangdong. Young rice grows often twice, even three times a year, in emerald fields; here also is the latitude of sugar-cane; vegetable-gardens are everywhere, stimulated by proximity to a big city. Trees are still few, though more than in the north, and in places there are disciplined orchards of fruit trees.

These snapshots of the immemorial Chinese countryside have followed the slow tide of Han Chinese spread and settlement southwards from the great bend of the Yellow River where, in a sense at least, Chinese history began. The localities may be readily recognizable to some as permitted haunts of foreign tourists, who usually see them in the opposite order. Such places, though now becoming more numerous, are still no more than a few tantalising chinks or windows set ajar in a great blank wall.

Notes

1. O. Lang, *Chinese Family and Society*, Yale University Press, New Haven, 1946, p. 100.
2. P. Gourou, *Man and Land in the Far East*, trs. S.H. Beaver, Longman, London, 1975.
3. Ibid., p. 31.
4. J.L. Buck, *Land Utilization in China*, Chicago University Press, Chicago, 1937.

PART TWO

HISTORY, SOCIETY AND ECONOMY

3 CHINA'S HISTORICAL INTEGRITY

> The question of the size of political units seems never to attract among historians and sociologists the attention which it deserves.
>
> Mark Elvin

Our thinking is block thinking. We are accustomed to seeing on maps, and to visualizing in our minds, blocks of uniform colour with linear boundaries, representing states. We even try by derivation to represent prehistoric cultures, or civilizations, in the same way. The modern idea of a state is block-derived, and, in turn, the block is derived from the (impersonal) rule of law: a state is founded on a constitution which is valid for a particular territory with fairly precisely-defined frontiers. Laws, when supreme, are impersonal, and show no favours. This of course is an overstatement of the character of modern states in actual practice, but it represents the tendencies of our thought about how they should be. Their jurisdiction, because impersonal, is clear-cut, and this dictates frontiers. Often, of course, they are not precisely defined, but then it is thought desirable to deal with neighbours so that they should be. Thus in theory a man standing one pace away from the frontier is just as legitimately subject to the laws of a particular country as if he were in the capital.

The same logic, incidentally, can be applied to social classes as to territories. Marxism is block thinking with a vengeance. So is Maoism. Mao wrote: 'Is there such a thing as human nature? Of course there is. But there is only human nature in the concrete, no human nature in the abstract. In a class society there is only human nature that bears the stamp of a class; human nature that transcends class does not exist.'[1]

This block thinking obliterates all the subtle chiaroscuro essential to the understanding of traditional political systems, of which most Asian ones have been a part more recently than Western ones.

The founding principle and legitimacy of a government lay not in the rule of law, and hence in defined pieces of territory, but in the magic of a person, a magic that, because it was personal, became weaker with distance, and left frontiers most imprecise. In him dwelled the favour of heaven. He was elected, not under a constitution, but by the gods, whose will could always be known by certain signs. The rules by which these signs could be recognized were often vague, but invariably, for example, the chief rule was birth: the son of a ruler, usually the eldest, succeeded his father.

But another mistake about the oriental 'state' is that in a simple sense, because it was theoretically absolute, it was therefore despotic. Karl Wittfogel's celebrated thesis of 'oriental despotism',[2] which postulated for much of Asia totalitarian autocratic states based on the rulers' control of irrigation works, though not a current issue in scholarship,[3] has some popular currency and appeals to stereotyped notions of exotic absolutism. But the historical record shows that traditional Asian states, including China, were seldom for long really totalitarian and autocratic. There were simply too many centrifugal forces. For example, the rules of succession always allowed differences of interpretation; there were always rival candidates; there were usually strong parties attached to the candidates seeking the accession of their patrons and power for themselves. In India and South-East Asia, and at many periods in Chinese history, disputes about the succession, often leading to warfare, were endemic. Rulers had many queens and concubines; sons made claims for themselves according to different aspects of the status of their mothers; local lords made claims according to the status of their ancestors; and rules were always sufficiently flexible to bestow legitimacy upon rebel commoners who seized power. In China the acknowledged principle was *tian ming* (*t'ien ming*), the 'Mandate of Heaven': if a man won, this proved that heaven wished him to win; therefore he was legitimate (the Communist Party now has the mandate, at least for mainland China).

The sociology of frontiers is all-important to an understanding of Chinese political traditions.

In the great tracts around the inland borders live sparse groupings scattered across the empty desert spaces. For the most part they are nomads. Han Chinese settlement has diluted their racial distinctiveness in places, but usually, in the proportion that they are nomads, they are non-Han. Their environment and their history have been decisive for the definition of China as it is. Their cultures and their societies frequently threatened to infect Han China in many ways, exerting an often subtle centrifugal pull on China which the emperors understood well enough: the Great Wall of China was intended as much to keep the Chinese in, in a cultural sense, as to keep the barbarians out. To understand China we must understand the nature of this pull.

To the north-east of the traditional agricultural zones lies the region we know as Manchuria, now called Dongbei (*Tung-pei*), the North-East, consisting of three great provinces. Its status in the classification of environments is ambivalent, for, despite the efforts of the partly nomadic Manchus in their hour of glory to keep their homeland distinct behind the 'Chinese pale', free of Han farmers, agriculture has crept into it and through it. Its potential as well as its propinquity tempted the Japanese, who made it, with Chinese labour, what it is today: a hearth of industry. But in China's history it has been a frontier zone, a series of regions shading into each other: farmland in the south, forests further out where huntsmen went on horseback; in the far north, reindeer were herded. Owen Lattimore emphasizes in his study of the frontier lands[4] that here, as frequently elsewhere, there was no stark chasm between peoples and ways of life: men could move between the cultural worlds of Han farms and the forests. Nurhachi, who laid the basis of Manchu might, could attract the support of forest tribes, Chinese neighbours or immigrants, and sinicized Manchu farmers alike.

A great part of the bleak inland frontier was taken up by Mongolia, which has several nomadic zones: wet pastures favouring sheep; limy soils suited best to horses; saline soils suitable mainly for camels. Goats and sheep crop the grass most closely and can feed where other animals have been. Camels predominate in the emptiness of the arid desert; cattle and yaks are most productive of meat and milk per acre; oxen are best for draft; sheep are best for the combination of products they yield: wool and skins for clothes and felt tents, milk, cheese, butter, meat and dung for fuel, made into bricks.[5]

Around the rim of the Taklamakan desert is oasis agriculture, very different from the life of the Chinese river valleys. Small communities congregate at points where rivers flow down from the mountains to waste themselves in the desert; men snare wild fowl and game in the hills, fish in the marshes. There are oases in the steppes too, where agriculture shades into herding. Different ways of life are seldom isolated from each other.

To the west lies Tibet, a huge plateau where the sense of infinite lonely space must be the most overwhelming in the world. There are pockets of agriculture around the south-eastern corner; in the uplands move small communities with their yaks.

All the way through these huge inland frontier zones, the lines between agriculture, pasture and forest have been blurred. They have shifted both with changes in the weather and with the fortunes of war.

The Chinese tried to draw a dividing line, but in vain. The Qin (Ch'in) dynasty joined together sections of their predecessors' fortifications and built the Great Wall of China. Today, tourists may go to a section of it by bus from Peking, and take photographs of each other smiling in front of the grey stone blocks whose erection cost the lives of countless conscripted labourers. The wall was a magnificent but hopeless gesture. Time and time again, nomadic hordes burst through, their horse-borne way of life making them terrible foes, too skilful and too mobile for the Han Chinese to match. When they had learned how to ride and fire arrows accurately from galloping horses they were sometimes almost invincible. Waves of conquerors made kingdoms for themselves — Wei, Liao, Jin (Chin), many more. As these Chinese names indicate, they were often assimilated culturally. Nomadic populations were too thin to remain long distinct when they settled down as rulers among densely peopled farmlands, though the Manchus tried. Most of them made kingdoms for themselves in the north, fighting the southern Chinese and each other. The Mongols (Yuan) in the thirteenth century, and the Manchus (Qing) in the seventeenth, succeeded in taking over the whole country and assuming the Mandate of Heaven.

But it would be false to see the relationship between these frontier peoples and the Chinese empire as one between two distinct cultural units each seeking to dominate and absorb the other. This view does not do justice to the cosmopolitanism, or the intermittent extraversion, of the Chinese, who willy-nilly were engaged in constant traffic with the outside world. Indeed the 'barbarians' can well be seen as a constituent part of this political order, which has been called 'synarchy'[6] — the joint product of Han Chinese and nomad activity. The very weakness of imperial authority in transitional zones virtually invited aggression, and just because no clear lines could permanently be drawn, aggression of this kind tended, for lack of limitation, to threaten the centre.

But it is important to realize that the threat could take other forms besides successful invasion. Even when the barbarians were kept at bay politically and militarily, the frontiers could work their influence indirectly.

Less directly sinicized barbarian lords could build up little empires across the transitional zone and become rival sources of authority. Han Chinese lords within the frontier could develop relations of trade and diplomacy with their barbarian neighbours, grow rich, support armies, and escape central control. Han Chinese marginal farmers could migrate or become herdsmen and thus pass beyond the scope of the Chinese tax-gatherers and magistrates. Merchants could come and go, building up networks of moneyed power independent of the Chinese empire. An example given by Lattimore illustrates the size of some of these operations.[7] At the beginning of the present century, Mongolian lamas were patrons of Chinese traders, and a symbiosis developed between the two. Lamaseries happily ran up huge bookkeeping debts at interest up to 500 per cent p.a. (the debt in Mongolia in 1911 was 15 million taels, or ounces of silver). The Chinese firm of Da Sheng Kui (Ta Sheng K'uei) alone took annually against interest 70,000 horses and half a million sheep. Clearly, the Chinese frontier problem was not simply one of resisting invaders: it was a problem of drawing an impossible line between interacting cultures.

It was, then, not only direct conquest by barbarian cavalrymen or loss of control in the outer provinces that threatened unity; a threat worked often subtly and indirectly to pull Chinese society apart, in the heartlands as well. When pressure mounted in frontier zones, rulers felt compelled to act: armies were raised, and taxes increased to support them. This impaired the government's ability to carry on the normal activities expected of it; civil and welfare operations were curtailed; the mandarins, especially, found that their licit and illicit sources of wealth, from which they supported themselves and their friends and relations in the style to which they were accustomed, diminished. Often the ruler had to resort to the raising of standing professional armies, sometimes armies of barbarians, which could easily become rivals to his own power. Ordinary people, fearing the tax gatherers and the press-gangs, betook themselves to powerful protectors, the owners of powerful estates. Disenchantment spread; semi-autonomous centres of local power developed across the countryside. It was not necessary for the local lords to be like feudal barons with armies; for the most part they were not; it was enough for them to be looked up to in their districts as the owners of land and wealth, the masters of huge bodies of serfs (who were happy with their status because of the protection from tax-gatherers and press-gangs it gave them), and the manipulators of gangs of bullies when the need arose.[8] Thus the emperor's real power was often effectively curtailed.

The essential integrity of a modern Western state seems fairly secure and is usually taken for granted. We therefore fail to ask, as often as we should, why a traditional Asian polity like China's should have been so well able to maintain its integrity in the long run: the factors of the vicious circle making for the rise of autonomous seigneurial estates, warlordism and fragmentation were always there, and in the early centuries indeed the vicious circle went far. Here is an extract from a Han dynasty governmental source, cited by M. Elvin:

The army was mobilized several times. Supplies were not adequate. Services were also exacted from the common people. The farmers suffered from these toilsome duties and did not go out to work in their fields but fled to the great households. The officials and the village heads were fearful, and did not dare impose responsibilities upon the latter, but instead harassed the humbler folk; and these, being unable to pay, absconded to distant parts. [Landlord] families of moderate means were able on this account to do uncommonly well for themselves. Those who fled later were those who had been held responsible for the services due from those who had fled earlier . . . Ever more people thus followed the example of the fugitives.[9]

It is an old story, told in the pages of every country's history: troubled frontiers entail the raising of armies, which entails the raising of taxes, which entails hardship and unrest in the countryside, which entails migration and banditry, which entail loss of revenue and the raising of more armies for internal security, which entails more loss of revenue, which entails national weakness and invites more frontier trouble. Whether the initial frontier problem was successfully solved or not becomes almost irrelevant.

The Chinese political order, then, took its shape from its foreign relations, paralleling the ancient Indian polity in which a king's power within the kingdom depended on his ability to win glory and loot outside it, though the mechanism was different. Relationships with the outside world were relationships of symbiosis. When rulers succeeded in laying down the terms of this relationship, they could preside over an empire more centralized than any other in the world; when they failed, networks of local power developed in the provinces and the empire fell apart. The remarkable thing about the Chinese record, which must now be further explored, is that at least since the seventh century the country has been politically unified much more often than it has not; and this prevalent unity has given to the Chinese tradition its distinctive character.

The secret of this success was not simply in keeping out invaders. It lay in creating institutions of control of such a kind that, even when invading 'barbarians' conquered, they should take over a centralized apparatus geared to the perpetual task of controlling the outer lands and preventing rival power centres from forming. The Mongol and Manchu invaders, though 'barbarians', took over this apparatus and worked it. That is why the Chinese political order was a joint creation: the co-production of inside and outside forces.

Despite its common culture and sophisticated institutions, India never developed anything comparable. Where India failed, how did China succeed? The question of China's long-term success in creating and maintaining a unitary state is rarely addressed directly. It is too big a question, and it leads the historian into minefields of speculation. But one answer deserves to be noticed here. In 1973, Mark Elvin produced his *The Pattern of the Chinese Past*, dedicated to an examination of broad (and dangerous) long-term questions about Chinese history. In it, the first of the three sections considers precisely the matter of Chinese imperial unity.

The second and third sections concern problems of economics in later Chinese history, and it is these that have attracted most of the critical discussion of Elvin's views.[10] The first has been relatively neglected. Yet, arguably, it is much more important than the others to an understanding of why China was the brittle and ramshackle structure that it was in the nineteenth and twentieth centuries when the energies of the modern world decisively impinged upon it.

The Chinese imperial tradition is often facilely supposed to be sufficiently accountable to the agency of orthodox ideological theory, as if the invention of a doctrine *ex nihilo* were capable of determining the structure of a society for centuries. But this will not do. As Elvin says:

> Anyone, moreover, who is tempted to ascribe more than a modest part in ensuring imperial survival to the myth of Chinese imperial unity — although the myth existed and was sedulously fostered — can see the limited applicability of this line of argument by reflecting on the ultimate impotency of the alluring and almost inextinguishable myth of the Roman Empire to realize any enduring imperial resurrection in the West.[11]

Elvin prefers to focus the search for an answer upon the relationships between three factors: the size of the political unit, the productivity of its economy, and the proportion of economic output appropriated by the state for administration and defence. If available wealth will not permit the government to bear the cost of sending armies to distant frontiers and controlling them without imposing too great a strain on the taxpayers, then the frontiers or the taxpayers will become intractable and equilibrium can only be restored with closer frontiers. 'In general, empires tend to expand to the point at which their technological superiority over their neighbours is approximately counterbalanced by the burdens of size.'[12]

On this view, the ability of China to maintain itself as a unified empire depended on its ability to keep ahead of its neighbours in military technology and organizational skill. This was not easy, and was never secured once and for all by a few inventions. Cultural diffusion across an ill-defined frontier benefited the 'barbarians', who could add to their natural advantage in horsemanship by becoming sinicized to the extent that their disparate quarrelling tribal groups were welded into cohesive engines of conquest with selected Chinese styles of weaponry and command. Often, they broke in and dismembered the empire, but never often enough to end it for good. From the Sui dynasty (AD 581-617) on, the foundations of unity were strong, and only during the latter Song dynasty (AD 1127-1279) was the north of China under separate control. Two of the last three dynasties were set up by foreign invaders, but the invaders took over the institutions of centralization intact.

This analysis is addressed to the relations between China and its neighbours, and for the purpose of the argument both terms are taken as given — a single Chinese state, and an array of threatening nomadic peoples. As such, it seems cogent. Further questions, however, arise about each of the two terms as soon as we decline to take them as given.

First, the pre-existence of 'China' demands an explanation. It might be objected that there is no reason why China should *ab initio* be one technical, cultural and social entity. It should be many. Before they coalesced into a single power dealing with distant barbarian foes, we need to know how it was that the various regions occupied by Han people were brought together under the control of one — the very question demanding an answer. The objection, however, misses the point that the logic applied to relations between China and the outside world is implicitly applied to relations between regions of China itself. The most wealthy and populous region has an edge over the others, and uses it to control them. This, indeed, is in effect the well-known theory of 'key economic areas' that was advanced a long time ago by Chi Ch'ao-ting.[13] In each period of Chinese unity, one major region was especially prosperous and acted as storehouse for the empire. It was eventually the Yangzi basin that performed this function.

But the analysis is still not complete. It may be a long time before information about the demographic and economic history of India and China are sufficient to warrant confident comparisons, but, on the face of it, the Ganges basin in India was as well equipped to act as a 'key economic area' for a unified Indian empire as was the Yangzi in China. Yet, though the Ganges basin was at certain times the heart of a large empire, it was much more often an arena of feuding principalities. The difference remains to be accounted for. This requires us to look more closely at the other term of the relationship, the array of threatening nomadic peoples. What comparative examination suggests is that, for a unified 'China' to come into being in the first place in obedience to the logic of key economic areas, it was necessary that the nomad frontier should be *relatively* peaceful and controllable. Otherwise, a putative key economic region would be confronted by too great a military and political combination to be able to assert its dominance. Of course, everything is relative. By some standards, the frontier was almost always turbulent. But, in the long run, it was not totally unmanageable. In the long run, Chinese civilization kept its edge more often than not. This is the point that matters.

Take India as another area where a homogeneous civilization was constantly threatened by nomadic invasions. Both areas suffered frequent invasions. Both were periodically united under strong rulers. But the profound and impressive contrast is that India was rarely unified, China frequently.

A bare listing of invasions, with dates and names of tribes, would give a misleading impression of similarity between the Indian and Chinese experiences. With some exceptions, the two series of invaders were very different from each other.

The nomads who pressed the defences of the cold marginal areas north and south of the Great Wall of China came from bleak, bare, arid lands. They had to learn the techniques of survival in the aching desert, in the stony mountains, in the wastes of Siberia where the wind is like ice.

From June to August the steppe is a green carpet of grass and flowers, whose growth is promoted by heavy rains; in September the cold is already severe, in October snowstorms sweep across the land, by November the water courses are frozen, and until the following May snowfalls are frequent and winds blow with such ferocity as almost to lift a rider from his saddle. The height and rarefied atmosphere sometimes induce giddiness and exhaustion, and the lack of oxygen often obliges the nomad to desist from his attempts to kindle a fire. The monotony of the steppe is notorious; as far as the eye can travel, it sees little but a flat wilderness, broken by occasional ravines and stony hills where no tree is visible.[14]

The nomads depended almost totally upon the precarious survival of their herds, which had to roam widely; they went in small groups, fearing each other. To China, they could oppose few of the skills and values of civilizations except those which they first learned from China itself. Upon their local shamanistic religion some of them grafted world faiths, successively Buddhism and Islam, but these faiths were rarely parts of a cultural parcel including literacy, science and elaborate social organization unless these things came second-hand from China. In the arts of 'higher' civilization, the nomads were perpetual pupils of the Han Chinese. Their way of life prohibited anything else, for they lacked the cultural resources of surplus-producing agriculture, urban life and leisured classes. Rarely were they sufficiently numerous and cohesive to build strong armies. The Mongols, for whatever reason (explanations of their rise from changes in climate have not won general acceptance) were exceptional; the Mongol phenomenon in world history is the more dramatic because it is isolated. China was surrounded by a great arid *cordon sanitaire*; in the absence of water the resources for flourishing economies were simply lacking.

The regions of central Asia from which came the invaders of India were very different. These people were ancient Aryans, Greeks, Scyths, Parthians, Huns, Turks, and many others. Few of them came in small groups of illiterate and desperate men; they combined with their nomadic life and their skill in war all the arts of civilization learned in Greek valleys or on the banks of the Oxus. They were cemented by cultural traditions that looked back to the glories of ancient Persian civilization, or to Homer, or to the words of the Prophet. They were numerous, cohesive, and well led. They came from large and productive base areas beyond the Khyber to which they could retreat, perhaps to plan next year's raids.

In India, a civilian ethos and an apparatus of centralization were therefore never able to dominate political culure. Society was almost permanently militarized. Local centres of power kept forming as a result of the sort of nexus betwen wealth and social influence that is favoured by a warlord society in which status can change rapidly, and as a result also of the clustering of men around protectors. Militarization was a vicious circle: rulers constantly had to lead armies against local lords, who had made themselves rebel barons. All those factors of decay, which in China were threats, became in India very institutions of society. The word 'ksatriya' could mean either 'warrior' or 'ruler'. In China this interchangeability would be impossible.

Dominant elements in Chinese and Indian culture typify two main kinds of power: the civilian and the military. Civilian power requires that local power centres should be prevented from forming, and it is exercised through a bureaucracy, whose loyalty must be bought. Military power needs success in gaining resources by conquest for distribution.

The task of a ruler in a civilian tradition such as prevailed for most, though certainly not all, of the time in China was to allow as little occasion as possible for the employment of soldiers. Barbarians on the frontier must be resisted if they attacked, but preferably they were to be neutralized, brought into a regular political relationship with the centre, such as was in fact represented by the Chinese tribute system, while allowing their autonomy. Merchants, being mobile and difficult to control, were always to be distrusted. Above all, links between money and social influence in the provincial towns must be weakened as far as possible.

The two types of tradition dictate characteristic attitudes to foreign relations. For the military ruler, like the Indian raja, foreign relations are influenced by *Realpolitik*. Alliances are mostly tactical. There is no objection in principle to aggressive expansion: it will provide congenial employment for the ruler's military party and yield new resources.

Perhaps, in a sense, Marxist-Leninist regimes are sometimes militarist-governments in disguise. But, to whatever extent their members have been taught by experience to value an impersonal code above particularist politics and to associate the military ethos with fragmentation and anarchy, they are drawn to the civilian tradition.

For the civilian ruler, the overriding purpose is to prevent centrifugal forces from appearing in society. In the absence of a traditional clearly-defined frontier, immediate neighbours, if they are not neutralized, will act like magnets to provincial power and wealth, which the ruler would thus no longer be able to control. When Europe ceased to be perpetually on the defensive against the Muslim and Mongol threats, the opportunity that would otherwise have arisen to create a new unified civilian order may have been removed by the coming of the maritime era: many new sources of wealth could be exploited overseas, and a ring of commercial maritime powers grew up round the coasts of Europe, their resources too distant to be controlled by any putative central authority. So, where possible, neighbours should be vassals. If they threaten, they may be attacked, but the reprisals must be swift, punitive, and cheap. As for the outer world beyond the neighbours, military involvement should *a fortiori* be avoided. But the values of a domestic culture, in the absence of war, may demand an aggressive diplomatic policy. If the mandate is divine and power is intensely personal, then the power should be seen to radiate outwards without limit; legitimacy is, ideally, acknowledged by the world.

This civilian order is specially characteristic of Chinese tradition, and is embodied in 'Confucian' values, but from time to time it has had to yield its turn, when the centre fell apart, to the military tradition.

Notes

1. Mao Zedong, *Talks at the Yanan Forum on Art and Literature*, Foreign Languages Press, Peking, 1960, pp. 31f.
2. K. Wittfogel, *Oriental Despotism: a Comparative Study of Total Power*, Yale University Press, New Haven, 1957.
3. But see J.H. Steward, 'Cultural Causality and Law', *American Anthropologist*, vol. 51 (1949), pp. 1-27. For criticism of the thesis, see W. Eberhard, *Conquerors and Rulers: Social Forces in Medieval China*, Brill, Leiden, 1970, and W.P. Mitchell, 'The Hydraulic Hypothesis: a Reappraisal', *Current Anthropology*, vol. 14 (1973), pp. 532-4.
4. O. Lattimore, *Inner Asian Frontiers of China*, American Geographical Society, Boston, Mass., 1940/51.
5. Ibid., pp. 73ff.
6. J.K. Fairbank, 'Synarchy under the Treaties' in idem (ed.), *Chinese Thought and Institutions*, Chicago University Press, Chicago, 1957, pp. 204-31.
7. O. Lattimore, *Inner Asian Frontiers*, pp. 94f.
8. See M. Elvin, *The Pattern of the Chinese Past*, Eyre Methuen, London, 1973, pp. 65-8.
9. Ibid., p. 30.
10. E.g. see Ramon H. Myers, 'Transformation and Continuity in Chinese Economic and Social History', *Journal of Asian Studies*, vol. XXXIII, no. 2 (February, 1974), pp. 265-76.
11. M. Elvin, *The Pattern of the Chinese Past*, p. 22.
12. Ibid., p. 19.
13. Chi Ch'ao-ting, *Key Economic Areas in Chinese History*, London, 1936 (Kelly, N.Y. 1970).
14. J.J. Saunders. *The History of the Mongol Conquests*, Routledge & Kegan Paul, London, 1971, p. 44.

4 THE TRADITIONAL ECONOMY

There is a time to fish and a time to dry nets

Chinese Proverb

Here, you see, it takes all the running *you* can do, to keep in the same place. If you want to get somewhere else, you must run at least twice as fast as that.

The Red Queen in *Alice Through the Looking-Glass*

China used to be, by the standards applied by outsiders, a remarkably rich country. In the eyes of visitors from Marco Polo to the eighteenth century, far Cathay was a paradigm of magnificence; to those who did not visit but only read, she was a legend of riches.

Nor was it only the wealth of China that was admired. It was China's arts and sciences, government, wisdom, ceramics, silks, tea and (eventually, and deservedly) cuisine.

One could write a history of China's economy from her cuisine. Most of it would make civilized reading, though not perhaps a few of the more arcane recipes, like the one for live monkey's brain. It would begin with the ancient pastoral days when the Chinese were not yet wholly farmers, and forests full of game were still there for the aristocrats to hunt. Different social order; different economy; different cuisine. The menus included sheep, oxen, pig, fowl, horse, dog, elk, deer, muntjak (a small Asiatic deer), quail, pheasant, boar and wolf. Bear paws were a delicacy.

Eventually, however, with many mouths to feed, land became too precious for hunting, too precious even for extensive pasturage; herds of goats or sheep had to be sought in the border areas outside 'China Proper'. Most of the animals listed above have disappeared from the table, though not the dog, and especially not the pig, for these can scavenge. Pigs, poultry and fish now dominate the non-vegetarian menu. The pig would figure very largely in our history (in the 1970s there were over 220 million of them in China, against a world total of less than 700 million), though roast pig may not have been invented in China in quite the way that Lamb fancied.

Eating of other types of meat, especially lamb, was sometimes grafted upon the cuisine of the intensively agricultural Chinese, particularly when it was imported by nomadic invaders. The Mongols brought flocks of sheep, but when the Chinese cook lamb they seek to disguise

39

the taste. (It can be done with sherry, and the result is delicious.) A proverb has it that 'Although lamb is good, you can't cook it to suit everybody's taste.' Chinese gourmets became finicky. Of Confucius it was said: 'When the food was not cooked right, he would not eat. When it was not in season, he would not eat. When it was not cut correctly, he would not eat. When it was not served with the proper sauce, he would not eat.'[1]

But it was an inclusive finickiness, not an exclusive one, and this is a very important fact about Chinese cooking. People experimented with anything. Everything that was capable of being eaten by humans (and, arguably, some things that were not) was brought into the kitchen and made the raw material of rare art. At different stages in their history, Chinese have eaten wasps, dog, bamboo shoots, pickles of ant larvae, hen's feet, fish lips, badger stew, whelps in liver sauce, sparrow broth, camel's hump, fried snake relish, magnolia pudding, birds' nests, snails, live monkey brain, live river shrimps, bear's paw, elephant trunk, veal tendons and seaweed. (It is of course the saliva cementing the twigs of the birds' nests that supplies the *je ne sais quoi* that is so highly esteemed.)

The rare delicacies of the rich man's table, in other words, obeyed the laws of a poor subsistence economy. For that is what, at base, pre-industrial agricultural economies have usually been. The gourmet's kitchen reflected, in artistic form, the miserliness forced upon society as a whole. Nothing must be wasted. Everything must be eaten, and made palatable if at all possible. By custom, the child who fails to eat up all the grains in its bowl is warned that its future spouse will have a pock-marked face.[2]

Whether poverty is actually a sufficient explanation for the inventiveness of Chinese cuisine is of course a different question. Gernet suggests that it is indeed the main determinant.[3] K.C. Chang points to th weakness of this argument: 'Poverty and the consequent exhaustive search for resources provide only a favorable environment for culinary inventiveness and cannot be said to be its cause. If so, there would have been as many culinary giants as there are poor peoples.'[4]

Whatever the explanation may be, Chinese cooks showed a degree of resourcefulness and imagination exceeded in no other cuisine. Every part of every animal or vegetable was exploited if it could be. Peking duck, the great northern delicacy, is not just a dish: it is a feast. The first course is the skin on its own, done to a perfect crispness after being dried out in a cold wind, and even the bones, in soup, make one course. A humble fish makes a symphony of tastes, for the Chinese are interested in the tissue at the base of the dorsal fin, in liver, in intestine, in gizzard, in maw, in tripe, each cooked a different way. Lin Hsiangju and Lin Tsuifeng further remind us that fat is a delicacy, that all oil is useful, that special uses are made of a pig's knuckle, kidney and brains, to say nothing of a duck's web. 'Savages eat all parts of animals too, but only civilized man will write about it or *choose* to eat parts.'[5] The Chinese also eat with chopsticks, which mean that the 'savage' part of cutting meat up has to be done in the kitchen and doesn't intrude upon a civilized meal.

Traditional pharmacology, incidentally, shows the same resourcefulness, which found uses for the dandruff of fat men and roast leeches among its specifics. Maggots from horseflesh were good for toothache (at least they would help the sufferer forget his toothache), maggots from rotting toads for infantile marasmus, carp macerated in boy's urine for bowel trouble, boiled carp brain for deafness, yellow-headed flatfish for drunkenness, alligator scales in butter and wine for toothache, lumbago and boils, terrapin urine for hunchbacks, and sea-snails for ingrowing toenails.[6]

The Lins say that Chinese virtuosity makes its home in the mouth, which we might expect in a race of gourmets. 'Chinese tongues and teeth are perhaps rather unusual. Many people can split a watermelon seed, extract the meat and carry on a rapid conversation at the same time, pausing only to expel the shell. Others, with a little practice, are able to tie one or two knots in a cherry stem with tongue and teeth.'[7]

It is important to recognize that Chinese traditional civilization valued *haute cuisine* as no other; it is one of the marks of culture. He who is tired of food is tired of life, as Confucius might have said. In fact, according to the *Analects* he did say: 'I have indeed heard about matters pertaining to meat stand and meat platter, but I have not learned military matters.' The superior gentleman gets his priorities right.

K.C. Chang, who cites this passage, put together a fascinating book on *Food in Chinese Culture* by soliciting articles on the subject from specialists in every period of Chinese history. As he comments, 'It may be an indication of something profound and significant – though I don't know what – that my invitation was accepted by every one of my colleagues on my first approach.'[8]

A paragraph from his introduction demands to be quoted:

The importance of the kitchen in the king's palace is amply shown in the personnel roster recorded in *Chou Li*. Out of the almost four thousand persons who had the responsibility of running the king's residential quarters, 2,271, or almost 60 percent, of them handled food and wine. These included 162 master 'dieticians' in charge of the daily menus of the king, his queen, and the crown prince; 70 meat specialists; 128 chefs for 'internal' (family) consumption; 128 chefs for 'external' (guest) consumption; 62 assistant chefs; 335 specialists in grains, vegetables and fruits; 62 specialists of game; 342 fish specialists; 24 turtle and shellfish specialists; 28 meat dryers; 110 wine officers; 340 wine servers; 170 specialists in the 'six drinks'; 94 ice men; 31 bamboo-tray servers; 61 meat-platter servers; 62 pickle and sauce specialists; and 62 salt men.[9]

Nowadays, no jet-set hotel, no oil sheikh's palace, is likely to lavish such benign attention upon the palates of its coddled inmates. Quite unambiguously, this catalogue demonstrates a labour-intensive economy. For millennia, the economy of China has been essentially one of concentrated labour-intensive agriculture. Wealth has depended primarily upon the produce of land, and labour to work the land has usually been abundant. Hence the problem perceived by Chinese farmers has usually been that of maximizing the return for a given unit of land rather than that for a given unit of labour. In Ming China, for example, the tension between available land and population growth was nothing like as critical as it is now, but frugal and efficient use of natural resources was even then a fine art:

Much of the land along the lakeshores in the countryside was swampy and overgrown. The country people had all left it to become fishermen. The fields that had been deserted could be counted in tens of thouands. Hsiao and Chao found the price negligible, so they hired more than a hundred of the country people, fed them, and had them make pools of the lowest-lying places, and open up the rest for cultivation by surrounding them with high dykes . . . Their ponds could be reckoned in hundreds, and in all of them they reared fish. Above the ponds they built grass huts on beams in which they reared geese and pigs. The fish fed on the manure and grew still fatter. On the dykes they cultivated all kinds of plum and peach trees. In the marshes they grew mushrooms, dye-plants, water chestnuts and water lilies. There were thousands of walled areas where they cultivated vegetables at all seasons of the year. They netted and sold all sorts of birds and insects.[10]

The drive has constantly been to make more and more efficient use of resources within the bounds of a traditional agricultural technology. This is well brought out by D.H. Perkins's important study of Chinese agriculture between 1368 and 1968.[11] He concludes that, before the period of his study began, most of the major technical advances within traditional agriculture had already been made; nevertheless, although population rose during the period from 65-80 million at the beginning to 583 million in 1953, agriculture was well able to cope for most of the time. 'By the nineteenth and twentieth centuries, changing cropping patterns and rising "traditional" capital inputs per unit of land had succeeded in doubling the national average yield per *mou* of all grains taken together.'[12] This increase in production by unit of land was of course only part of the story, but it was important. It was achieved by a number of piecemeal improvements, none a major technical advance: the use of new seeds, the extension of water control measures for irrigated agriculture, and the increased use of natural fertiliser. Increased population per *mou* meant increased availability of nightsoil. Also, as people kept more pigs and draught animals, the application of animal manure roughly doubled.

However, what chiefly served to maintain the standard of living of the Chinese was (apart from occasional Malthusian checks on the population) migration to new areas and pioneering of new land, increasing the area under cultivation. It is perhaps only in the present century that saturation was finally reached, and no sustained advance could be initiated within the limits of traditional agriculture by opening new land or technical expedients. In most previous centuries, rich land was waiting, ripe for cultivation as the population grew and spread this way and that. Accustomed as we are to thinking of China as a victim of the grinding poverty that has afflicted the nation in the last century or more, we may too easily forget that, in earlier times, this sort of traditional economy, run with vigour and imagination, laid the basis on which was erected a highly sophisticated superstructure of commerce and made China's prosperity the envy of the world. Here is Marco Polo's description of Hangzhou (Hangchow), the former Song Dynasty capital and a major port city:

> At the end of three days you reach the noble and magnificent city of Kin-sai, a name that signifies 'the celestial city', and which it merits from its pre-eminence to all others in the world, in point of grandeur and beauty, as well as from its abundant delights, which might lead an inhabitant to imagine himself in paradise ... Accord-

ing to common estimation, this city is a hundred miles in circuit. Its streets and canals are extensive, and there are squares, or market-places, which, being necessarily proportioned in size to the prodigious concourse of people by whom they are frequented, are exceedingly spacious . . . It is commonly said that the number of bridges, of all sizes, amounts to twelve thousand. Those which are thrown over the principal canals and are connected with the main streets, have arches so high, and built with so much skill, that vessels with their masts can pass under them, whilst, at the same time, carts and horses are passing over their heads, — so well is the slope from the street adapted to the height of the arch . . . In a direction parallel to that of the main street, but on the opposite side of the squares, runs a very large canal, on the nearer bank of which capacious warehouses are built of stone, for the accommodation of the merchants who arrive from India and other parts, together with their goods and effects, in order that they may be conveniently situated with respect to the market-places. In each of these, upon three days in every week, there is an assemblage of from forty to fifty thousand persons, who attend the markets and supply them with every article of provision that can be desired. There is an abundant quantity of game of all kinds, such as roebucks, stags, fallow deer, hares, and rabbits, together with partridges, pheasants, francolins, quails, common fowls, capons and such numbers of ducks and geese as can scarcely be expressed; for so easily are they bred and reared on the lake, that, for the value of a Venetian silver groat, you may purchase a couple of geese and two couple of ducks . . . The streets connected with the market-squares are numerous, and in some of them are many cold baths, attended by servants of both sexes, to perform the offices of ablution for the men and women who frequent them, and who from their childhood have been accustomed at all times to wash in cold water, which they reckon highly conducive to health. At these bathing places, however, they have apartments provided with warm water, for the use of strangers, who, from not being habituated to it, cannot bear the shock of the cold. All are in the daily practice of washing their persons, and especially before their meals.

In other streets are the habitations of the courtesans, who are here in such numbers as I dare not venture to report; and not only near the squares, which is the situation usually appropriated for their residence, but in every part of the city they are to be found, adorned with much finery, highly perfumed, occupying well-furnished houses, and attended by many female domestics.[13]

As far as science and technology are concerned, the centuries-old pre-eminence of China (until quite recent times) has long been recognized by students of its history. It is just not the case that the Chinese stumbled upon a few inventions like paper, gunpowder and printing and failed to see how they could be exploited. Chinese people were responsible for hundreds of other inventions besides, and exploited them for all they were worth. The research team headed by Joseph Needham has been performing a monumental task in collating the record of these achievements and making it plain: immunization techniques; seismographs; drilling apparatus boring to depths of 2,000 feet with steel bits; the iron chain suspension bridge; the segmental arch bridge; the principle of the crank (applied to winnowing machines in Han times); the double-acting piston bellows, important in metallurgy; the conversion of rotary to longitudinal motion; gunpowder used in flame-throwers, bombs, rockets and grenades (not just fireworks); the barrel gun; the trebuchet; ironclad warships; the sternpost rudder; the paddle-wheel boat; magnetism, and the use of compass bearings in navigation; the mechanical clock; the horse stirrup; the efficient collar harness (making it possible to use horses for draught); wheelbarrows; rotary milling; silk reeling machines; iron and steel, with large scale nationalized production − most or all of these are world firsts for China, some by many centuries, and all of them are inventions which were applied by sophisticated engineers and craftsmen.[14]

Yet, somehow, all this wealth, all this organization, and all this inventiveness did not lead to an industrial revolution. Why not?

There are many answers; there is no answer. Some of the proposed partial explantions that have been advanced include shortage of the accumulation of capital necessary to invest in industry, the limited home market available to industrial products, and the stifling of private commercial activity by government control and corrupt official interference.[15] For the most part such explanations raise more questions than they answer.

The latter sections of Mark Elvin's study referred to in the previous chapter attempt a more convincing account of the problem. Part of the explanation offered uses the idea of a 'high-level equilibrium trap', according to which the very excellence and adaptiveness of the Chinese *traditional* economy made it increasingly difficult, as pressures increased, to make a qualitative change: no steps could be taken towards mechanization that would actually improve on the highly sophisticated cheap-labour system in existence. By the eighteenth century, economic success had assisted population to increase to a point where material resources were becoming relatively scarce and expensive. Given the traditional technology, resources were already maximally used, so that, for example, enhanced irrigation in one area might starve another. Thus the facilities and materials for industrial development became much more expensive — even wooden machinery had to work hard to be competitive with manpower.[16] The theory, though much more elaborate than these few lines can convey, has to battle with many critics, particularly economists.

Looking at the whole problem from a different point of view, Joseph Needham speculates that those features of social structure which in Europe combined with the technological advance to foster the industrial revolution were, in China, simply lacking. Thus, various inventions could assist, in Europe, in destroying a feudal order or building a capitalist one, but both these orders were alien to China and the same repercussions could not follow. Gunpowder spelled the end of the feudal era because castles and knights in armour ceased to be impregnable; thus the way was cleared for the rise of a new capitalist order. In China there were no heavily armoured knights or manorial castles to be outdated by the new warfare; there was only the emperor's bureaucratic apparatus, which did not change. Or again: in Europe, efficient horse harness cut the cost of land haulage, speeded transport, led to the improvement of vehicle design, encouraged long-distance travel and commuting to and from commercial centres, thus assisting the rise of the city state, womb of capitalism. In China, a centralized bureaucratic empire inhibited the rise of city states; the terrain (seamed in the south by waterways) was inappropriate for cavalry, and there was no improving on water transport anyway.[17]

The difficulty with all explanations of China's failure to engender a primary industrial revolution is that Europe's success in doing so is so far unexplained, and the expression 'industrial revolution', while unexplained, cannot be properly defined. There are piecemeal theories, some appealing, but there is no agreement upon a list of conditions that were severally necessary and jointly sufficient. Nobody can say why Europe had an industrial revolution; therefore nobody can say why China did not. (Much the same can be said about the same vexed question in the economic history of India.)

No answer need be attempted here. However, the analysis in the previous chapter of the peculiar form taken by China's symbiosis with the outside world does help to identify a relevant condition of economic change whose significance is rarely observed.

After various fits and starts, China's social and political colouration tended prevailingly to be influenced by civilian values rather than by a warlord ethos. Traditionally, China's civilian regimes have been distrustful of foreign contacts, seeking constantly to limit and control them. Some emperors were anxious to promote foreign intercourse, but more were not; most were influenced by the mandarin outlook and fearful of the centrifugal forces which might be generated by an uncontrolled increase in private trading empires, naval expeditions, and international politicking. Any sort of frontier entanglement was anathema, and threats of war were seen as problems to be solved quickly and cheaply, giving the military no chance to tread the corridors of political power, rather than as opportunities for loot and glory. Dealings with foreign ambassadors and traders needed to be institutionalized as far as possible under the rigorous protocol of the imperial Tribute System. Frontiers must be sanitized. On occasion, attempts were made to shift whole populations bodily inland away from the contamination of smuggler-infested coasts.

During a short period in the early fifteenth century, indeed, great Chinese fleets went out repeatedly to traffic with all the lands around the Indian Ocean, but it was a final fling. The admiral in command of these spectacular voyages was, incidentally, not a member of the regular scholar-gentry bureaucracy, but a Grand Eunuch, and a Muslim. The whole exercise reflected the values and interests of the palace, as opposed to the government as such. At the end of the century, when the Portuguese rounded the Cape, China had turned decisively inward once more, and its voyages to India and Africa were a misunderstood memory.

Now, it is clear that, to the extent that it became dominant, this sort of civilian tradition must seriously constrict the exploitation of foreign trade and resources which were, let us assume for the sake of argument, necessary to the sort of qualitative economic change that took place in Europe. There is surely something plausible in the bureaucratic oppression theory, even though this same 'oppression' was consistent with an extremely vigorous commercial life.

On the other hand, it appears just as likely that a warlord ethos such as India's, while it allowed plenty of opportunity for unfettered economic contacts with the outside world, did so at the cost of constant fragmentation, invasions, civil war, and the insecurity and waste of resources thus entailed that could only militate decisively against the rise of a new industrial order.

The prospects for China's advance, that is to say, could be glimpsed, if at all, only between the Scylla of stagnation and the Charybdis of chaos. If so, it is not surprising that an industrial revolution did not occur in China. It is only surprising that one should occur anywhere.

The conditions necessary for the industrial revolution may include a particular and paradoxical combination of some features characteristic of a civilian order (political stability, relatively long periods of peace, bureaucratic institutions capable of protecting trade) with others characteristic of a feudal-military order (outside trade and the rapid expansion of sources of raw materials).

It is understandable that this combination should be rare and difficult. To the extent that a society reaches out for new fields outside itself, it invites insecurity and fragmentation, and many of its resources are tied up in the support of aristocracies and armies. To the extent that it is peaceful and centralized, it denies itself the means to expand. In Europe, perhaps, the progress of fragmentation went so far that some of the outer fragments, prospering on their naval and commercial achievements, were able to develop, paradoxically, stable civilian orders within themselves. However this may be, it is clear that China did not follow a path that could lead to such a marriage of assets.

Speculation on such lines can of course only be tenuous and provisional. Even so, it does suggest one last thought, however precariously founded.

It is common in the West nowadays to regard China as a land of economic opportunity, possessed of a 'disciplined workforce' (it isn't) and rigorous economic planning (it is inefficient), capable of enormous industrial progress so long as the government forgets its ideological scruples and follows outward-looking economic policies. But perhaps, even with the passage of centuries and the spread of a new international scientific culture, the difficulty of combining involvement in the world at large with peaceful, rational and controlled internal economic development has not disappeared. The danger which needs to be seen is that, in the context of Chinese culture, openness to the outside world spells corruption, fragmentation and insecurity. The Chinese instinctively recognize this much better than we do. It is a gamble some of them have decided to take.

Notes

1. Lin Hsiang-ju and Lin Tsuifeng, *Chinese Gastronomy*, Nelson, London, 1969.

2. K.C. Chang (ed.), *Food in Chinese Culture*, Yale University Press, New Haven/London, 1977, p. 10.

3. J. Gernet, *Daily Life in China on the Eve of the Mongol Invasion, 1250-1276*, Stanford University Press, Calif., 1962, p. 135.

4. K.C. Chang, *Food in Chinese Culture*, p. 13.

5. Lin Hsiang-ju and Lin Tsuifeng, *Chinese Gastronomy*, p. 39.

6. B.E. Read (ed.), 'Chinese Materia Medica', *Peking Natural History Bulletin*, 1937; see *Far Eastern Economic Review*, vol. 107, no. 1, (January, 1980).

7. Lin Hsiang-ju and Lin Tsuifeng, *Chinese Gastronomy*, p. 16.

8. K.C. Chang, *Food in Chinese Culture*, p. 5.

9. Ibid., p. 11.

10. Cited by M. Elvin, *The Pattern of the Chinese Past*, Eyre Methuen, London, 1973, pp. 237f.

11. D.H. Perkins, *Agricultural Development in China 1368-1968*, Aldine, Chicago, 1969.

12. Ibid., p. 188.

13. Marco Polo, *The Travels of Marco Polo* Dent, London, 1908 (Everyman's edn), pp. 290-5.

14. J. Needham *et al.*, *Science and Civilization in China*, Cambridge University Press, Cambridge. A series of volumes, still in progress. A useful summary of many of the data appears in J. Needham, 'Science and China's Influence on the World' in R. Dawson (ed.), *The Legacy of China*, Oxford University Press, Oxford, 1964, pp. 234-300.

15. These theories are cited by Ramon H. Myers in 'Transformation and Continuity in Chinese Economic and Social History', *Journal of Asian Studies*, vol. XXXIII, no. 2 (February 1974), pp. 265-76.

16. M. Elvin, *The Pattern of the Chinese Past*, pp. 285-316.

17. J. Needham, 'Science and China's Influence on the World' in R. Dawson (ed.), *The Legacy of China*, Oxford University Press, Oxford, 1964, pp. 234-300.

5 THE GOOD EARTH

It is better to let your mother starve to death than to let your crop seed be eaten up.

Chinese Proverb

China has a land area of 3,657,765 sq. miles. This is roughly 2,340 million acres. But the greater part of this consists of the vast interior tracts of desert, semi-desert and pasturage where, despite what has been done to develop extractive industry, garrison the frontier and pioneer new land, agriculture is almost non-existent and population is extremely sparse. China proper, the inner 18 agricultural provinces, is about three-sevenths of the total, occupying 1,532,800 sq. miles. Inner Mongolia occupies 747,366 sq. miles.

Figures for the proportion of the area under cultivation, or irrigation, or double cropping, usually refer to agricultural China. Buck in the 1930s estimated the proportion of land under cultivation as about 27 per cent of China proper.[1] Only in the North-East and Manchuria (where the poor man's maize and sorghum will grow where other crops cannot) and Sichuan (Szechwan, China's ricebowl) does the proportion exceed one-half; in much of the south it is down to a quarter or a tenth. In 1959 it was said that 105.6 million hectares were arable (a hectare is 2.471 acres). Nowadays, about 30 per cent of China proper is under cultivation (about 12 per cent of all China).

The simple division of China into two zones, north and south, may over-simplify, but it is certainly useful. The division is apt to the realities, and an approximate frontier is the Huai River. To the north of it, China is cold, very densely populated in relation to resources, and poor. Wheat and millet are the most common staple crops. To the south, China is somewhat better off and warmer, and the most important crop is rice.

Within this great divide, however, are many sub-divisions. The famous survey made by J.L. Buck in 1929-33,[2] for all its faults, remains a useful source. At the extremities of China, the agriculture of the Han has over the centuries extended into areas once dominated by the nomadic or forest economies of other peoples. In the southern part of the north-east, agriculture has long thriven with maize and sorghum, grain alternating with vegetables and especially with soybeans; spring wheat is combined with oats, millet and various oilseeds. In the north-western provinces of Shaanxi and Shanxi, which belong to 'China

Proper', millet and maize prevail, with winter wheat. In the north-east, winter wheat, barley or peas are followed by maize; sorghum and cotton are widespread. Sichuan (Szechwan) in the west, isolated by battlements of mountains, is extremely densely populated but also extremely fertile. In the war against Japan it was the stronghold to which the government retreated, along with millions of refugees from the occupied zones. Here rice grows in alternation with sweet potatoes, maize, wheat and peas. Across to the east, in Hubei, Anhui (Anhwei) and Jiangsu (Kiangsu, part of which also belongs to the north-eastern zone) are rice, winter wheat and cotton. In the south-east is rice, sometimes grown twice a year, sometimes alternated with wheat or cotton. In the south double-cropping of rice is common, but sometimes it alternates with wheat or vegetables; in Guangdong sugar-cane. Finally, the south-western provinces grow rice with wheat, beans and rapeseed.

In many areas, then, farmers may choose between different proportions of food crops for immediate consumption and industrial crops. Since 1949, the *locus* of decision-making about the sowing of the broad fields has varied; most of the time it has been transferred from the individual household to larger encompassing units, although the recent trend has been back to the household. In quick stages, as agriculture was collectivized in the 1950s, the decision came to be made by bigger and bigger collectives. When the communes were introduced in 1958, the plan was to have all such decisions made by the central commune management itself, but from at least 1961 day-to-day policy-making began to be passed down again to a collective known as the 'production team', something a little more like a face-to-face group of people who know each other. At the level of abstract ideology, it is the aim continually to raise the level of collectivization, but for some time now this idea has been put in cold storage.

The chief industrial crop now is cotton, which grows over huge tracts of China, but cotton cloth is still rationed. Historically, silk has been very important in the Yangzi valley and southwards, techniques of worm-breeding, mulberry culture and spinning being zealously guarded and handed down over the generations. Silk, with porcelain and later tea, was among China's chief surplus-producing trade goods with the West: as early as ancient Roman times, across central Asia, lay the Silk Road.

Tea is still important. Traditional skill goes into the nice judgement of the point when the leaves are withered to exactly the right degree. Legend identifies the tree-bush as a miraculous growth from the eyelids of the Dhyana Buddhist monk Bodhidharma, who tore them out and threw them upon the ground so that he could meditate sleeplessly. In the eighteenth century, as Pierre Gourou records,[3] Zhen Fu (Chen Fu) prescribed that for the best result one should put tea, in a little muslin bag, into a lotus before it closes in the evening; then when the lotus opens the next morning the tea should be taken out and infused with rainwater.

These are cash crops. For direct food consumption, the grain staples are millet, sorghum and wheat in the north, rice in the south. In prehistoric times, millet was probably the first crop brought into regular domestication. Cattle-fodder and the poor man's grain, millet and sorghum, are not as nourishing as wheat, but in many areas millet and sorghum do so much better that they must be grown. Survival sometimes depends upon originally imported crops that have lodged in an ecological cranny which nothing else will fill. Notable among these are maize and sweet potatoes. The Chinese do not particularly like potatoes, which they cut into slices and dry, but they fill a gap.

Despite the supererogatory abundance of ingredients in Chinese cusine, most Chinese really have little to sauce their grain staple, and may be glad even of a few vegetables. Every household does its best to produce what vegetables, and sometimes fruit, it can on its private plot, which may also support pigs or poultry. So-called Chinese cabbage, actually related to mustard, is common. So are peas and beans, particularly the nourishing soya bean, which supplies the extract that does so much for Chinese cuisine as a whole, and has a number of uses besides (its flour makes *doufu* (*tou-fu*); its sprouts are on the menu as bean-shoots; its residue is fodder or manure). Oil, essential in cooking, comes from the seed of sunflower, mustard, rape or sesame.

The most important single crop in China is rice. But Asian civilization did not in fact arise from riziculture. Rice is relatively recent. When the Chinese first developed agriculture, it is likely to have been millet that they grew near the Yellow River, far from the southern latitudes where rice, that vastly superior grain, was later added to the farmer's technology. Early Indian farmers grew wheat, barley and such vegetables as lentils. In South-East Asia, even though prehistoric men there lived in or around the home of wild rice where the grain could be domesticated, it appears likely that vegetables remained more important than grain well into the historical period (which began, in South-East Asia, in the first few centuries AD), and there are areas where rice has penetrated only in the last few centuries. As in China, it is still spreading.

But there can be no doubt about its prominence today. Rice is a folk science. There are more than 3,000 types, and over the centuries farmers have learned which of those available to them are most suitable to their particular stretches of land. Some varieties are better adapted than others to dry conditions, or to deep or shallow water, or to water that is pure or brackish. Some rice ripens earlier than other rice, so that the farmer (or the collective management) can plan to stagger the harvest in different fields and thus diminish the harvest manpower crisis. This is not to say that Chinese famers are bold experimenters and scientific innovators. The common view is rather the reverse; reformers have usually met with caution and often surly suspicion. The reason for this is that people living at the very threshold of subsistence, depending for their survival from one year to the next upon a successful harvest, cannot afford to experiment. If they make a mistake, in principle they should benefit from the knowledge that this brings; in practice they may not live to enjoy the benefit.

The conservatism of the Chinese farmer is real enough, but it is not the conservatism of a dull, bovine spirit. It is the conservatism of people part of whose accumulated wisdom is to distrust the exhortations of enthusiastic amateurs set in authority over them. In the imperial past, records show that there were indeed many mandarins who were conscientious, diligent and anxious to import into their districts improved agricultural methods pioneered elsewhere; but there were also many who attempted to impose upon their subject peasantry methods that were unproved and positively harmful. Such behaviour does not belong entirely to the forgotten past. Many farmers now living must have vivid memories of what happened when in 1958 and 1959 new methods were vigorously pressed upon them, yields diminished by unwise close-planting and deep-ploughing; tracts of land made alkaline by reckless irrigation. Villagers cannot be expected always to discriminate between the pronouncements of properly trained agriculturalists who in fact deserve to be trusted and those of harassed and ignorant officials implementing hasty and uninformed orders from above.

The annual round is governed rather by the wisdom of forefathers than by technical manuals. It is a round that has not changed very much in a long time. The cycle begins with ploughing. Water buffaloes in flooded fields, oxen in some areas, or men anywhere, may draw the plough. The rice is not planted in the field: it is grown first in special nursery gardens. This is partly so that, while the young shoots are growing, the fields can be used for the last part of some other crop cycle. But this method also makes for economy in the use of seed, and lets the rice be given special intensive care in the beginning of its growth. Then it is planted out, a long and arduous task that may involve making myriad little holes for the shoots with sticks. For most of its growing cycle, ricefields need to be flooded. This indeed is not the only way of growing rice, but it is the most productive. Rice, like many other crops, has been in the past, and in parts of Asia still is, grown in dry fields. In Indonesia the term *sawah* (for flooded fields) and *ladang* (for slash-and-burn cultivation) are used to distinguish the two types of cultivation, and have a general currency. It has been found that, contrary to expectations, the yields of *ladang* cultivation per acre are not necessarily always below those of *sawah*. There is an overlap between the ranges. *Ladang* requires a very much smaller expenditure of effort in maintaining the fields, and suits the usages of a number of tribally organized hill peoples in South-East Asia and parts of southern China very well. But without irrigation a field's fertility is quickly exhausted and the cultivators must move on; the system therefore supports only a very sparse population whose required *Lebensraum* is spacious.

Dry-field swidden cultivation of this sort probably represents a stage in the history of man's relationship with rice, but, equally probably, not the origin of it. Wild rice occurs most abundantly in an area incorporating parts of eastern India, northern South-East Asia, and southern China, and it is likely that the first men to make the plant serve them lived in this general region. The plant which they set to work for them throve in marshes, and the first steps towards cultivation may have been elementary measures to encourage its growth, perhaps weeding out competitors and diverting water to it. Only much later, after a long period of domestication and selection of varieties suitable for *ladang*, was rice included in the calendar of settled agricultural peoples who had first developed intensive methods with other crops.

It has been argued that irrigation, first of the crops such as millet in the loess region where Chinese agriculture appears to have begun, later of rice in the south, has always been a leading architect of society. The argument, in its most uncompromising form, is associated with Karl Wittfogel, who considers that as communities of farmers became more numerous and their irrigation methods more sophisticated, it eventually became necessary for a controlling power to co-ordinate the elaborate waterworks, allot shares, and marshal the hordes of labourers whose toil the massive earthworks entail. Thus there comes into being what he called a hydraulic society, and the leviathan of the central state — 'oriental despotism' — is born. In the despot's hands lies awful power, for his domain compasses supreme authority over the life-giving waters on which all his subjects depend. On this view, China, its survival mortgaged for millennia to big irrigation works — the first recorded public work for irrigation was the Shih reservoir in Anhui — has always been presented as a prime example of a hydraulic society.

Yet the link between political power and irrigation is not likely to be as simple as this. For one thing, the first centralized states in Asia did not invariably depend on large-scale irrigation: in ancient China, large-scale irrigation works developed later than states.[5] For another, power in China was never so monolithic, shared as it was between emperor, his advisers, and dominant sections of the local gentry. Even the *esprit de corps* of the imperial civil service itself was such as to provide in some ways a diminution of the emperor's powers.

Irrigation is nevertheless politically important, along with flood control. The present government has constantly attempted to enlist the country's rural manpower in the promotion of hydraulic works, not only in the Great Leap Forward of 1958-60 but in uncounted national, provincial and district programmes before and since. The farmer's work is not at all evenly spread over the agricultural calendar, and accordingly there should be a reservoir of under-used labour especially in the winter months. Governments have acted upon this theory. The results have not always been happy, for of course farmers had not previously been accustomed to laze away the cold season, or other slack times, in complete idleness. They had engaged in a host of occupations designed to better the next year's yield or earn money in other ways. Mass-labour projects could perhaps be beneficial if they were carefully and realistically planned, but if they were hastily made they could upset delicate patterns of activity important to the survival of farming families.

Buck estimated that 46 per cent of all cultivated land, and 69 per cent of the riceland, was irrigated by all methods — from wells, ponds and ditches.[6] This includes primitive and inefficient irrigation; methods may have improved without expansion of the irrigated area in places. But there is no doubt that considerable efforts have been made to increase the area under irrigation as well as to improve it. In the Great Leap Forward, huge labour-intensive projects were undertaken, involving the labour of 100 million people, to construct dykes, canals and wells among other things. (Some of these projects were badly planned and counter-productive as they caused salinisation and ruined land for many years. In the 1970s, it appeared that North China had 50 million *mou* (nearly eight million acres) of alkaline land.)

The vicious circle of poverty has been at work in the matter of irrigation as in the economy generally. If China's agriculture could support more industry, manufactures might become cheaper; earth-moving equipment and electric pumps might become more widely available, and serve the needs of an agricultural prosperity that in fact is necessary before the machines can become cheap.

Throughout China's history, all manner of contrivances have been adopted to bring water from its source to the fields. Canals along the sides of valleys gently conduct it horizontally to points far above the river. Big tanks trap rainwater. China pioneered mechanical devices of many sorts long before they were thought of in the West. Tilt-hammers minimized the effort of lifting water in a bucket at the end of a counterpoised pole. Men pedalled, and oxen turned wheels, to drive water up chutes from river to field. The *noriah*, the endless chain of scoops or buckets that ladles matter up at one point and deposits it in another, was invented in China. Water-power itself was thoroughly exploited in imperial times, and a water-wheel could drive a *noriah* for irrigation, as well as it could drive a mill for polishing rice or a loom for making cloth. Even the corkscrew pump, in which a sealed rotating corkscrew forces water up a tube, was pioneered in China, though not widely applied.

For many centuries the life of the Chinese rice-farmer has been intimately bound up with the water on which he depends. Irrigation meshes with politics, for so much of the energy of government in the countryside has been directed to the management of water.

More subtly, it influences a farmer's view of the world, for his dependence upon rains and rivers has led him to perceive instinctively the intricate relationships between all the forces of nature; he feels himself to be a tiny and dispensable part of a grand organism in a way that is not possible for a city-dweller for whom the seasons themselves may be kept at bay.

Again, socially, the strings that tie him to his flooded fields rob him of much of the independence enjoyed by people with simpler methods of producing food. The immense labour that he invests in the creation and maintenance of his fields makes them expensive and him reluctant to leave them; given the low level of technology the agrarian population is anyway so dense that movement to another village would be most hazardous. Thus he loses mobility, rooted to the source of his subsistence and vulnerable to the demands of tax collectors and bandits. Unlike the sparse mobile bands of nomads who used to come as invaders, he is wholly preoccupied with his immediate economic tasks; he is dependent on others to protect him from outsiders and to sell him the tools he needs: he is a social being, part of a large community.

However, while the water in which a farmer works so much is helping to ensure that he will have enough to eat and that his family line may be continued, it is also in many ways insanitary and plays dice with his health. Schistosomiasis, for example, is widespread, and is contracted from tiny snails harbouring viruses that enter the body in these flooded fields. It is one of the rural afflictions which the 'barefoot doctors' were instituted to combat.

The most important thing, however, is to stay alive. Many risks must be taken. Chinese agriculture may once have been the best in the world, but without a breakthrough to a qualitatively different type of technology its practitioners need to use more and more ingenuity in squeezing survival from the soil. *Sawah* cultivation, in particular, is extremely responsive to labour, so that, up to a point, the yield of any one acre will increase at a rate something like the rate of increase in the number of hours of labour put into it. But so long as methods and materials remained the same, returns had to start falling off eventually. In the last 100 years or so, different parts of China have reached crisis point at different times, the northern provinces generally earlier than the southern. Traditional agriculture reached the point of sharply diminishing returns. The rural population became more vulnerable to adverse conditions, and famines became more frequent and more tragic in their ravages, many costing millions upon millions of lives. In parts, famine conditions became almost normal. In his classic essay at the beginning of the 1930s, R.H. Tawney wrote: 'There are districts in which the position of the rural population is that of a man standing permanently up to his neck in water, so that even a ripple is sufficient to drown him.'[7]

Artifice combined unwittingly with nature to turn the screw upon the suffering population. As D.H. Perkins writes in the conclusion of his study:

Just as China was running out of new land, her population growth began to accelerate. It is probable that this acceleration began early in the twentieth century with the coming of the railroad and the consequent improvement in transport and famine relief. But the biggest push came after 1949 with the systematic application of modern public health measures. The rate of increase in the number of people jumped from under 1 per cent a year in the decades prior to 1949 to over 2 per cent after that date.[8]

After a century of rebellions, civil wars and invasions, the country could begin to attend realistically to the amelioration of its people's lot; yet, ironically, that amelioration worked against itself.

The few decades of peace (relative peace; we must not forget the hideous turmoil of the Great Proletarian Cultural Revolution or the appalling famines partly consequent upon the ill-named Great Leap Forward) have brought changes to the countryside, of course. What is remarkable is how few and late they are, for until very recently governments have been, at best, equivocal in their attachment to the modernization of agriculture.

What changes have taken place in the rural scene in the present century?

They include new strains of wheat developed for the growing conditions of western China, strains of rice that will grow farther north than before, contour ploughing which slows down erosion, afforestation, which may serve the same among other purposes. Chemical fertilizer is still inadequate, but is produced in a myriad local plants wherever it can be; it, and whole plants to make it, are also imported. It is indeed possible that fertilizer production is the most important factor in Chinese agriculture today. Between the 1950s and the 1960s, local production increased sevenfold, and the importation of fertilizer and fertilizer production plant has recently been a priority.

Another sort of change, difficult to measure, may be in the decline of traditional cosmological notions. These, commonly called *feng-shui* ('wind and water'), envisaged a cosmos of correspondences in which all elements had to be kept in mystic harmony with each other if disaster was to be kept at bay. Not only wind and water but hills, roads, houses, towns, and all the doings of men were parts of the grand pattern whose transcendent symmetry must not be vitiated. Every locality had its diviners, full-time or part-time but usually recompensed, who chose the auspicious dates for weddings, journeys or other important undertakings and read the portents to choose the sites of graves or houses. Quite often, it could be conveniently determined that an auspicious grave site might lie upon a stony hill; often it could not. Graves are still to be seen in the fields. In the 1930s it was calculated that graves occupied about 2 per cent of the farmland and 1 per cent of the crop area. It is likely that *feng-shui*, which probably militated against efficient production, has a somewhat less assertive part to play in the management decisions of collectives, though this has no doubt been a source of friction between farmers and officials.

The novelty that one might expect to be most conspicuous in the countryside is in fact among the least: the mechanisation of farming. In a poor country, labour is cheap as machinery is dear. Occasionally one sees threshing machines in the fields, and fortunate areas have tractor stations (which have seldom been free of spare parts and maintenance problems), but for the most part still men and women work with locally-made tools, moving slowly through fields with their scythes or hoes in human chains, or carrying baskets of earth from cuttings for irrigation works. It is the old bootstraps dilemma. Mechanization is one obvious route to a big increase in productivity; but a big increase in productivity is necessary to mechanization. The role of mechanization is controversial, however. The productivity it affects is productivity per man; but what is scarce is cultivable land and it is above all productivity per acre that must be raised; hence, perhaps, the special importance of fertilizer production.

Terraces are pushed up steep mountainsides, at a huge cost in labour both in their initial construction and in irrigation. Water is carried uphill in hand-held containers. Marginal areas are desperately brought into cultivation even where two years out of three they would be more productive as pasture. Every last speck of potential fertilizer is assiduously garnered. Dust from the village street is more fertile than field dust and so is carefully scraped up and carried out to the crops. Topsoil is completely dug up, dropped in a canal, dredged out again and put back in its field. All these are the characteristics of an essentially traditional type of agriculture, driven in the present century to its utmost ·limit and beyond, in a process that has been called 'agricultural involution' — a technology that, unable to make any big qualitative change, strives to achieve its effects with greater and greater complexity of old patterns. Chemical fertilizers, tractors, pumps, threshing machines, even aerial spraying — all the elements of modern agriculture may be seen in China, in the right places, and in the picture magazines, but they have only just begun to make an impact on the total scene. Their influence has not yet brought about a total change in the face of the countryside, where farmers for the most part walk, as they move about their fields, carrying the same sorts of implements that their ancestors wielded.

The most dramatic twentieth-century change in the rural scene lies, of course, in the consolidation of each village's grain fields into a cooperatively owned and managed venture. In the 1930s, when J.L. Buck's survey was made, it was calculated that each farming household farmed on average 5.6 parcels of land; these averaged half an acre each and were on average half a mile away from the homestead. Chinese farmland was a mosaic. Every farmer tilled whatever land he could get rights over, leasing or buying patches as the opportunity offered, and selling titles or relinquishing leases when necessity dictated.

Many of the small patches have gone, but many remain. The traveller still sees a mosaic of small fields, often separated by bunds. These bunds have traditionally been causes of dispute; they could be improperly breached to obtain a neighbour's irrigation water, or shifted bodily at night. They occupied a significant proportion of the arable land; but, quite apart from the area occupied by the bunds themselves, the square corners of the fields, suitable for hoeing, did not lend themselves to the plough. A possibly over-optimistic Japanese estimate during the war was that a radical reorganization of the fields could lead to a 15 per cent increase in yield.

Yet, from the individual farmer's point of view, the separate parcels often had their advantages. They were in different areas with different growing characteristics, so that the risk of general crop failure was spread. Further, they lent themselves to multiple treatment, each patch having perhaps a different sort of grain so that they would not all have to be planted or harvested at once.

The merging of private fields into communal property seemed of course to be a sensible plan, for reasons often described as economies of scale. Unevenly distributed assets like tools and draft or plough animals could be pooled and their use made more readily available to all the land and people. The savings of a large body could serve as an insurance fund, or as a fund for the purchase of assets that individual families could not afford. Manpower could be efficiently and apparently rationally organized, especially at harvest-time, apportioned in the best interests of the land as a whole. Irrigation could be managed centrally, and would not suffer from a competition of interests between small private farms each seeking to maximize its own water portion. The advantages of buying and selling in large quantities, at a chosen time, could be secured. All the minor logistic operations ancillary to farming (accounting; trips to shops; cropwatching; many more) could be more efficiently carried out. The list could be extended.

Yet most of these advantages could, in principle, have been secured by *ad hoc* arrangements made by groups of families, and the first stage in the organization of the rural population, into 'Mutual Aid Teams', did not go far beyond this. Traditionally it was already common for groups of farmers to pool their labour and perhaps tools and draft animals at busy times of the year in the interests of efficiency. This did not involve any surrender of ownership or even weaken the link between the individual farmer and the particular fields which were his by ownership or tenancy. But the first step towards collectivization was taken, after the land redistribution of 1949-52, by organizing farmers into permanent, year-round, mutual aid groups under (sometimes discreet) official pressure.

In many cases this was resented, and the situation was unstable. Responsible officials felt either that pressure should be relaxed and advance towards collectivization postponed, or that the only way to avoid slipping back was to go forwards. The latter view soon became, if not unanimously, government policy. Mao wanted it, perhaps in part because he wanted to take Stalin as his model and adapt him to China.

The next step was to form first-stage co-operatives, the lower Agricultural Producer Co-operatives, equivalent to the *dui* (*tui*) or team, in which the permanent pooling of land and animals was institutionalized and the new unit was managed as a whole. Each farmer was given work to do by the co-operative and his pay was, at least largely, a dividend on the value of the assets he had contributed, reckoned as a share of group profits.

The next stage was the higher APC or *da dui* (*Ta tui*, large team or brigade), in which the logic of this development was carried further. Collectives were large units, commonly corresponding to natural villages, in which members were no longer paid much if anything as dividends on assets contributed. Thus the link was broken between the farmer and the particular fields which he had previously regarded as in a real sense his. He had little say in farm management and distribution, and little incentive except for private plots. Pay was henceforth by labour, under the work-points system which has since prevailed. This system is largely based on the piece-work principle, but pay may be varied according to other factors including notably, in periods of political activism, 'revolutionary consciousness'. The element of discretion involved in the administration of this system opens avenues of corruption, nepotism and client-gathering to village officials.

In 1958-9, with the Great Leap Forward, came the organization of rural society into communes. According to the original directive drawn up by the Politbureau meeting at Beidaihe (Peitaiho) in August 1958, communes were to consist normally of about 2,000 households but could be up to 6,000 or 7,000 and not more than 10,000. In the frenzy of the Great Leap, when overfulfilment of targets was felt to be almost obligatory and all orthodox standards of reform and consolidation were in abeyance, village populations were at first regrouped into commune units of great size, some being reported that contained 24,000, 26,000 or even 27,000 families. At the peak of the movement the rural population was grouped into only about 26,000 communes. In the years after 1960, however, the worst mistakes of the Great Leap Forward were unscrambled; more powers were delegated to the component parts of the commune, and the biggest communes were broken up. By 1964, there were 74,000. This brought them back to the original specification, following which they corresponded to 'administrative villages' (groups of real villages) and contained 2,000 households or fewer. G.W. Skinner, in his important study, associates the revised smaller communes with the natural marketing areas, each a discrete group of villages around a market centre; considerations of distance and communications made these marketing areas appropriate units of local administration.[9]

The situation thereafter long remained fairly stable. In the 1970s communes accounted for 95 per cent of cultivated land though, within them, private plots occupied a significant proportion. The residue came into other categories of which the chief was state farms, mostly pioneering marginal farmland on the outskirts of the agricultural area.

During the Great Leap, indeed, it was claimed that communes should be 'sprouts of communism'. This meant ideally that rural society was to live communally to a high degree, and that there should be free supply of some commodities. But communes rapidly became unpopular because of the bungling, the attempts at regimentation, the mass labour on land reclamation, irrigation works, and small industries set up in the villages, and because of the confiscation of private plots. These officially consisted of 5-10 per cent of the land, on which individual families worked for themselves.

The retreat began even in 1958. In 1959 the private plots were returned, and in the summer many functions of the commune devolved to brigade (*da dui*) level. By 1961 there was further devolution to lower levels, and a half of the inefficient industrial enterprises established by communes more or less as spare-time activities were closed.

The production brigade, *da dui*, is roughly equivalent to the former full collective or higher APC, commonly corresponding to a natural large village or several small ones, with 100 to 300 or so households and perhaps a couple of hundred acres. The production team, *dui*, averages 20 to 30 households, and in practice more recently it has been within the team that many or most of the practical decisions have been made about the planning of the farm calendar, the disposition of labour and the distribution of communal income, while schools, nurseries and industrial enterprises are run by brigades or communes. But by 1980, even the teams were in many cases fragmenting.

The private plots, restored after the Great Leap, averaged about 20 to 50 sq. metres per head, and were allocated to families. They were supposed to account basically for 5-7 per cent of the land, but following a series of provisions made in 1961-2, could be augmented by a further 8 per cent for individuals to grow fodder for animals, and individuals could cultivate reclaimed land on their own account. Thus in practice private farming could amount to effectively distinctly more than the 5-10 per cent of the farmland commonly designated as constituting private plots. In places, the proportion could have been over a third of the cultivated area by the end of the 1970s. Certainly, it is difficult to exaggerate the importance of these plots to the livelihood of farming families. In 1970 it was calculated that they produced more than four-fifths of the meat and vegetables that were consumed. And the local markets for private trade, conducted since the 1960s with interruptions in times of political activism, are the chief means by which the farmer may earn a little cash to put in his pocket.

The grain grown on the public fields under communal auspices was divided several ways. There was a large retained category labelled 'tax-and-purchase' which went to the state compulsorily, and included the unpaid-for 7 per cent tax on communal crops; a further variable quantity of surplus could be sold to the state, and some could be a commercial asset, to be sold in the nearest urban market.

Of the division within the team, about 70 per cent was normally kept to ensure minimum subsistence rations for all. Those whose workpoints accumulated by field labour through the year entitled them to more than basic rations were paid the excess in cash or kind. Reserves were kept for seed, for fodder, and as a welfare fund for those families who needed it — the chronically sick, the old and the very young without able-bodied breadwinners working for them.

Where the value of a family's labour, as measured in work-points and whatever other supplementary criteria, exceeds its basic foodgrain entitlement, the difference is paid to it, as we noticed. Not every family's labour exceeds the minimum, and some must make do with the basic foodgrain entitlement paid in kind; in such cases cash may be earned only by private trade. Private trade may account for 10 to 25 per cent of income, sometimes less or more. The basic minimum entitlement is determined by the number and age of people in each family; theoretically it is supposed to guarantee subsistence. The actual value of this minimum varies substantially according to the wealth of the production team concerned. It is not surprising that farmers lavish their most tender attentions upon the private plots, which are still reserved for them to grow vegetables and fruit trees, keep pigs, and do whatever else they may to add private appetising nourishment to their collective rice. It is not surprising that the property of collectives mysteriously disappears. It is not surprising that great campaigns have been waged, with the full panoply of state publicity, to encourage farmers not to 'forget' to bring in the harvests of collective grain.

Rural wages reckoned in cash illustrate the differences that obtain between relatively well-off and relatively poor areas. In prosperous farmland near a city, adult males might each earn about 1.5 *yuan* (Chinese dollars) a day in the 1970s, about 0.60-0.90 in a more typical plains village, and as little as 0.30 *yuan* in poor hill villages. These wages would be determined according to the value of work-points accumulated by work clocked up; a change in the value of work-points could diguise a change in cash income, as when, in a Fukien village, a point was worth 40 cents in 1971, 20 cents in 1974.[10] Of two adjacent villages in Kwangtung, in 1979 a work-point was worth 0.05 *yuan* in one, 0.5-1.0 *yuan* in the others.[11]

Simple and obvious answers are not available to the questions how China's agricultural problems arise and how they ought to be solved. It might be argued that Mao Zedong's vision of a revolutionary army of farmers moving mountains, sometimes quite literally, by perseverance and willpower was a cogent understanding of the needs of the times. But there was a great deal, both in Mao's obsessive apriorism and in the circumstances in which decisions became practice, which muddied the lucidity of this vision. It could be argued that, if it is true that the growth in Chinese food production has exceeded rising population even by a small margin, this alone is a creditable achievement. Perhaps, in the long run, it may be the success or failure of population control that matters most.

Notes

1. J.L. Buck, *Land Utilization in China*, Nanking, 1937, p. 166. For cautions about the reliability of this survey see D.H. Perkins, *Agricultural Development in China 1368-1968*, Chicago University Press, Chicago, 1969, pp. 241-4.
2. J.L. Buck, *Land Utilization*.
3. P. Gourou, *Man and Land in the Far East*, Longman, London, 1975.
4. K. Wittfogel, *Oriental Despotism: A Comparative Study of Total Power*,

Yale University Press, New Haven, 1956.

5. See, for example, W. Eberhard, *Conquerors and Rulers: Social Forces in Medieval China*, Brill, Leiden, 1952. The 'oriental despotism' thesis is not generally accepted or debated. Actually, the Cambodian kingdom of Angkor in ancient times would have provided the thesis with a better example than the evidence which Wittfogel chiefly used.

6. J.L. Buck, *Land Utilization*, p. 186.

7. R.H. Tawney, *Land and Labour in China*, Allen & Unwin, London, 1932, p. 77.

8. D.H. Perkins, *Agricultural Development in China, 1368-1968*, Aldine, Chicago, 1969.

9. G.W. Skinner, 'Marketing and Social Structure in Rural China', *J.A.S.*. vol. 24, no. 1 (1964), pp. 3-43, no. 2 (1965), pp. 195-228; no. 3 (1965), pp. 363-99.

10. *China News Analysis*, December 1974.

11. Elena S.H. Yu, 'Overseas Remittances in South-Eastern China', *China Quarterly*, no. 78 (1979), pp. 339-50.

6 SOCIETY

This history recorded no dates, but over every page were scrawled the words 'benevolence, righteousness, truth, virtue' . . . but written between the lines all over it was the sucession of two words: 'Eat men'.

Lu Xun

I hope eagerly to live in a rational society. I want to smash this world where men hate men.

Chinese student, answering questionnaire

You can buy a party branch secretary for a few packs of cigarettes, not to mention marrying a daughter to him.

Mao Zedong

There is a view of the distinctive character of Chinese society which is widely shared, embedded in the self-perception of Chinese culture itself, explicit in the venerable precepts of 'Confucian' orthodoxy, and essentially false.

This is the view that in traditional China, and in traditional Chinese families today where they survive, one may find little trace of individualism, but rather self-abasement, hierarchy, dependence and an obsessive need to dissolve the raw promptings of the ego in a soothing and harmonious concert under the direction of unquestioned authority.

Confucian teaching, especially when it became orthodox, demanded that men should prize and render loyalty and obedience to those in authority. The 'five great relationships' were those between king and subject, husband and wife, father and son, elder and younger brothers, and friend and friend. In all cases except the last, the relationship was supposed to be one of respect and obedience rendered by the second term to the first.

Some modern observers, indeed, have substituted for individualism a special quality technically known as 'individuation' as a Chinese characteristic; but this 'individuation' consists of the development of the individual's potential specifically as a co-operative unit in a web of duties and relationships, and it is therefore essentially a part of the 'harmonious' model of Chinese society.[1]

Richard Solomon gives considerable attention to the Chinese ideas of tranquillity and harmony as values governing traditional social behaviour, and opposes sharply to this inherited style of life the individualism represented by the leadership and policies of Mao, whom he sees as an alien agent standing outside Chinese tradition and acting upon it in the interests of progress:

> Rejection of the dependency social orientation finds varied expression in the Maoist political style. Where Confucianism lauded the virtues of tranquillity and interpersonal harmony, Mao has made activism the key to the behavior of the ideal Party cadre. Where fear and avoidance of conflict characterized the 'cultivated' response to social tension in the traditional society, Mao has stressed the importance of criticism and controlled struggle in resolving those issues which block China's social advance.[2]

Solomon gives weight to the 'ambivalence' which he sees in the traditional attitude to authority. When authority seemed to be abused (forfeiting the Mandate of Heaven), wild and anarchic insurrections might break out. But his repeated emphasis upon the 'dependency social orientation' as a principle of behaviour (and not simply Confucian philosophy) confirms Solomon's substantial acceptance of the interpretation that denies individualism to the traditional Chinese *persona*.

This interpretation is partly true, because it accords both with certain elements of traditional Chinese perceptions of their own society and with the character of the dissimulations often exacted by requirements of politeness or expediency in a great deal of social and political outward behaviour. The part which is false is, however, more important.

Let us paraphrase an aphorism of Hobbes and lay down this principle: there can be no better proof of the scarcity of a thing than that it should be dearly cherished. Now, we notice that conformity and submission were dearly cherished in 'Confucian' tradition.

C.P. Fitzgerald has seen it clearly:

> It is difficult to escape the feeling that Confucian doctrine is based on a shrewd appreciation of the real character of the Chinese people, and endeavours to stimulate by precept and regulation the qualities which are not naturally well developed in the national character. Like the reformers of the modern age, Confucius deplored the particularism of his countrymen, and emphasized the virtues of filial submission and loyalty, virtues which, as he himself attests, were all too rare among his contemporaries. The Confucian insistence on

filial duty and the strict training of the young would seem harsh until it is realized that the Chinese, a people naturally over-kind and indulgent to children, are also averse to discipline.[3]

Chinese society was atomized: people gave respect and obedience one to another when they had to; when they did not have to, they looked to themselves.

We should not seek evidence that society was atomized from Confucian literature, except by the process of reverse inference. Literature is the deposit of realities filtered through minds, therefore selected and rearranged according to preconceptions, which are influenced by a theoretical world view.

Let us start with proverbs, which owe their currency to their aptness to realities.[4] (Some 'Confucian' sayings are virtually proverbs.)

It was, and is, a *sauve qui peut* society. Each man's hand was turned against his neighbour; when it wasn't, it was because he was too busy looking after himself.

Sweep the snow in front of your own door.
An enlightened person looks after himself.
More trees are upright than men.
Everyone gives a push to a tumbling wall.

Nobody could be|trusted:

A man who has a furtive glance and a laughing face hides in his heart a murderous sword.

— even those who (like Mao) looked venerable:

Of ten bald men, nine are deceitful, and the tenth is dumb. [Probably the reference was to Buddhist monks, though.]

In a hectic, back-stabbing rat-race, life at the top was not necessarily enviable:

He who aspires to rank and fame has not as much enjoyment as the one who does nothing.

High office is necessarily dangerous.

It was a rich man's world:

Gold is tested by fire; man by gold.
Money makes the blind man see.
With money you can move the gods; without it, you can't move a man.

In such a society, prudence was the better part of valour. The less a man did or said, the less likely he was to get into trouble. This lesson was re-learned, if it was ever forgotten, after the vicissitudes of political campaigning under the Communist Party. Here are some catch-phrases popular in the 1970s:

The beam that sticks out rots first.
When you collide with a problem, go round it and walk away.

There are countless traditional saws about the wisdom of keeping one's own counsel. In recent years they have been life-or-death principles:

Say what will please. Straightforward words provoke dislike.
When you talk on the road, remember there may be a man in the grass.
What comes out of your mouth goes into a man's ear.
Close your mouth like a bottle; guard your thoughts like a fortified city.
If your thoughts are unacceptable, keep back half of them.

In the 1970s people were saying:

When you meet a problem, be slow to open your mouth.

You might expect that, even if the warm and loving qualities of traditional morality are missing in society at large, they are to be found nevertheless around the family hearth. After all, the family is always regarded as the bastion of Chinese society.

In the 1930s, O. Lang studied social organization, and collected some views about family life.[5] How does the traditional myth of family affection and solidarity measure against the experience of some articulate writers?

The nineteenth-century reformer K'ang Yu-wei said: 'Filial piety exists in name only. In my village hardly one out of a thousand people provides for his father, hardly one out of a hundred provides for his mother.' Nor was it the poor alone who were unfilial – they had some excuse; but the rich were as bad.

Rich families were sometimes big ones, large joint families, which 'present a harmonious picture from the outside, but inside there is an inescapable and overwhelming atmosphere of hatred'. When family solidarity existed, it was solidarity in cheating the outside world. 'Their cupidity is boundless. They lie and forge documents. They become corrupt – one step more and they steal, kill, betray.'

Hu Shih, the early-twentieth-century liberal and one of the chief figures of the literary renaissance, wrote that joint family life was marked by 'frictions, suspicions, intrigues, oppression, and even suicides . . . In those rare cases where (filial piety) was consciously cultivated the price paid for it was nothing short of intense suppression resulting in mental and physical agony.'

Lin Yutang, the writer and thinker, said:

> Seen with modern eyes, Confucianism omitted from the social relationships man's social obligations towards the stranger, and great and catastrophic was the omission . . . In the end, as it worked out, the family became a walled castle outside of which everything was legitimate loot.[6]

The picture is surely very clear. The unit of interest was the atomic individual. Family links were valued so highly for the very reason that nobody could be trusted. People who had to live with each other perceived the tactical necessity of maintaining among themselves a certain minimal solidarity as protection against the outside world. To a lesser extent, the same logic applied to groups of related families linked in clan organizations.

The family was one sort of molecule; political groupings were another. Men of power formed a symbiosis with men of wealth. The whole point of entering the bureaucracy was to gain wealth and status – to be, oneself, the central atom in a big molecule.

Under the emperors, the salaries of the district mandarins commonly did not cover the expenses of maintaining office staffs, and it was understood by all that what we would regard as corruption was not an option – it was a necessity.

In 1426 an official inspector reported, of the grain administrators of Suzhou (Su-chou), Songjiang (Sung-chiang) and Huzhou (Hu-chou): 'They take about five times as much from the common people as they are entitled to.'[7]

Innumerable proverbs commemorate the way of life of the mandarin and lackeys:

An honest magistrate cannot succeed.
An honest magistrate cannot avoid having dishonest clerks.
Before a man comes into office he reproves a thousand faults; after he has come into office he commits the same himself.
If the magistrate is upright his *yamen* will be poor.
Yamens[8] are deep as the sea and their corruption lofty as heaven.

In this sort of society, power and influence fed each other. Around every official clustered people who hoped to be able to perform services, however small, in return for favours. Presents were given; friends and relatives were introduced and recommended for jobs; intelligence of the district was collected, secrets shared. The atomization of society moulded politics. Small men sought patrons; big men sought clients.

There is good shelter under great trees.
With friends at court it is easy to get into office.

To be a mandarin was to have opportunities of all sorts thrust ceaselessly at one:

Even an honest prefect may during a three-year term of office save 100,000 snow-white taels (ounces) of silver.
An official with his dogs and his chickens rises straight to heaven.

Society was divided between those who had connections and those who had not. For the latter, politics turned sour:

In life beware of *yamens*; in death beware of hell.

The relationship between theory and practice in social organization can only be obscured if we start with any perceptions contrary to those of this traditional folk wisdom. There is a sort of received wisdom that Confucian tradition entailed and imposed 'conformism', and that this stands in contrast with the 'individualism' which Western society and culture (and perhaps Maoism) have to offer. The truth, however, is that successive orthodoxies have striven, more or less hopelessly, to materialize ideals of co-operation and voluntary acceptance of legitimate authority and fit them upon a ruggedly individualistic kaleidoscope of recalcitrant humanity.

In a word, the Confucian myth needs to be dispelled. There is a communist myth also.

When the Chinese Communist Party extended its authority over the whole country, it was obliged to represent its social policies to itself and to the world in the terms prescribed by Marxist-Leninist theory — class terms. In the new government's view of the situation demanding rectification, the proper names must be applied and conformed to. According to this view, rural society was dominated by a class of landlords. who exploited the rest, and other classes entered into relationships of co-operation or antagonism with the landlords according to perceived interest. It is important to recognize that, according to the theory, it was classes as such that were the units of social behaviour. Other aspects of psychology were all secondary. Class was sovereign.

Of course, in some respects this analysis could be useful as a predictor of behaviour. Given Chinese rugged individualism, wealthy people tended to exploit poor people; *ergo*, as a tautology, wealthy classes tended to exploit poor classes. But it over-simplifies and obscures more than it reveals.

There is no novelty whatsoever in saying this. However, it is worth pausing to see how the way of looking at China as a unitary state with a civilian tradition, suggested in previous chapters, makes the class analysis particularly unsatisfactory.

In the particular circumstances of Chinese history, as we noticed, imperial governments were eventually able, in the long term, to forestall the institutionalization of local autonomy and large private liveries. So long as the challenge of baronial castles does not arise, a degree of social manipulation can be attempted that would be impossible for a feudal overlord. The first dynasties to unify China sought to ensure the equal division of landholdings among sons. This meant that the big estates of the aristocratic families (which, being the richest, were in that measure likely to have the most sons) were broken up and did not threaten the emperor.

No mere paper enactment could, of course, suffice to set a pattern for thousands of years of Chinese culture. But this particular enactment was effective because, more often than not, local estates did not turn into petty kingdoms that could flout the emperor's law. So the partition of property among sons remained until 1949 as a distinctively Chinese tradition of tenure, and the accumulation of big estates kept intact under powerful families by primogeniture over the centuries, as in England, did not come about. Big estates at times there certainly were, with hordes of retainers: but they took the decisive last step, and become vassal states with armies, much less often than in other countries such as India, even in ancient times. In recent centuries, it has been much more normal for family estates to be relatively small and without armies. M. Elvin called it 'manorialism without feudalism'.[9]

Under the emperor and his bureaucracy, therefore, by the nineteenth century, local power centres were miniature, consisting most often of those families in each village which happened, for a few generations, to rise well above the average in wealth and property, and thus to become nodes of clan allegiance and patronage.

The pattern of social mobility in China is important to the way the structure worked, and is obscured by the conventional categorization of 'gentry' and 'peasants'.

There were several routes to elevation, none with the guarantee of security for the family. One was success in farming. By hard work, good weather, good luck, low cunning, or a combination of these, a family might so increase its affluence as to employ servants. But a few bad years could ruin it all, and, in the long run, usually did. The legendary profligacy of the spoiled sons of wealthy parents, and the division of property among sons likely to be numerous because affluence favoured survival, made it difficult for a family to stay powerful for more than a few generations. At certain periods of Chinese history, though not in recent centuries, there were indeed large family estates; they did not, however, in the long run turn into miltary power centres.

Two routes to respectability lay through its opposite. Merchants and criminals were not respectable. By orthodox standards, commerce was considered ungentlemanly and ranked below farming; and once a man had made his money by trade, it was his natural ambition to buy land, engage a tutor, and merge himself with the gentry.

Similarly, there was always an underworld of gangsters, secret societies, wheeler-dealers, smugglers, and outright criminals. It attracted younger sons and the destitute, and for the lucky few it brought riches and, when a man chose to retire, respectability. Memories could be short.

But the most important avenue to advance was success in the examinations and appointment to office. The Chinese have traditionally valued education so highly, not because of the sovereign influence of an arbitrary cultural value, but because it was the way to get on. The attitude has, to some extent, perpetuated itself in the modern ambition of poor parents to have their children become officials (though it has seldom been more true than in the last three decades that 'high office is necessarily dangerous').

Up to a point, office could be self-perpetuating. It was a certain way to riches, and riches allowed a good education to be bought for sons — who would have the added advantage, presumably, of a cultured home atmosphere. Mandarins cultivated long fingernails and wrote poetry. There was a very good chance that one son at least would follow his father's footsteps.

But even this was much worse security for a family than a gilt-edged English country seat. In bad times the jobs available were far too few for well-qualified applicants. There was thus something of a lottery about it. Turnover in families with members in the mandarinate there certainly was, although it slowed down a great deal in the latter part of the Qing dynasty.[10]

These circumstances matter to the analysis of any social engineering that the present regime may have wrought.

In Chinese villages, the circumstances we have reviewed did not, at least in the last couple of centuries, allow families to climb very high before they fell; the range was small. L. Pye writes: 'In general, the gentry had pathetically small landholdings, and only those who got into government could hope to amass fortunes significant by any standards.'[11]

For the earlier part of the present century, there are various discrepant estimates made of the distribution of property among landlords, smaller farmers and tenants; some of them are guesses influenced by theoretical preconceptions, and it is impossible to believe them all simultaneously. It is arguable that the most reliable calculations are those of J.L. Buck's survey in the 1930s.[12] Some would dispute this claim; it must be acknowledged that the sample areas examined were small and not necessarily representative; but the examination was thorough. According to Buck, farms cultivated directly by their owners average 4.2 acres, while tenant farms averaged 3.56 acres. More than half of all farmers were owners of the land they cultivated; something under a third were part-owners; 17 per cent were tenants. Owner-farmed land was over four-fifths of the cultivated area in the northern plains, three-fifths in the Yangtze basin and about a half in other major areas. According to M. Elvin:

> The amount of land held by landowners who did not themselves farm was clearly too small to serve in and of itself as an adequate basis for a distinct and dominant class. This picture is confirmed by the Com-

munist land-reform documents from Kiangsi province during the same period. The differences between those catalogued as 'landlords', 'rich peasants', 'middle peasants', and 'poor peasants' were so fine that there was constant difficulty in assigning persons correctly. In Sheng-li county, for instance, the initial investigation turned up 1,576 'landlord' and 'rich peasant' households. When Mao Tse-tung did a follow-up survey, he uncovered 536 more such households. Subsequently however 941 of the new total of 2,112 managed to clear themselves of 'landlord' or 'rich peasants' status. Mao also complained that: 'The majority or the great majority of landlords and rich peasants in many places . . . have not yet been found out.' Such a statement only makes sense given a social continuum with a restricted overall range.[13]

The village communities to which land reform came at the beginning of the 1950s (earlier, in Communist-held areas) were, then, not squirearchies. The social change to be wrought upon the 80 per cent of the Chinese population living in the countryside was not the suppression of an upper caste but the bestowal of rewards upon an often arbitrarily designated winning side at the cost of those identified as losers. Power, wealth and mutual assistance were distributed in each village according to the tactics of constantly scheming factions; the better-off found themselves patrons of parties, and the parties waged Corsican vendettas against each other. Each party had its clan links and its richer and poorer members; some parties were richer or poorer as a whole than others. Certainly, the haves oppressed the have-nots – not because they were a conspiring class, but because in principle everybody was prepared, pre-emptively, to oppress anybody else, and the haves were temporarily in a better position to do so. Individual villagers were not congenital rogues – they were trapped into a situation not of their own making.

Alliances shifted according to tactical exigency among struggling families of varying wealth but common Machiavellian views. This year's winners could be next year's losers; a lawsuit, a gift, an inheritance, a theft or a cunning piece of business could make an underdog into top dog, or *vice versa*. That something like this was (it still is) the prevailing social order is dramatically illustrated by W. Hinton's vivid documentary account of a village during the land reform campaigns, *Fanshen*,[14] and all the more impressively in that it was not exactly the author's intention to do so.

Into this tangle of bucolic Montagues and rustic Capulets came the

Communist officials, often strangers from distant areas, to decide who were the exploiting landlords and who were the deserving poor.

Ostensibly, between 1949 and 1952, a minority of wealthy 'landlords' were expropriated and their land given to the poor and landless. Not surprisingly, the labelling was difficult, because lines were hard to draw. Officially, a 'landlord' rented out land and did little or no labour himself; a rich peasant engaged in *some* labour; a poor peasant had *little or no* land of his own.[15] Elaborate and artificial rules had to be drawn up to decide whether a man was a rich peasant, or a middle peasant, or whatever. How many members of a man's family could engage in manual labour if he was a rich peasant? Should the assessment be based on the amount of land that people had then, or had the previous year, or had the year before? Barrack lawyers had a field day, and the final assessment − which often did not come until several years after it was officially all over, after appeals and revisions − was likely to be determined as much by alignments of village politics as by the realities of any 'class' system. In the long run, certainly, genuine poverty genuinely helped, and the new rules, for a game with big rewards and fearsome penalties, accelerated a realignment influenced by actual wealth and poverty; but the spectrum was so narrow, and the local politics so confused, that a straightforward and uncontroversial resolution could seldom be achieved.

But, if a class sytem did not exist, it was necessary to invent one. Those labelled as poor peasants were supposed to remain poor peasants ever after, even though officially, in the collectives and communes that have come since, there was supposed to be no significant private property.

Whether or to what extent the new government actually succeeded in creating an egalitarian society is another question, influenced by many complicating factors. Much depends on one's terms of comparison. Martin Whyte has shown that differences between various classes and occupations in education, wealth and opportunity for advancement have diminished in some ways, but that very marked inequalities persist.[16]

What happened to Chinese society was only partly that the weak rose up and overturned the throne of the strong. It was partly that an attempt was made to freeze village politics at a particular point, to draw a line around those parties considered potential friends of the regime and another round those considered potentially hostile, and to make a regular aristocracy of the first, regular outcastes of the second. The mechanism is very like that of the Japanese Tokugawa Shogunate's institution of a special class of lords considered friendly, the Fudai daimyo, who were given central estates, while the less reliable daimyo were given outer estates. It is an attempt to embalm society in the posture of an ancient victory.

It is necessary to recognize that the purpose behind these manipulations was to make the government's writ effective. Like emperors of the past, the policy-makers were confronted with the all but impossible task of enlisting the co-operation of a poor and obstinately individualistic populace in programmes of welfare and betterment that by their nature require the acceptance of authority and the merging of private interest with the general good as perceived by those in power. In a way, this analysis reverses Solomon's.

Like mandarins expected to keep order in turbulent cities, the officials have found themselves constrained to make their weight felt by recruiting allies. Mandarins could keep order after a fashion if they bought the co-operation of powerful underworld bosses. The present regime has succeeded in promulgating far-reaching innovations that make an impact on the life of every individual in the country by enlisting the support of local power constellations. But the underworld bosses remained underworld bosses; and the parochial parties remain parochial parties. The history of political campaigning has been in large measure a history of doomed efforts to change their nature. After each phase of each campaign, the governors have seen that the officials directly concerned behaved parochially, and instituted a new phase in which they would be criticized and reformed by the level of officialdom directly above them. W. Hinton's *Fanshen* exhibits this seismic rhythm clearly, showing how by a natural impetus tremors rise upwards towards the government.

The vocabulary of politics grew to incorporate the jargon-names of many heresies of which officials might be guilty. They are all names for varieties of traditional behaviour. 'Commandism', for example, is the tendency of officials to throw their weight about. 'Tailism' is any tendency for officials to do as little as possible, to fit in with local expectations.

From the very beginning, those who were given authority saw no reason not to use it, much as the secretaries and treasurers of clan or temple organizations or the bosses of secret societies used theirs. One of the first major enactments of the new regime was the marriage law, under whose compassionate provisions men should dispense with second or later wives and concubines, in the interests of the dignity of woman. But there was sometimes a want of compassion in the execution. Local officials, often yokels with rubber stamps, used rank to compel unwanted divorces. For them, there were old scores to pay off; there was fun to be had; there were wives to be seized for themselves. In many provinces there were literally scores of suicides a month in the years 1950-2.

The Great Leap Forward was not conceived as a lucky dip for rural officials, but many of them saw the opportunity to make it so. In the general turmoil of the reorganization there were pickings to be had. Since the policy was to create everywhere canteens, crêches and kindergartens, local bullies with rank could confiscate household utensils and possessions from hapless farm families on the pretext that they were to be made anachronisms by the new communal living. On the orders of petty despots, crêches were made compulsory, and mess halls established, even where there had been no planning and there was no proper equipment.

The Cultural Revolution frightened Party members and officials of all sorts, but when it had faded away life returned to normal. In every enterprise or institution of any size, in every city ward, in every village or production brigade, there was a 'revolutionary committee' and wherever possible a party branch. All of the men and women in these bodies carried weight. But it was the party branch secretary whose word counted for most. It still is.

He is the man who can decide, if he plays his cards right, which instructions from above are carried out and which not. He can manipulate the allocation of work-points. He can turn a blind eye to smuggling and profiteering. He can arrange transport for a trip into town, or admission to a good school or university for a client's child, or free medicine. He can require 'landlords' or any other counter-revolutionary elements to spend long hours in tedious study sessions, or arraign them for petty offences, or let them off if they can give him something for it. He is not, of course, an absolute despot; he is harnessed by multitudinous rules and conficting orders and supervision from above; he knows that if the political wind changes direction he may without notice become the target of persecution and officially sanctioned abuse; this may have happened to him before; he has seen it happen to others. Perhaps indeed he is honest and conscientious and does a good job. But the pressures on him are great, as they were on mandarins. If he began his career as an honest man, he may have become embittered by callous vendettas against him. He is unlikely to be blind to the prudence of salting away a few savings, forming discreet friendships with the breeders of pigs, or the managers of government car pools, or the smugglers of wristwatches, or the fathers of beautiful girls. It is an old game, though the rules are written in a new language. He does not cultivate long fingernails; and he does not write poetry; but he is in a way the heir of the same traditions as the mandarins.

One of the white hopes of agricultural modernization used to be the tractor stations, on the Russian model, which maintained pools of tractors for the surrounding countryside; but in the 1960s many reports spoke of corruption among their staffs, who could cook the books and pocket the income from the 'squeeze' which they put on communes hiring their vehicles. On the farms, brigade and commune officials used their position to benefit from the possibilities of private enterprise far beyond the prescribed limits, rearing ducks and pigs, using collective land, borrowing collective possessions for their own use. At the higher levels, official connections were valuable in obtaining educational advantages. There have been many reports of officials getting their children into university illegally, by the back door.

Officials are not all bad men. They are often the victims of circumstance. Many have been the reports of inefficiency, laziness and avarice on the part of the good citizens whom the officials were supposed to infuse with revolutionary zeal. They are not necessarily culpable inefficiency, laziness and avarice — they may be those of people, disillusioned by China's continued poverty and by persecutions and switches in policy, whose folk wisdom and bitter experience convince them that no good will come of man's officious striving to improve on the natural order of things, that to conform outwardly to what is required and get away with doing as little as possible is the only sensible policy, and that if a man doesn't pick up a dropped cash, somebody else will. In the Great Leap Forward, grain was consumed more or less on the spot or stowed away for the benefit of production teams who were supposed to hand it over to the state. Disorder broke out in many places as officials sought to re-organize the population on a huge scale. Wells were poisoned; officials were attacked; animals were slaughtered for private consumption.

Again in the Cultural Revolution rural discipline weakened. In Jilin (Kirin), there were reports of trees on the forested slopes being illegally cut down and sold; property of all sorts belonging to collectives was sold; truancy increased in the villages. Villagers would prefer busying themselves in private trade to working in the collective fields, where their labour was less well rewarded, and adjusted by a number of factors other than the amount of work they put in; it was even worth a fine of two yuan a day to go and trade in the city. Farmers lacked incentive to work on communal fields unless compelled; in 1971, a report from Hunan said: 'Where the party's policy does not drive the peasants on, the spring sowing is lax.' Official instructions have frequently exhorted farmers not to 'forget' the harvesting of grain on collective fields.

In the cities, workers took advantage of the turmoil of the Cultural Revolution to take holidays and (for a while in 1967) to go on spending sprees with the firms' money disbursed to them by managers. In the 1970s, the many disgruntled former red guards in the labour force were a constant inducement to strikes, absenteeism, disobedience and riot. The black market has thrived, with high prices for gold, silver, opium, lighter flints and many little luxuries.

There is still an underworld. Foreign visitors do not usually see the black market at work (they do in Russia), because they are usually under constant official scrutiny. When they are not, their foreignness is unmistakable, and they tend to attract attention. It is probably still sometimes the case, as it certainly has been in the past, that everybody who comes into contact with them, from hotel managers and interpreters to laundrywomen, is subject to rigorous supervision by anonymous superiors, to whom they make reports on every trifling incident; but the extent to which this would happen would vary a great deal with the campaigns and political climate. In accordance with the world view described above, to have contact with foreigners is, after all, to go beyond the Great Wall: there must be a scrupulous quarantine for the possible infections. It is therefore not surprising that the property of foreigners is as safe as if they had arrived in flying saucers with a luggage of inscrutable Martian electronics. But to whatever extent the liberalization of the years following Mao should lead to foreigners being a common sight in the cities, and to closer and less restrained contacts as part of the policy of learning from foreign things, it is to be expected that foreigners should increasingly experience both the benefits and the disadvantages of being an accepted part of the scene.

Among the Chinese, the millennium of honesty has not arrived. The doors of town flats have locks, because of course 'we are still living in the socialist phase' — it will take full communism to supersede locks and keys. Crimes are still committed, as in every other country. Mass executions have recently been known.

The atomism and individualism of Chinese society, so screened by myths as to be too little recognized by the outside world, have an important bearing on the prospects of the modernization programme vigorously prosecuted in the late 1970s and early 1980s.

As was suggested tentatively above, the long course of Chinese history demonstrates a paradox: openness to the outside world has hindered economic development by enhancing the conditions of fragmentation, corruption and insecurity, but, on the other hand, insularity has also hindered economic development by restricting the activity necessary to it. Under Mao, there was a period of insularity. After Mao, there began a period of openness.

Now, whenever a big prestige building is bought for an overseas embassy, whenever a mammoth contract is drawn up with a multinational firm to build factories, whenever a licence is bought to manufacture a Western product in China, or whenever battalions of skyscraper hotels are built for foreign tourists and armies of interpreters, cooks and drivers are trained to deal with them, money is moved about in large quantities: and whenever this happens another blow is dealt at the precarious edifice of the Chinese 'revolution', shallow as its foundations are.

For the 'revolution' has been able to move towards its goals only to the extent that it has been able to suppress the countless centrifugal impulses of a naturally atomized society.

Mao's men introduced a puritan ethic difficult to sustain. Every army commander, every factory manager, and in the measure of his rank every official was and is surrounded by temptations to self-aggrandizement, corruption, 'squeeze' and influence to which it has always in the past been traditional to succumb. The puritan ethic, if it was to be enforced, needed constant encouragement, example and (especially) correction from above, but from 1949 onwards the question arose, as it always must, *quis custodiet ipsos custodes?* (This is indeed a problem inherent in Marxism-Leninism. If morality is only class morality, and if only proletarian morality is correct and the party expresses the will of the proletariat, then there is no need for custodians.)

The prosecution of Mao's 'revolution' encountered diminishing returns. By the 1980s there were men sitting behind desks in all parts of China to whom the new movement of 'modernization' spelled not so much (as it does to Western minds) pragmatism, sensible decisions and emphasis upon technical problem-solving as the accelerated revival of a whole traditional ethos – the *sauve qui peut* ethos of entrepreneurialism, bribery, jobs for nephews, carefully nurtured business friendships, and what by Western standards is termed corruption, though it is traditionally an accepted way of life. It is an ethos in which a huge gap opens between government plans and real life. The plans are made, but little happens as a result of them except that some officials become richer and some army officers become more powerful.

Power corrupts. Wang Dongxing was accused (and if such abuses did not occur, there would have been no point in making the accusation) of requisitioning over US$4.2 million equivalent to build for himself a luxury residence in Peking with a gymnasium, a cinema, and 17 suites of rooms for his children. Officials at all levels certainly used their positions to get the best housing available; theoretically state-owned houses tended to turn into the family property of officials. And housing is just one of many illegal perquisites. An official delegation to Japan included 600 'delegates' of whom two-thirds were family members going on holiday for the shopping. Officials going on tours of inspection in less exciting rural areas could still expect to be treated well by those on whom they reported. A tour in Guangdong by 70 officials (surely one or two could have done the job, and told the rest when they got back) was banqueted with 50 kg of pork, 15 snakes, one cow and two sheep.

Teachers, recovering from the humiliation and trauma of the Cultural Revolution period, began to feel safe enough to return to the practices which had made them victims of militant pupils. Evidence mounted of fraud in getting favoured pupils through the university examinations. Officials who wanted to get their children 'through the back door' in this way doubtless gave a few presents to those who assisted. Humble shop employees found pickings: half of a consignment of 50 foam rubber pillows (a scarce luxury) disappeared before it hit the front of the shop. Even those in charge of groups of urban youth sent to remote country areas had power to sell favours (for upon their word depended their charges' chances of ever getting back to civilization), and one enterprising Casanova in Heilongjiang caused all the 96 girls under his care to visit him privately in turn for special political education sessions. A girl who had been a heroine of the Cultural Revolution, now employed as a cashier in a fuel enterprise, embezzled 350,000 Chinese dollars in seven years.

Such reports could perhaps be paralleled anywhere; remember though that what is reported as news in China is reported for a purpose, not because it is interestingly exceptional, and the purpose is often to identify and solve widespread problems. The villainess of the last case above was shot.

Very well known to be widespread is the bribery involved in getting business transacted. Overseas Chinese dealing with local authorities, regularly had to make presents. One, visiting relatives in the countryside had to give a colour television set (the most favoured form of *pour-boire* these days) to a brigade head to avoid having to wait forever for an exit permit. Another foreigner had to make a present to a shipyard foreman to get his vessel repaired. Such cases are innumerable; they are taken for granted.

That officials could be expected to use their influence to set justice aside is demonstrated with especial clarity by the way in which their children behaved. These were the young aristocratic bloods whose tastes for the sweet life it was the responsibility of the world to gratify. Twin sons of one official in Hangzhou (Hangchow) perpetrated 106 rapes. Plebeian youths discovered that merely by pretending to be sons of the great they could attract a dream-fulfilling servility from all and sundry. One, claiming to be the son of a provincial First Party Secretary, easily got free first-class train travel and a promise of betrothal by a father anxious to be well connected. In another famous case, a young visitor to Shanghai, representing himself as the son of a deputy chief of the General Staff, was able to spend two months living the life of Riley. Shanghai dignitaries who thought that he would be able to bring his father's influence to bear on their behalf showered him with favours. He was given free theatre entertainment, introduction to actresses, the use of a car, spending money, and not least a girl friend whose parents were enthusiastic about the connection. When the case came out, the *People's Daily* aptly commented that what was alarming was not so much the specific episode as the fact that it could happen. If a youth could expect such favours from strangers, it is obvious that the whole ethos was one in which officials threw their weight about as a matter of course. There would be no point in publishing the news that Hua Guofeng went to his daughter's school on foot (not in a sybaritic car, of course) and insisted that she be sent to the countryside like any normal school-leaver unless it were common for politicians to use their influence on their children's behalf. Again, the lesson of the swamping of Peking in 1979 by provincial petitioners, who were sent back home with 1,000 crack troops to solve their problems, is that provincial authorities were too corrupt for justice to be available locally. We had a look at the behaviour of rural officials above. There was no reason why the passing of the Maoist era should reform them. Many of them continued to use power quite arbitrarily, imprisoning factional enemies, levying fines for trivial or imaginary offences like sowing seedlings the wrong way. Illegal levies were exacted from co-operatives who were compelled to part with 10 per cent of their profits for 'public construction'.

Public construction was for purposes decided by local officials, often to the benefit of themselves and their friends, who hankered after the relaxation of club rooms with abundant recreational facilities. An official in Hebei conscripted the labour of 600 farming men to build party committee offices and halls for no pay; another in Shandong conscripted 150 schoolboys quite illegally to cut over 200 acres of sesame and beans on commune land.[17] Officials could expect to get their way with impunity in all matters, great and small. A story published about Lin Hujia is that, while he was a mayor of Tianjin, he went to a bakery and stood patiently in the queue (noblesse oblige). Some officials jumped the queue, expecting to be served first and given the best bread. Lin remonstrated with them, and they arrested him. What is significant about this story is that it is regarded as plausible that arrests should be made in such circumstances and on so slight a provocation.[18]

This then was the social background for the modernization of industry, and it is not surprising that it made for inefficiency. The economy got the worst of both worlds: overplanning directed by officials with political and personal rather than professional motives, leading to waste and lack of co-ordination, and separatism on the part of individual enterprises, which were often able to keep going only by defying the intentions of the planners and which became little empires working against the best interests of the econmy as a whole. They withheld taxes whenever they could. It was estimated that in one city taxes not paid to the province totalled 38 million *yuan*. Illegal transactions abounded between different enterprises. In 1977 it was picturesequely estimated that the successfully detected illicit deals in Hunan and Shaanxi alone were worth enough to pay twice over for the cost of the Peking-Tianjin railway line, while in the Jilin banking area idle and misappropriated funds amounted to 61 million *yuan*.[19]

All this is the dark side. But obviously the whole picture was not so dark as to drive away the canny overseas Chinese businessmen who were thoroughly aware of all the pros and cons, and rushed to invest in China when the chance came. Indeed, they were enthusiastic, and saw the long-term prospects as sufficiently alluring to compensate for the teething troubles made inevitable by an underdeveloped industrial culture. Small businessmen subcontracted the stitching of shirts; giant conglomerates waded in with contracts to build monstrous luxury hotels that would (like the Chinese official with his chickens and dogs in the proverb) rise to heaven. What matters about the social background to industry is not that the push to modernization must fail –

though it may well succeed more slowly than many optimistic observers, including some governments, think. What matters is that the centrifugal forces in society are a threat to the integrity of the state that must be carefully skirted.

Notes

1. Derk Bodde, *China's Cultural Tradition*, Holt, Rhinehart, Winston, New York, 1959, pp. 65f.

2. R. Solomon, *Mao's Revolution and the Chinese Political Culture*, California University Press, Berkeley, 1971, p. 513.

3. C.P. Fitzgerald, *China. A Short Cultural History*, Cresset Press, London, 1935, p. 88.

4. Chinese Proverbs, including many of those cited here, may be found in W. Scarborough, *A Collection of Chinese Proverbs*, Shanghai, 1927; J.F. Dawson, *Chinese Wisdom and Wit*, Melbourne, n.d.; H. Dawson-Gröne, *Ming Hsien Chi*, Hong Kong, 1911.

5. O. Lang, *Chinese Family and Society*, Yale University Press, New Haven, 1946. For the samples which follow, see p. 113.

6. Lin Yutang, *My Country and My People*, Heinemann, London, 1938, p. 180.

7. M. Elvin, *The Pattern of the Chinese Past*, Eyre Methuen, London, 1973, p. 92.

8. 'Government Office'

9. Ibid., pp. 69-83.

10. Ho Ping-ti, *The Ladder of Success in Imperial China*, Columbia University Press, New York, 1962, pp. 102-25.

11. L. Pye, *China, an Introduction*, Little, Brown, Boston, 1972, p. 78.

12. J.L. Buck, *Land Utilization in China*, Chicago University Press, Chicago, 1937.

13. M. Elvin, *The Pattern of the Chinese Past*, p. 255.

14. W. Hinton, *Fanshen, a Documentary of a Revolution in a Chinese Village*, Vintage Books, New York, 1966.

15. See W.L. Parish and M.K. Whyte, *Village and Family in Contemporary China*, Chicago University Press/London, 1978, p. 98.

16. M.K. Whyte, 'Inequality and Stratification in China', *China Quarterly*, no. 64 (1975), pp. 684-711.

17. *Asia Week*, 5 October 1979, p. 18.

18. *Asia Week*, 17 October 1978, p. 15.

19. *China News Analysis*, 9 December 1977.

7 THE FAMILY

A man thinks he knows, but a woman knows better.
There is no such poison in the green snake's mouth or the
hornet's sting, as in a woman's heart.
If you love your son, give him plenty of the cudgel; if you
hate your son, cram him with dainties.

Chinese Proverbs

An interesting trend noted at the beginning of the 1970s was the resurgence of 'clan-ism', which one might have expected to be long dead by this time.[1] Officials in Hubein (Hupei) villages were said to be corrupted by 'feudal clan relations', and gave favours according to family connections. In a Guangxi (Kwangsi) brigade, control of the leading offices was seized by a single kin group. In a brigade in Fujian (Fukien) there were two one-clan villages which had been in the past, and remained, mortal enemies to each other. In Ningxia (Ninghsia) a commune party secretary was lauded for his success in reconciling three clans, the Yang, the Ma and the Zhang (Chang), which had been at daggers drawn, the Yang having been able to monopolise most official positions. In Zhejiang (Chekiang) a dispute between two clan villages prevented the materialization of an important project for an irrigation canal. In Fujian, it was found that clan groups were appropriating for themselves collective property such as chemical fertilizer, insecticide, timber and grain. In one commune, 'clan-ism' went with bribery and theft; kin groups were able to make themselves bastions of corruption and illegality. These cases were singled out as 'negative examples' in the press; they were not regarded as trivial, for obviously the practices which they represent were sufficiently widespread to receive serious attention.

Nepotism, the unfair preferment of one's relatives, is a term not happily applicable outside the celibate eclesiastical order in which it originated, but it has become so widely current with an extended sense as to be indispensable. In a society dedicated to the values of family and lineage, it is of course sons rather than nephews that benefit from the survival of family loyalty and the solidarity of clan groups; but brothers, uncles, nephews, and even these days sisters or aunts may come in for a share of whatever pie is on the family hearth. There seems to be no shortage of evidence of family solidarity in modern China, and examples such as these described by John W. Lewis could easily be multiplied:

> In the No. 6 Production Team, related members of the Wang family
> (not just individuals with the surname 'Wang') appear in all parts of
> the hierarchy, while in the second team the Yang family predomin-
> ates. In still another production team in Kiangsu which received
> national recognition in 1960, moreover, the team leader is Liu So-
> chin. His first elder brother is a secretary of the party branch, his
> second elder brother is a work group leader, his fourth younger
> brother is an 'advanced worker', and his two sisters are Young Com-
> munist League members. For a team of 105 households, it is highly
> revealing that this single family has attained such a pervasive leader-
> ship position. The 'proletarian' relationships among family members
> must be of an order different from the strictly neutral relationships
> dictated by Communist ethics.[2]

To be sure, William Parish and Martin Whyte, in their major study of
modern Chinese society, wisely distinguish between unfair preferment
and family tradition. That sons should follow fathers into positions of
authority, or that several members of a family should hold public office
in a village, need not of itself entail collusion or nepotism. It may
reflect what they describe as 'common socialization into a strong ethic
of public service',[3] particularly when public service involves hardships.

This caution needs to be borne in mind. Village officials, particularly at the level of the team (a small village or a group of households
within a village) stand to gain little from their service, have few strings
to pull, and must suffer the obloquy of those whose farm labour they
supervise. But at the level of the brigade (a large village or a group of
villages) things are different. The brigade leader has his feet on a ladder
of real power. (Reporting a local power conflict, Parish and Whyte tell
us that 'If the attack on the brigade secretary failed, he could make
their lives miserable.'[4]) Some of the statistics presented by these
authors conflate information about team and brigade officials, yet it
seems desirable to draw a line below the brigade secretary but above
team officials if we are to detect the characteristics of power politics.
When we learn, for example, that 100 per cent of brigade leaders in the
(admittedly very small) sample studied had sons with at least a junior
secondary education, as against 72 per cent or fewer of other officials
and 54 per cent or fewer of parents who were not officials,[5] the
suspicion does obtrude itself that those with power in the village seek
preferment for their own families. We would need more information

than is given before any conclusions could properly be drawn about this sample, but in connection with nepotism there is no need for it – at all higher levels of politics the proclivity of those in authority to seek advantage for their children by the 'back door' – by unfair preferment – has long been notorious.

None of this is surprising if we recollect that what happened in 1950-2 was not exactly the abolition of an old society; it was to some extent, in effect, an attempt to impose new rules on it in the interests of a new regime. The old antipathies, often dominated by clan connections, have continued ever since; sometimes the originally disadvantaged clans have learned how to work the new rules.

So far, we have been concerned here with the social order as a whole, and we had discovered that traditional alignments, such as kin, are still important. The survival of 'clan-ism' bears this out. It is therefore desirable to narrow the focus and turn to the micro-society of the family.

The traditional values of submissiveness, conformity, harmony and so forth might well appear to reflect the equally traditional patriarchal family institution in which the authority wielded by the father and husband is paramount. In an ancient agrarian civilization like China, the household was controlled by the father, and at least in theory his authority had traditionally to be accepted unquestioningly by his wife and all younger members of the family. If his own parents were still living they had a claim on his obedience as long as they were active; when they retired from work and became dependent or senile a less simple relationship could develop in which he had to exercise responsibility tactfully and continue to show outward deference. Status can be exchanged for power.

This much is traditionally accepted theory, and to some extent it is practice – even now, in the rural areas. Despite all the campaigns against old family ties, the antique patterns persist to a much greater degree than is often realized. But it follows from the conception of social atomism offered here that the submissiveness and conformity in the family may often be extremely precarious, founded on considerations of interest and property.

Bottled-up frustrations would, certainly in the past, often explode into passion, suicidal or murderous. Individual temperament might override *mores*; hen-pecking wives and insubordinate children were well enough known. We should not assume that the naked authority of the father automatically made for harmony and contentment. On the contrary, the relationship between father (seeking to control and retain his patrimony) and son (seeking to share and succeed to it) had rivalry built into it. To some extent, order of birth would affect family relationships: oldest sons, though not benefiting from primogeniture, were usually favoured, getting preference over others in education and in choice of bride.

Traditionally, high value was put on having many sons and large households; but this does not mean that the average family size was in fact large, though the myth that the Chinese extended family was universal still has some popular currency outside China. Kinship ties have always been important — more so than consideration of 'class' in the Marxist sense — but actual household sizes among all but the wealthy have been modest. Census figures from former dynasties (Han, Tang, Yuan and Ming alike) indicate an average of five to six members. This would probably not take account of all infants in many families, but in most families many children died in infancy. The same average holds for the present century, with the most typical household patterns being the nuclear family (parents and their dependent children) or the stem family (nuclear family with the father's parent or parents still living). The extended family (brothers with their wives and children living in their old parents' household), though idealized, has been realized chiefly only by wealthy families, which might have up to eleven or twelve members or even more. In such families, wealth could create the conditions in which infant mortality was less common. But it was normal for grown sons to take their wives and their shares of what little family property there was and set up on their own as soon as possible. Families of four were, as well as are, common among the poor.

The question of family size is relevant in various ways to the prospects for success of the present regime's demographic policies.

Although from time to time Chinese politicians have made statements implying that the more Chinese there were the better it would be, in line with Marxist orthodoxy, the dangers of overpopulation have been recognized in China since the time of the Qin Minister Han Feizi (Han Fei-tzu) and are certainly not neglected now. On the other hand, ordinary Chinese people have long been in the habit of wishing and trying to have as many sons (and therefore, in the absence of selection methods, as many children) as possible. The task for the government is therefore not simply to make family planning possible; it is to change people's habits of thought. When birth control was first encouraged by the present regime, it was often said to be directed to the physical well-being of mothers (not to any economic goal); more recently the economic reasons have been openly stated.

A reason that has often been given for the desire for many sons is that, in a religious culture dominated by ancestor cults, men believed that the happiness of their spirits after death depended totally upon the availability of sons and descendants ever after to conduct the ancestral rites before their tablets. If this were the whole truth, the present government's undoubted concern to suppress traditional religious culture would of itself be a sufficient strategy.

But there is more to it than this. The farmer's desire for sons is compounded of various elements, and is by no means a product of ignorance or superstition (not that Chinese folk cults should be dismissed in such terms anyway). Despite the common view, there are few more hard-headed and rational beings than farmers in poor countries. They have to be if they are to survive.

In the first place, even quite small children could in the past, and still can even in collectives, make an important economic contribution to a family's welfare. For one thing, by performing simple routine tasks like weeding, or tending pigs and chickens, or keeping an eye on babies, they can release adult earning-power for productive labour that yields work-points on the collective fields, or cash from the state purchasing co-operatives or profits at the frequent free fairs for private produce. For another, many of the tasks performed by children could contribute directly to the family income. The gathering of grass for fuel, or herbs for medicine, or of snakes for sale, as well as the care of animals kept for private profit and help with money-earning sidelines like mat-making could make a very welcome increment to the family's resources.

Again, good health can never be taken for granted, and many parents deliberately chose to have children as early as possible with the thought that, if in their thirties they contract TB or any other of the protracted illnesses (such as bilharzia) which are a permanent hazard of the simple rural life, the children may well be old enough to earn work-points and exploit the private plots. Production teams have scant welfare funds to protect the sick and the old; poor ones frequently have very little if anything left in the kitty to spread around after making the basic grain provision to keep people alive.

The same considerations apply even more obviously to old age. A man or woman too old to work and without children is entitled to support under the 'five guarantee' system (food, clothing, medicine, housing and burial expenses), but especially in a poor area this is a very feeble second-best to being properly looked after by filial sons; rural welfare is administered not nationally but locally, largely at the level of the team, and its standard necessarily varies enormously with local conditions. If old people have daughters but no sons, welfare provisions may be made grudgingly or not at all; but even today for various reasons daughters have much less earning power than sons, so the traditional preference for boys in the family is fortified. In the sample studied by Parish and Whyte, only 6 per cent of those over 60 were receiving 'five guarantee' maintenance. 'Most welfare assistance in rural localities depends upon kinship roots or upon the limited resources and willingness of the team.'[6]

Another traditional motive which may not have lost all its force is the desire to have a son who will get on in the world and bring wealth and honour to the family. In the imperial past, this meant a son lucky or clever enough to pass the examinations and become a mandarin. The more sons, so it was believed, the greater the chance that one at least would be successful. Even for the poor, this was not necessarily always a totally fanciful daydream. There was always the chance that a few good years or an unexpected inheritance, or a kind, rich kinsman, might bring a family from below to above the average condition of wealth, and that with hard work and help from clan finances an education could be provided for a sufficiently promising boy. (This used to be recognized as a good cause and was a popular type of charity, for all members of a clan or even a village, and their friends and relations, stood to gain by the elevation of one of their sons.) During the earlier republican period, the path to advancement was uncertain and dangerous, but with the rapid and gigantic expansion of desk jobs in the 1950s the old motives must have revived. Even though the spin-off from the earnings of an official is not so great now as were the prospects of largesse from association with a mandarin, there are more officials than there were mandarins and the ambition is now more realistic.

And there was always little to lose. At each new conception, there was always a substantial likelihood that the child would die at birth (umbilical cords used commonly to be cut with grubby pottery shards, to mention one of innumerable hazards), or die in infancy. It would add little, by itself, to the family's economic burden during infancy, and it would soon start being useful, either releasing adult labour or earning money directly.

As for the real possibility with each birth of death for the mother, we must not forget that there were often decisive psychological compensations for her. She lived in a man's world, was bound to the house, had a great deal of work (often under the sour and despotic autocracy of her mother-in-law), and enjoyed little share in the occasional luxuries that could be afforded. Her children, after their first few years of life, came under their father's authority and ceased to regard her as the dominating source of love, comfort and guidance. What has made life worth living for most country women has usually been the pleasure of looking after babies and watching them grow.

Things have changed in recent years, but the changes, though now gathering pace with many sanctions such as the withholding of ration cards for non-conformists, have not been immediate and complete. Later marriages have been favoured, to keep the birth-rate down and to maximise the mobility and efficiency of young workers; but people still like to marry in their early twenties and have children early as insurance for the future. Still, as in the past, they prefer sons. Young daughters have a way of marrying and going to live in or near their husband's families' houses soon after they have begun to earn adult wages to put in the household kitty; young men can rarely afford at once to set up house on their own and continue to contribute their work-points to the family welfare, with the assistance of their wives. When they move out, they usually stay nearby and are available to help their parents. Besides, whatever may be official about equality, men earn more then women — about eight to ten work-points where women earn six to eight.[7] Naturally sons are preferred to daughters. It is not surprising, then, that birth control programmes in China have been slow to bite. While an extra child entitled a family to a higher basic grain allowance and more land to cultivate as a private plot, government policy, even without intending it, offered incentives to multiply children. The campaigns of the 1950s and 1960s were half-hearted and abortive.

But, since the 1970s, something has at last been happening. With better publicity, more widespread information, new methods of birth control and improved administration of the programme, Chinese parents have begun to heed the wisdom of having fewer children. A particularly effective part of the system is the levying of sanctions against those who have too many children; for example, a fourth child may entitle the family to no more rations of grain, cotton, sugar, oil or fish; and positive material incentives are offered for volunteering for sterilization or abortion.[8] Parish and Whyte in their study of rural society survey the suggestive evidence that birth control has been catching on, however belatedly. In some cases, practical experience was teaching the need for population control to the villagers. One informant said:

> No one opposed the movement — they have learned their lesson. Before, the brigade population was only 600, but now it is 1,400 plus. So there has been an increase of over 100 per cent in recent years, and everybody understands the need. The economic difficulties of actual life persuade them. Now people don't think that many sons will pay off later . . . Now the concept of 'more sons more wealth' is already undermined by practical experience.[9]

If Chinese parents should cease to desire sons as the *summum bonum* of felicity, the consequences are bound to be favourable for the position of women. Such favour would be not before time.

The sage Fu Xuan (Fu Hsuan) said: 'How sad it is to be a woman. Nothing on earth is held so cheap.' In hard times, female infanticide was often practised, though in the nature of the case figures are not available to measure its prevalence. But even in good times girls used to be neglected much more than boys, who attracted more and better food, more medicine, more warm clothes, more attention generally and greater expenditure whenever scarce resources made it impossible to give good care to all the children in a family. As recently as the 1930s, Buck's figures showed a ratio of boys to girls of 108:100,[10] which probably reflects differential attention as well as infanticide.

Though differential attention is unlikely now to have disappeared, it has probably been much reduced. Another traditional handicap inflicted upon women which now belongs to the past is the curious custom, for which the Manchus may have been largely responsible, of footbinding. This involved binding up a girl's feet in infancy so that as they grew the toes were forced beneath the foot and broken. Women were crippled for life, barely able to hobble out of doors. The custom was so widespread as to be normal in the wealthier households; economic necessity prohibited it for poor peasant families, who could not dispense with the labour of their womenfolk in the fields, but otherwise it was accepted and proper.

One type of explanation of the custom is social: if a man had a wife with bound feet it showed that he could afford to do without her labour, and thus possessed a mark of status whose absence would have been a brand of poverty

Another is sexual: Chinese men happened to like women with tiny feet, which featured in sex play. *Chacun à son goût.*[11]

Both these explanations leave it surprising that half the population, the disadvantaged half, should acquiesce and participate in self-mutilation for centuries. A third type of explanation, also social but less obvious, points to its survival value. Like some other customs, it can be seen as the institutionalization of habits that will carry society through hard times. Just as it can be argued that the Indian sanctity of the cow helped, among other things, to dissuade starving farmers from slaughtering all their stock in a famine and blighting their prospects of surviving beyond it, so it could be argued that, where small children faced death from cold in the north and disease in the insalubrious paddies of the south, nothing was more important to the rise of each generation than that children should be properly looked after indoors. The contribution made to a family's posterity by the housebound mother is obvious.

The status of women is of course another matter in which the success of government policy must wait on slow social adaptation to changing realities which are complex and often difficult to identify. The subjection of women cannot be legislatively 'abolished', any more than can the Indian caste system.

Government policy is embodied pre-eminently in the marriage law of May 1950. This did many things. It set minimum marriage ages of 18 for women and 20 for men (thus outlawing the institution of 'little daughters-in-law'). Divorce could be obtained by mutual consent. Compulsory betrothal by parents was made illegal, as were infanticide, bigamy and concubinage. Wives could keep their unmarried names; husbands and wives had equal rights of property.

Whatever the intentions, the immediate consequences were not totally felicitous. The implementation of policy, however wise, lay in the hands of junior officials who did not necessarily have emancipated views. Many well-off men had second wives or concubines who were relatively happy with their lot, at least when they contemplated the alternative to it, which might be destitution. All these were abruptly, often callously, flung out of their homes. Suicides were numbered in the thousands.

Girls were often treated as chattels as in the past. In the early 1960s, work teams discovered numerous abuses in the countryside:

> In the Hua-wu brigade at Ao-chiang, eighteen girls of an average age of fourteen years were sold at an average of 750 yuan each. In Pai-sha there is a girl who has been married thirteen times. In some places girls are sold like hogs at so much a catty. Even worse is that some people make a business of buying and selling girls. They get

fifty yuan merely for making an introduction.[12]

In the long run, no doubt, women have benefited, though much more in the towns (where expensive facilities and sophisticated officials are more likely to be found) than in the villages. The differential is not new. From the earlier stages of modernization, there have been, in the families of the urban well-to-do, many politically active and well-educated women (the Soong sisters are a notable example) determined to enjoy an occidental style of freedom in their studies, their employment, their dress, and their marriages.

Now, in larger towns, women are freed from many of their burdensome household chores by the provision of kindergartens and crêches in factories; and working mothers have two and a half hours off a day to nurse their babies. In the early years of the present regime, the number of women working in factories rapidly grew.

In the countryside, where of course the overwhelming majority of women live, the case is not always the same. Crêches and kindergartens are relatively few. Possible reasons for this that have been suggested are that the chaos and disorganization that attended their institution as part of the commune movement of 1958-9 put people off them for good, and that even the modest cost of putting a child in a nursery, often one work-point a day, can ill be afforded by poor farm women who prefer to use any babysitter, however unsatisfactory, and save the money.

Changes have occurred, but the traditional family has not been destroyed. Probably the biggest agent of social change is urbanization, but the country cannot yet afford any dramatic increase in the proportion of the population that can be spared from the farmlands (for centuries it has been about a fifth). Some people think that since 1950 there has been a net transfer of population from towns to country. This, if true, would be remarkable, and could not augur well for industrialization. Since the 1950s, certainly, the government's concern has been to keep people from migrating to the cities, lured by the false promise of a more comfortable life, only to turn into an uncontrolled and unproductive class of unemployed. The frequent rustication campaigns, involving the transfer of large numbers of officials and students or ex-students to the countryside, represents among other motives the desire to keep the cities from growing unmanageably. Migrants need certificates to move into cities, and cannot get ration coupons without certificates. Even when they take up jobs in cities quite legally, they frequently have to leave their families behind.

The condition of life enjoyed by factory workers in China, in comparison with that of farmers, makes them something of an elite as well as a minority. Obviously we should not judge the country as a whole ·from a partial knowledge of urban conditions without taking into account these differences between China and Western countries. The slowness of urbanization is one reason why the traditional family is not dead. Most young men still live in or near their parents' homes. There are other reasons. The family is the significant unit in production; the welfare system treats the family as a whole in applying criteria to select recipients for benefits; the private work which is often all-important in putting cash in farmers' pockets between harvests is conducted by families, largely on their private plots – pigs, chickens, fruit and the products of scavenging (for fuel, herbs and so forth) or handicrafts. Cash paid for a pig may equal the cash obtained over a whole year, over and above the basic grain allocation, for collective work; the pig is known as the 'farmer's bank', and the obvious pun is appropriate. Certainly, the position of the paterfamilias as owner of the soil or as contracting tenant has been very much weakened; but he is still the owner of his house and nearly all that is in it, and usually the biggest earner. A big campaign in 1969-70 to change family relationships, with the old accepting the guidance of the young, fell flat. And the old spirit of clan allegiance is not dead either.[13]

Continuities in Chinese social history there obviously are. But it would be a rather sterile game merely to juggle with evidences of continuity and change; obviously there are both all the time. The Chinese family is living in an age of transition; this is not remarkable, because all ages are ages of transition. What matters is that for want of good evidence we should not imagine the present transition to be more rapid than it actually is.

Notes

1. *China News Analysis*, December, 1971.
2. J.W. Lewis, *Leadership in Communist China*, Cornell University Press, Ithaca, NY 1963, p. 238.
3. W.L. Parish and M.K. Whyte, *Village and Family in Contemporary China*, Chicago University Press, Chicago, 1978, p. 113.
4. Ibid., p. 109.
5. Ibid., p. 110, Table 15.
6. Ibid., pp. 74-7.
7. William L. Parish, Jr. 'Socialism and the Chinese Peasant Family', *Journal of Asian Studies*, vol. 34, pt. 3 (1975), pp. 613-30.

8. W.L. Parish and M.K. Whyte, *Village and Family*, pp. 138-42.

9. Ibid., pp. 152f.

10. J.L. Buck, *Land Utilization in China*, Chicago University Press, Chicago, 1937, pp. 375-6.

11. See H.S. Levy, *Chinese Footbinding: the History of a Curious Erotic Custom*, Walton Rawls, New York, 1966.

12. W.L. Parish and M.K. Whyte, *Village and Family*, pp. 160f.

13. W.L. Parish, Jr. 'Socialism and the Chinese Peasant Family'.

PART THREE

BUDDHISM AND THE COMMUNIST POLITICAL ORDER

8 BUDDHISM AND POPULAR CULTURE

This Part begins with a prediction. However irrelevant Buddhism may seem to modern Chinese culture now, it will in the coming years emerge bit by bit as an influence of no mean order upon the national psyche; and the forms of its influence will appear, not to have re-emerged after long eclipse, but to have been always there. It is therefore proper to give it special attention.

This attention is unusual, because it is usually Confucianism that commands our notice. There are those who say that in China the past refuses to lie down dead, but their argument is usually nothing to do with Buddhism. It is the mandarin, not the bonze, who has discarded his robes; and he has put on the new-pressed uniform of the commissar.

Let us list those characteristics which can most easily be twinned with those of the 'Confucian' tradition:

1. The country is run by an essentially civilian regime, not a military dictatorship.
2. The government depends on a bureaucracy of commoners, not aristocrats, who are ideally at least recruited on the strength of their presumed familiarity with, and devotion to, an established orthodoxy of state.
3. This orthodoxy embodies a code of social morality, deprecates all other-worldly religious belief and practice, denies the legitimacy of any alternative claims on the citizens' intellectual loyalty, and seeks to inhibit or control any form of spontaneous communal organization that is not expressly licensed by the state.

These parallels are not coincidences or conceptual artifacts. But how useful, after all, is such a game of continuity-hunting? Perhaps it is just a *jeu d'esprit*. Levenson disapproved of the attempt to identify the present with the past:

There are those, with a taste for paradox, who feel that the new regime is 'in spirit', in real content, whatever the surface forms of revolution, Confucian forever . . . From this point of view it is enough to remark that (give or take a few degrees) both Communist and Confucian China have been institutionally bureaucratic and despotic, intellectually dogmatic and canonical, psychologically restrictive and demanding. And for those who balk at forcing Confucianism and Communism to match, there is still the 'Legalist' label for Mao's China . . .

 If, in such a timeless, noumenal version of continuity, China were 'always China', the place of Confucius in Communist China would be pre-ordained, and empirical inquiry gratuitous or fussily misleading. Yet, if only out of piety to history (or, less grandly, in defence of his occupation), a historian has to assume the authenticity of phenomenal change . . .[1]

 This is well put. But 'the authenticity of phenomenal change' is a vague notion, as protean as, say, 'Chinese character'. Obviously, some things change, and other things stay the same. It is certain that the regime established in China since 1949 (so far as one can generalize about a series of governments over such a long period) is not 'really' just an old-style Confucian system in disguise. It is equally certain that it is not a new materialization *ex nihilo* of some exotic monster without kin or affinity to anything that has gone before.

 What is not legitimate, or at least is no good answer, is the appeal to 'Chinese character' as an explanation of apparent continuities. Some things stay the same, it might be said, because they belong to the native genius of the race. Chinese culture is so distinctive that the 'Chineseness' of China has always exercised a fascination upon outsiders. Even those who most assiduously certify the ways of old China to be irrelevant to the understanding of the 'revolutionary' present bear witness to this fascination: the more studiously we ignore a thing, the more homage we do to it.

 But to say that some things have stayed the same because they belong to the Chineseness of China is a tautology, not an explanation. What is this Chineseness? Is it in the soil, or in the genes, or in a racial ideology which, once hatched in the mists of time forgotten, has ever since governed the psyche of the race that begat it? None of these is plausible. We can only say that some of the circumstances which influenced the development of Chinese culture in the past continue to be effective today; what these circumstances are remains to be discovered.

 Let us add to our list of the features of modern Chinese politics. The resemblances to Confucian orthodoxy soon disappear when we examine such elements as these:

4. The philosophy of state, however much adapted to the Chinese genius, is in essence and origin an exotic creed, begotten in the West and imported as an alternative world view.

5. It is a philosophy specially calculated to appeal to those who have suffered; it is nothing like a code of behaviour for prosperous and contented gentlemen; on the contrary its protagonists can argue that it is a gospel of compassion for the wretched of the earth.

6. It offers a total and self-contained cosmology, an account of how the world and its history work in which the individual can discover a meaningful and satisfying place for himself.

7. History has shown that, by whatever adaptations, it has in at least some periods — notably periods of crisis — acquired the active allegiance of broad masses of ordinary people, however tenuous their understanding of its higher principles.

8. It is pre-eminently associated with dissidence, rebellion and social upheaval.

9. It looks forward to an ideal state in the future, rather than backward to a golden age from which all good values are to be derived.

10. Whatever may be the corruption of its principles in its practical working out, it preaches a social equality that can give hope to all men.

11. In particular, it offers emancipation to women, who can find in it a new self-respect and opportunities for worthwhile careers.

12. Those who dedicate themselves to a political career under its dominion are expected to cut themselves off from the family bonds and cultural pursuits of their past life and take on a new identity.

13. They are expected to display in public an austerity of life-style that is almost puritanical.

14. In ridding themselves of the taint of their old life under the influence of traditional culture, they may be required to undergo induction processes and periodic study sessions leading to severe psychological stress.

15. The philosophy of state declares that man is subject to the conditioning forces of past history, but at the same time offers to those of its practitioners who gain true insight into the forces of history the hope of breaking through its constraints and rising to a higher plane.

16. It preaches, and constantly impels people towards, a form of collective community living that is almost monastic.

Some of these elements, of course, represent a rather idealised view of Chinese Communism; they take little account of all the confusion and half-measures that characterize the living reality forming the matter of earlier chapters here. That does not matter, for the present concern is with ideas. What we can observe from this list is that the Chinese political order is quite unlike the traditional Confucian orthodoxy. Indeed, it is just such features as those just listed which generally seem to identify the Chinese Communist regime as in important ways distinctively 'modern', and for precisely that reason best studied with the tools of political science rather than history.

That is as may be. What follows may help us to see how true it is, and it may later prove useful to refer back to this list. Here, we are not going to examine further the similarities, or the differences, between Confucianism (or Legalism) and Chinese Communism. This subject, it might well be said, has already been done to death. But what modern observers of China have accorded little or no attention, and what therefore will prove of special interest here, is the part played in China by Buddhism and the questions to which many Chinese have seen it as the answer.

Confucianism and Legalism have often enough been taken seriously as factors in the 'old society' commonly now thought to be abolished, or being abolished, because they are in an obvious sense political. Buddhism is not usually taken seriously as a clue to Chinese culture either old or new because it does not look political enough to count. Therefore it is generally ignored, or dismissed with generalizations of careless simplicity. This is a mistake.

There can be no doubt of the importance of Buddhism to China down to modern times. In 1948 an observer wrote:

> The one thing which is certain is that Buddhism has so affected the character of the Chinese as a whole that it will continue to bear fruit even if the tree from which it grows is no longer clearly identified.[2]

Here is 'Chinese character' again, but we need not cavil at it. The expression is harmless so long as it is regarded as a label on a sealed box — a set of observed continuities in Chinese history whose causes remain unspecified. It is dangerously unhistorical only if it is taken to imply some particular theory about the causes, such as the autonomy of ideas or the genetic inheritance of national character.

Buddhism, then, is a part of the Chinese character in a sense, and, however transmuted, it survives still. It represents an outlook, a psychological need, a distinctive way of addressing the obstacles that impede the yearning for fulfilment. It is not a separate exhibit in the museum of culture, standing alongside equally separate exhibits identified as 'Confucianism' and 'Taoism'; rather it is more like a colour woven into a tapestry. Its influence, then, cannot be measured by counting the heads of a distinct 'Buddhist' congregation, or by listing the supposed achievements of the enthusiastic educated laymen responsible for the so-called 'Buddhist revival' earlier in the present century. Chinese Buddhism has exercised its influence as a set of memories and aspirations, not just as an institution; and the memories and aspirations might well persist (indeed they do) even when the institution is in eclipse.

Take the counting of heads in congregations. In a generally very valuable sociological study, we meet a neat tabulation of the religious affiliation of a population sample in a particular *xian* (hsien) or county. From it we derive the impressive intelligence that (among other things) 14.4 per cent were Buddhist, 13.6 per cent subscribed to the ancestor cult, and 43.6 per cent professed no religion.[3] What a misleading exercise! Chinese religious life is a blend of traditions which is the possession of the whole community. At most periods during many centuries past, a typical family in the countryside would be quite likely to conduct its own ancestor rituals, pray and make offerings at Buddhist shrines, consult Taoist priests, solemnly pass on Confucian precepts, and tell its children stories from the rich native mythology of adventures with demonic spirits and celestial journeys. Some families might have special links with particular temples and therefore come to profess a particular allegiance; most would not. It is not surprising that 43.46 per cent of the sample assigned themselves to the category called 'no religion'. It is as if a sample of the general population were asked to identify itself exclusively as followers of science, engineering, arts or 'don't know'.

It would likewise be misleading to identify Buddhist influence with the institutional activities of the educated evangelists who sought to fit Buddhism for the modern world. These activities, however pious, were sometimes eccentric; and their effects have often been exaggerated.

In 1928, a Western visitor, James Pratt, gave this description of the Buddhist New Youth Society in Peking (as cited by Holmes Welch):

Its headquarters were in one of the rooms of the Kuan-in Ssu, near the Parliament Building, and its equipment at the time of both my visits consisted of a set of teacups . . . On my first visit to the headquarters I was told that they had two hundred members; on my second that they had five hundred. I do not think the membership really more than doubled during my absence. I think both answers were prompted by hope rather than by statistics, and that at my second visit hope had more than redoubled. For hopes should be mentioned along with tea cups as a part of the really very useful equipment of the association. The officers of the association, I was told, planned to have several schools, a Buddhist university, and many preaching places . . . On taking my leave I unfortunately inquired as to the size of the audience at their bi-weekly preaching service, and was told that in the spring they hoped to have a large attendance; but that as a fact just at that time they hadn't any preaching services at all. Since my visit (I am informed) the association has been temporarily disbanded.[4]

Many Western missionaries or Buddhist sympathisers who have investigated the Buddhist revivalist activities of the 1920s and 1930s have taken the claims of the revivalists too much at face value. In fact, they have much the same relation to reality as have all the monumental plans for the transformation of economy, education and society drawn up by successive governments in Peking or Nanking throughout the republican period (and, one might almost add, the Communist period as well).

It is best to judge the institutional strength of Buddhism not by the count of congregations or the manifestos of dreamers but, in a safe traditional way, by the population of the monasteries and convents where the acknowledged professionals of the religion were to be found. Buddhist monasteries have dotted the Chinese landscape since the period of the Three Kingdoms at least, in the third century AD. Chinese Buddhism is as Chinese as rice or noodles. In 1930 there were said to be about half a million monks and a quarter of a millon nuns living in about 233,000 foundations scattered all over the country. Clearly, the proportion of ordained monks to lay population compared well with that of a typical general practitioner or a parish priest to his flock in a Western country today. We must remember, though, that the distribution through the country was very uneven — monks were particularly numerous in eastern central China, and very sparse in some other areas — and that they functioned not as parish priests but as coenobites, congregated in communities in each of which the majority would make no pretension to sanctity, wisdom or even education, and would have very little contact with the lay world.

Here our concern is with the cultural forces with which in China

Buddhism came to be largely though not exclusively identified. It is not with Buddhism as doctrine or soteriology. The original or 'essential' content of Buddhism as a belief is too often and too easily misunderstood – perhaps it is not even prudent to claim to understand it – to be seriously examined here. But this omission raises a vexed question: is it legitimate at all for a student to look upon a religion as a play of social forces and ignore its meaning as an often passionately maintained belief in the minds of its devotees? Some scholars see religions as languages which groups of people use to express their vision of themselves and their society; some insist that religions must be seen from the inside as sets of ideas with a life of their own. Hobsbawm sees religious movements as representatives of a pre-political stage of social development; Cohn sees them as outlets for the despair of the deprived; Wilson sees them as instruments giving solidarity to social classes; Weber wrote about Chinese religion (often with valuable, though uneven, insight) as evidence for his social theories. Against the sociologists, Y. Talmon maintains that we must recognize the autonomous causal agency of religious beliefs, which do not simply express people's ideas, but form them; Eliade argues that we should investigate the actual meaning of a religion for its devotees and recognize the independent exercise of its influence upon them; D. Overmyer, examining folk Buddhist religion in China, asserts that each movement must be taken as a whole and that it is not legitimate to siphon its real religious meaning out of it by artificially subdividing it into separate categories.[5] Here then is a dichotomy: social scientists want us to look at religions from the outside; religious historians, from the inside.

If it is really necessary to take sides, perhaps it is better to side with the religious historians. But is it necessary?

Obviously, a religion that influences anybody at all influences some parts of the world and not others; it spreads in one direction, not another; it influences people at one time and not another, in one way and not another. There are necessarily specific historical cirumstances responsible for all these differences (perhaps geographical, economic or social), whether we can recognize what they are or not. It is legitimate to investigate these circumstances. Such an investigation treats a religious movement as a social phenomenon, from the outside. It is more likely to succeed if the investigator first makes some attempt to understand it from the inside. Some investigators, seeing their material more as sociological theory than as human beings, produce results that are crass or glib. What is wrong then is the glibness or crassness, not the attempt to analyse a religious movement as a social phenomenon.

Here we shall briefly review the sects of Buddhism that grew in China and the influence they exercised upon popular religion. Such an exercise must look upon these sects as social events rather than as autonomous ideas, but this circumstance does not automatically render the exercise valueless. Its value here lies in the conclusion that, after the passage of many centuries, the elements of popular religious aspiration which Buddhism chiefly endowed were messianism, millenarianism and utopianism. This is not a negligible lesson. It is a lesson which might help us to make better sense of the history of the last 40 years in China than a great deal of narrowly political analysis.

There is another element, which is not a part of popular Buddhism but which matters historically because of its status in the Buddhist community. The generality of village laymen certainly did not imitate or understand, but they certainly respected, the demanding exercises to which the most dedicated and holy of the monastic brethren addressed themselves in the quest for salvation. These exercises consisted pre-eminently of the rigorous courses of meditation prescribed by *Chan (Ch'an)*. The very fact that these monks enjoyed such prestige entails that whatever they were trying to do must have had some special resonance in the unsophisticated cosmology of everyman. Now, *Chan* is a discipline of meditation that deprecates discursive thought and preoccupation with material things. It is so far nothing like the ideology of People's China. Let us note, though, that it enjoins austere self-control, seeks to point directly to the soul of the practitioner so that he may see into his own nature, and promises enlightenment in a flash of insight, independently of any mere mechanical expertise. There may, in all seriousness, be something to ponder here.

Chan transliterates the Sanskrit *dhyāna*, 'meditation', the name of the original Indian school. Its twenty-eighth patriarch, Bodhidharma, reached China from India in AD 520 and became the first patriarch in China. It is said that a Chinese ruler boasted to him of his generous patronage of Buddhist foundations. 'After all these endowments that I have made, how much merit have I earned?' asked the ruler. 'Nothing at all', replied Bodhidharma, and turned away. It is also said that Bodhidharma spent nine years in meditation sitting facing a blank wall. These may not be the most important facts about *Chan*, though they illustrate its contempt for conventional standards. But what facts can be said to be important? The whole point of *Chan* is wordless intuition independent of anything that is written in books. To state facts is to use words; to use words is to falsify. (Taoism says the same thing: those who know do not speak; those who speak do not know.)

Chan is one of the eight sects conventionally reckoned to constitute the establishment of Buddhism in China during the early period between the Han and the Tang (T'ang). Another is *Qing tu* (*Ch'ing t'u*), 'pure land'. Based on a group of scriptures describing the pure land or Western Paradise in which all true believers are to be reassembled after death, this sect was founded in the fourth century AD and became influential in North-Western China in the sixth century. Eventually it became extremely popular in China as a paradise religion — and, as *Jodo*, in Japan. The loving detail in which it dwells on the felicities of heaven, and the simplicity of the means it offers to get there, endeared it to generations of poor men leading drab lives in a bleak landscape. All too facilely, it matches the image of religion as the opium of the people, but there is more to it than that.

Zhen Yan (*Chen Yen*), the equivalent of the Sanskrit *mantrayāna* school, was the last arrival of the Indian sects transplanted to China, being founded there in the eighth century. This is the school of esoteric doctrine and secret ritual, using *mantras* (spells) and *mudrās* (secret signs). By its nature, it did not seek a broad popular following, but the tantric type of religion it represents became extremely influential in Tibet.

The *Hua-yan* (*Hua-yen*) sect, *Kegon* in Japan, takes the *Avatamsaka sūtra* as its scripture; its chief early teacher in China was Fa Zang (Fa-tsang, AD 643-712). Its strong suit is the distinctively Mahāyānist philosophy of immanence which declares the cosmos to be non-composite: each part of the universe is actually identical with the whole of it. In such apparent contradictions we find the logic of paradox which, like *Chan* though in a different way, defies conventional patterns of thought. This sort of thing is strong meat for the ordinary villager; among studious monks, however, *Hua-yan* gained a considerable following.

Fa-xiang (*Fa-hsiang*) represents in China the *yogācārin* school which was founded in the fourth century and introduced to China in the seventh by the famous pilgrim monk Xuan Zang (Hsuan Tsang), whose odyssey to India in search of authentic Buddhist scriptures inspired the sixteenth-century fantasy story *Monkey* which has been translated by Arthur Waley and is well known in the West. Institutionally, this sect did not long survive as a major force in the Chinese Buddhist community. It dependended for its early success chiefly upon the prestige of Xuan Zang himself, but its doctrines were Indian or central Asian recipes deliberately chosen by the master for their authenticity, not for their aptness to Chinese taste, and they did not prove popular in the

Chinese kitchen. For all that, their essential teaching of 'mind-only' or subjective idealism was in the long run a very important ingredient in Chinese Buddhist thought. Life is just a dream; therefore monkeys are as important as emperors, and ghosts are just as real as palaces and revolutions. Where nothing is real, everything is possible. Mountains can certainly be moved. Here there is much to appeal to the poetic imagination – and also, let it be said, however indirectly, to the political.

Tian-tai (*T'ien-t'ai*), *Tendai* in Japan, was named in China after the mountain where the sect had its headquarters. Its great teachers in the sixth century were the patriarch Hui Si (Hui-ssu) and his disciple Zhi Yi (Chih-i). It offered a synthetic Mahāyāna doctrine based upon the *Lotus Sutra*, the widely popular scripture which offers vivid descriptions of the ethereal splendours of the Buddha worlds and declares that the Buddha exists, has always existed, and always will exist. Here lay the potential for a devotional religion. In the ninth century, the Tian-tai patriarch developed the teaching that the Buddha is in everything – in every grain of dust – giving special emphasis to the Mahāyāna doctrine of the immanence of the sacred or ultimately real in the phenomenal world.

The *Lü* sect, founded by Dao-xuan (Tao-hsüan) in the seventh century, is devoted to the study of the *lü* or discipline (Sanskrit *vinaya*), the rules which a monk must obey. There were 250 rules for monks, 348 for nuns. Writings on Buddhism, in China or elsewhere seldom give very much importance to the nature of the training of monks as a formative influence upon the character of the religion. In fact, it is the living heart of the faith. Some monks in Theravada countries, where Buddhism is still unfettered, will tell you that the doctrines can be ignored (after all, they are just words); what matters is the self-aware acting out of life itself in accordance with the rules. Perhaps fortuitously, there is an echo here of some of the ideas thrown up in the history of Marxism-Leninism-Mao Zedong thought. We shall see later on something of the significance of monastic training.

The *San Lun*, finally, is based on three texts of the Indian *mādhyamika* school. Nāgārjuna is generally recognized as its founder around AD 200; the three most influential texts of the school were translated into Chinese early in the fifth century by the great translator Kumārajīva. The doctrine of this school seeks to point the believer towards direct intuitive or mystic insight by purporting to prove that rational thought is impossible: no logical arguments about the universe are coherent; all views whatsoever contain latent contradictions. Nāgārjuna was aware of the paradox, which the reader may have spotted, to which this argument may seem to commit him (it is like the well-known Cretan Liar paradox)[6] ; he argued that it did not follow.

Now, these eight sects are not the only ones which grew on Chinese soil, but they are conventionally reckoned as the basic ones belonging to the formative period. During this time, up to and including (very irregularly) the Tang dynasty, Buddhism was frequently patronised by rulers, particularly rulers of foreign origin during the period of disunity (AD 221-589) when China was dismembered and nomad warriors founded dynasties in conquered territories in the north. Under the Tang, when China was reunited, some rulers (especially the Empress Wu) gave Buddhism special favour, though there were others who, spasmodically and arbitrarily, persecuted the faith. In its heyday Buddhism enjoyed the august status of national state orthodoxy. It alternated uneasily with Confucianism, which always remained *par excellence* the ideology of the Han Chinese scholar-official class, and with Taoism.

From the Song (Sung) dynasty onwards (Northern Song AD 960-1127; Southern Song AD 1127-1279), things changed. For the first time, the majority of the Chinese population lived in the fertile south, which supported China's frequent periods of prosperity and the entrenchment of her tradition of imperial unity which was interrupted only during the Southern Song. For most of a millennium, the country had a centralized administration staffed by a regular civilian bureaucracy. Almost without intermission (though the Mongol invaders gave their preference to Buddhism), Confucianism was firmly established as state orthodoxy. In large measure, it is true that many of the country's best talents were attracted to the service of the state. Confucianism attracted their intellectual loyalty. The Neo-Confucian movement of the Song dynasty poached on the domain of Buddhist philosophy to add a dimension of metaphysical speculation to the secular social morality to which the name of Confucius was attached. Buddhism continued to feed the imagination of educated Chinese, in their leisure hours; but its most conspicuous influences were upon the religion of ordinary people, who found in it a rich mine of colourful ritual, myths and magic. Above all Buddhism came to be the nation's psychopomp. While Confucianism had no medicine for death, and Taoism offered medicines that did not work (some emperors had died of Taoist potions for immortality), Buddhism had much to say about the hereafter and taught people how to cope with the tribulations of their passage to it. It therefore came to busy itself particularly with the rites of the dead.

Perhaps the dichotomy is too facile, but let us make it all the same:

Confucianism was official, Buddhism was popular. Today, Communism is official. It is obvious that there is no simple isomorphism between Buddhism and Chinese Communism; but that is not to be expected anyway. We should expect, rather, to find parallels between Chinese Communism and Confucianism, and as we have noticed above they exist, however many differences there may be. This does not mean that we may not hope to find in Buddhism, as an ingredient in popular culture, some interesting clues to the workings of modern Chinese minds, including the minds of politicians.

The dichotomy may help us to see what may reasonably be expected and what may not, but it carries a snare with it. The line between the official and the popular is not the same as that between high culture and superstition, or between the pure and corrupt. The distinction has too often been overlooked. Those who have studied Chinese Buddhism have found the earlier centuries more interesting, and concentrated upon them to the neglect of the more recent period. This has encouraged the rarely examined supposition that, after the Tang, Buddhism declined. Students of modern China, usually little interested in religious affairs, have noticed that Buddhism in popular Chinese religion has been often corrupt, venal and ignorant, and have taken these indications as a sufficient index to the character of Buddhism in general. A totally misleading picture of the status of the faith in China has therefore become current.

Every faith has different levels of practice; it is usually thought proper to judge a faith by what is distinctive of the higher levels. We do not assess Christianity by the sanctity of a sexton, or the theology of a grave-digger, or the morals of a vagrant or ragamuffin attached to an army in the Crusades. Such people as Jesuit missionaries may seem more representative, though they are less numerous. Chinese Buddhism has always had its conspicuous and substantial contingent of loafers, criminals and nitwits. Many monks took ordination to avoid paying taxes, or to evade the arm of the law, or to desert from an army, or to escape destitution, or because they couldn't think of anything better to do. Many laymen, and, particularly, laywomen would make their ritual offerings at Buddhist temples with no more sophisticated motive than to secure the fulfilment of a selfish wish by the purchase of a little apotropaic magic. But there was more to Buddhism than any of this.

Here are two contrasting cases presented by a sympathetic Western observer. They are of monks that he met during his travels.

It was in this monastery that I met a monk who had only recently entered the Order. He had been an officer, and relished a gay life to such an extent that he still put on military uniform from time to time and went out in search of pleasure. It was well known that he indulged himself in meat and wine, possibly in still more dubious pleasures. Though the officials of the monastery complained about him, nobody thought of turning him out altogether. 'Poor fellow. Where would he go?' they said.[7]

The second case is also of a former soldier, an educated man who became an officer in a warlord army. This army was pulverized in 1927 by the Kuomintang, and he, now a beggar and a fugitive, entered the order, though he had previously had no interest in Buddhism whatsoever. There could be no less promising beginning to a religious career. Yet little by little, and chiefly through the friendship of a wealthy lay patron of his monastery who helped him in his studies, this man was drawn in. Earnestly and piously, he devoted himself to an austere course of study and meditation. Slowly, he made progress. In his own words,

> From then onwards I have found myself making good progress in the practice of meditation. That, again, is something which I cannot describe; I can only say that my life is full of peace and of that true happiness which is to be distinguished from the empty pleasure of desire fulfilled. In the silence and stillness of my own mind I find the answers to all the riddles of life.[8]

For the purposes followed here, it is desirable to look at those forms of Buddhism which have had the widest influence; so we must look at some of those practices which are most liable to seem debased or corrupt. But this is not to deny the continuing potency of a tradition of piety, erudition and sanctity that has always been at the core of Buddhist life. The wanderer through the temple precincts may see an uncouth and ignorant monk fit only to beat a wooden fish for a dollar a day, but should not forget that in the meditation hall there may be other monks who sacrificed comfort and status to wrestle, as they sit cramped and chill in the dawn, with the ultimate enigma of their own existence.

But the Buddha's way was never intended to be the possession of a privileged few. As he said himself, the teaching is not clenched secretively in a closed fist. In India, folk tales were enlisted as seasonings to tickle the palate of lay audiences: the *jataka* stories, which draw freely on the vivid fables and fantasies of popular legend, point a Buddhist moral by representing their heroes, human or animal, as the Buddha in previous existences. In China, monks with propagandist gifts would mesmerize crowds of listeners with popular lectures given at bustling festivals and ceremonies. Stories based on episodes from the sutras, *bian wen* (*pien wen*), passed into the lore of oral tradition and vernacular literature. Folktales, plays and novels commemorated Buddhist cosmological myths and moral doctrines. Buddhism inspired many popular religious movements, such as the Maitreya (seventh to sixteenth centuries), the White Cloud (twelfth and thirteenth), the *Lo* or *Wu-wei* (sixteenth to twentieth), the White Lotus (twelfth to twentieth), and the *Yiguan dao* (*I-kuan tao*), a sect sharing certain eschatological notions with the White Lotus that was still carrying a torch for folk belief in the early years of the Communist regime.[9]

Such movements were often not so much organized sects as traditions. They bought their resilience and longevity by taking on the very hues and textures of immemorial popular culture, with its polychromatic melange of dogmas. The distinctively Buddhist was stirred into one great pot with the distinctively Taoist and the distinctively classical; the result was distinctively Chinese. The cosmology of the Former Heaven sect, as described at the turn of the present century by de Groot, combined in itself the Taoist doctrine of non-activity or *wu-wei* (intuitive oneness with nature), the ancient theory of cosmic harmony regulated by the interplay of two great principles, *yin* and *yang*, the divination praxis of eight trigrams bodied forth in the *Book of Changes* and sanctioned by Confucian orthodoxy, and a powerful leavening of Buddhist myth.[10] The White Lotus movement, like others, adopted a cosmogonic theory of probably prehistoric folk origin which ascribed the creation of the world to a mother goddess, Wu-sheng Lao-mu or 'unborn mother', possibly representing in part the influence on the White Lotus movement of aboriginal culture in border areas whither it was hunted by government persecution. The adepts of the Great Way, a cluster of sects that could still be studied among Chinese communities in recent years, were said to be able to fly through the air like Taoist sages, building fortresses in the clouds. The sect of the Golden Elixir, claiming to have been founded in Tang times by one of the eight immortals, used the Confucian eight trigrams and propounded a subtle psychologized alchemy obviously influenced by Taoism; for its practitioners it prescribed a course of meditation that was very much like Buddhist yoga, but distinguished itself from Buddhism by the signs and confirmations of progress that the devotee could recognize.[11]

Chinese religion is essentially syncretic. Every doctrine had to come to terms with the rich native mythology that established manifold continuities between the seen and the unseen. Behind a temple near Hangzhou, reported Dr Leo Wieger, were huge stacks of unburied coffins. Why did not the ghosts of these wretched dead create a great nuisance? The bonze of the temple explained: they were all well-fed prosperous ghosts, even though in life they had been destitute. Therefore,

> being filled and content, they are without malice. Do not you, who are a mandarin, know that whoever steals or kills, does so because he is hungry or cold? The *kuei* (*gui*, ghost) who appear to the sick or who perform evil tricks, are they well-clothed and well-nourished *kuei*? No! They are wretches, with dishevelled hair, naked and emaciated. They make demands, because people have not given to them. – I thought to myself that this bonze was perfectly right. And in fact, during a month that I spent at the temple, neither I, nor my attendants, nor by children, heard even a hiss.[12]

The moral of the story is that, if you honour the ghosts of the past, they will not come back to haunt you. There is a lesson here for every revolutionary leadership.

Ghosts are taken very seriously. Even in a monastery where *Chan* Buddhism is at its most sophisticated, it remains important to give proper attention to the unseen spirits. Senior monks ritually feed hungry ghosts. At the latrine, the rules as cited by Welch specify that the monk must first 'snap the fingers of his right hand three times toward the opening of the pit. This is to avoid having the excrement dirty the heads of the hungry ghosts, thus incurring their revengeful wrath. It is terribly important.'[13]

It was Paul Mus who warned orientalists against mistaking a library for a civilization. The Western student investigates Buddhism through books, and if he is unwary, may come to think that Buddhism consists only of what the books say. Of course it depends which books they are. But Buddhism is as much a civilization as a doctrine. In its baggage it took to China not only the high-flying quest for nirvana but techniques for restoring an ostensibly severed tongue, for spitting fire and for burning objects without destroying them. These are magic tricks, but we must be careful how we define magic. It is whatever technology seems to be effective. Our magic is modern scientific technology. Anybody who is unfamiliar with scientific technology, however erudite and intelligent, may quite legitimately subscribe to another sort. The evidence available to him for the success of his magic may not be much worse than the evidence available to us for the success of ours. Thus a powerful motor for the invention of printing in China in the sixth century was the belief that the multiplication of religious merit could be magically secured by the multiplication of auspicious written words. (Something like this logic lies behind the principle of the prayer wheel popular in Tibetan Buddhism.) The first known printed book anywhere in the world was a Chinese *Diamond Sutra*, a Buddhist text printed from wooden blocks in AD 8 68 and discovered a whole millennium later in the Thousand Buddha Caves at Tunhuang. Mass production was born in China. And in the eyes of the oriental Henry Ford who hit upon the idea, the engine of progress served not Mammon but Nirvana.

Pre-scientific magic is not dead in China. In a work, that, though it has attracted criticism, is full of provocative thoughts, Wolfgang Bauer explicitly grounds the *rationale* of Mao's spuriously 'modern' or revolutionary style of government in traditional magic. 'The East is Red' is a religious hymn. *Dong* (*tung*), the last syllable of Mao's name, means 'East'. Mao is mystically identified with the East and with redness.

To demonstrate a religious component in the attitude of contemporary China hardly requires the enumeration of further indications such as the many, prayer-like letters sent in to Chinese newspapers by readers, the well-known, no less numerous reports about the miraculous effects of the 'Thoughts of Mao Tse-tung', or the anthology, the 'Red Bible', originally intended only for the army and published with a red cover. The billions of reprints of Mao Tse-tung's writings brought out since 1966 and whose publication took precedence over that of all other material point in the same direction. Involuntarily, one is reminded of the early period of Buddhism in China where the mass distribution of sacred writings was so firmly believed to be a good deed that it resulted in the invention of printing in the sixth century.[14]

Perhaps this sort of parallel seems forced — worth a smile, perhaps, but essentially frivolous. If so, it is worth a pause to reflect. What better standards of interpretation are there? If we insist upon regarding the behaviour of China's modern leaders as characteristic of modern man, *homo politicus*, explicable by the canons of a psychology basically like our own, then we must interpret such fads as the Little Red Book either as irrational bouts of mania, which is insulting to the intelligence of the Chinese leaders, or as efficient techniques of political organisation, which is ingenuous. Politicians in any country are usually shrewd enough to attune their policies to the resonances of popular culture. Chinese popular culture, whatever some observers would like to think, was not manufactured *ab initio* by a band of revolutionaries standing in an exotic tradition of European origin; it had always been there, and, the secularism of Confucianism notwithstanding, it was religious through and through (or, which comes to the same thing, it did not distinguish between 'religion' and other categories of thought).

Notes

1. J.R. Levenson, 'The Place of Confucius in Communist China' in A. Feuerwerker (ed.), *History in Communist China*, MIT Press, Cambridge, Mass., 1968, pp. 56-73, at p. 57.

2. J. Blofeld, *The Jewel in the Lotus: an Outline of Present Day Buddhism in China*, Sidgwick & Jackson (for the Buddhist Society), London, 1948, p. 193.

3. Chow Yung-teh, *Social Mobility in China: Status Careers among the Gentry in a Chinese Community*, Atherton Press, New York, 1966, pp. 14f.

4. Cited by H. Welch, *The Buddhist Revival in China*, Harvard University Press, Cambridge, Mass., 1968, pp. 27f.

5. The literature is reviewed by D.L. Overmyer in *Folk Buddhist Religion Dissenting Sects in Late Traditional China*, Harvard University Press, Cambridge, Mass., 1976, pp. 14f.

6. Parmenides, the Cretan, said that Cretans always lie. If what he said is true, it is false.

7. J. Blofeld, *The Jewel in the Lotus*, p. 63.

8. Ibid., pp. 84f.

9. These are listed by D.L. Overmyer in 'Folk-Buddhist Religion: Creation and Eschatology in Medieval China', *History of Religions*, vol. 12, no. 1 (1972-73), pp. 42-70 at p. 46.

10. J.J.M. de Groot, *Sectarianism and Religious Persecution in China* (Leiden, Brill, 1901), 2 vols in one, pp. 176ff.

11. R. Wilhelm (tr), *The Secret of the Golden Flower*, Harcourt Brace, New York, 1938, *passim*.

12. L. Wieger, *A History of the Religious Beliefs and Philosophical Opinions in China from the Beginning to the Present Time*, Paragon, New York, 1969 (reprint), pp. 619f.

13. H. Welch, *The Practice of Buddhism*, Harvard University Press, Cambridge, Mass., 1967, p. 62.

14. W. Bauer, *China and the Search for Happiness*, Seabury Press, New York, 1976, p. 415.

9 BUDDHISM AS HERESY

A special contribution of the Buddhist component in this religious culture was to offer to the Chinese a cosmology, an explanation of their place in the universe in its totality which might give meaning to the phenomenal world. Men have always needed to see order, system and meaning in the brute facts of existence that mould their lives, and Buddhism provided a reassuringly systematic account of the integration of the here and now into the suprasensible immensities of space and time. In this, it surely answered the same need as does the orthodoxy of today. Marxism-Leninism goes far beyond the needs of political philosophy alone: it purports to offer a theory of mundane existence, a key to open all the doors of human thought. Mao's excursions into vapid metaphysics ('the one becomes two') represent not the arrogance of the would-be polymath but an acute sensitivity to the need of a new orthodoxy for a total explanation of the universe. Such an explanation had its greatest value for the half-educated and the tradition-bound rather than for the governors themselves, for a science is most convincing to those who do not properly understand it.

Buddhism gave man a universal context by mapping space and time. Every monastery, for example, was mystically, and therefore effectively, a mirror of the cosmos. The visitor to the monastery, approaching the first shrine, would encounter the four heavenly kings, two on each side, symbolizing the sacred energies of the four cardinal points which govern the order and stability of the world. The Guardian of the East, with black face and beard, held a sword and a golden ring; the Guardian of the South, with a white face, held a 'balloon guitar'; the red-faced Guardian of the West held a snake or dragon and a jewel; and the pink-faced Guardian of the North held an umbrella and a rat. Every symbol had a meaning, which concentrated the powers of unseen forces into a tangible and manipulable form. The pagoda itself was replete with symbolism:

> The Chinese name of the pagoda also denotes a deep meaning. It is composed of the two characters 'earth' and 'answer' . . . the earthbound soul shall get, through meditation, an answer to the deepest questions of life. Another symbolic idea is this: the square foundation on which the pagoda rests represents earth, the round

storeys the air, and the top storey, with the four openings, represents heaven and the four heavenly guardians. The ball at the top is perfection, becoming one with Buddha.[1]

In the elaborate Hindu-Buddhist cosmology of India, the majestic stride of time was divided into cycles of awesome length called kalpas. Each kalpa was a day of Brahma, a period of four thousand, three hundred and twenty millions of years of mortal men, demarcating the lifetime of the world between each renewal. For Buddhism, kalpas were of uneven length. In China, kalpas played an important part in the doctrines of popular movements, giving their followers a sense that they could transcend the enormity of history and make direct contact with the Buddhas. Many sects gave an important place to the teaching of three successive cycles, past, present and future. The past cycle is the one in which the Buddha Dipankara appeared, incarnated in China as Fu-xi (Fu-hsi), alleged to have invented the eight trigrams of divination. His lotus throne has three azure petals. The present cycle is that of the historical Buddha, Sakyamuni, who sits on a lotus throne with five red petals. The long awaited Buddha of the future is Maitreya, on his throne with nine white petals. Each kalpa ends in violent catastrophe, perishing by deluge, by fire and by wind respectively. One sect believes its patriarch to be Maitreya already incarnate on earth, and the hydrogen bomb to be the apocalyptic wind.[2]

Men long for a better future. Iron determinism feeds optimism: a theory which precisely describes a series of past ages, and necessarily entails the foreseeable coming of a better age ushered in by a messiah who may indeed be already present in the flesh, gives scientific certainty to hope. The parallel to modern Chinese orthodoxy is too obvious to deserve remark.

In the sometimes garbled cosmology which Buddhism brought with it, we must recognize, men saw a science. When the science of the West came in its turn, it seemed to some that Buddhism must have something to say to it, complementing its crabbed materialism with a transcendent cosmological dimension. The egregious evangelist Tai-Xu (T'ai-hsü), earlier in the present century, liked to talk at length about Buddhism and science, and some Western sympathisers were impressed. In 1945 a former abbot, talking about the same subject, said:

Now, isn't this the space age we are living in? In twenty years scientists are going to start visiting other planets. And how will they talk to the people who live there? Obviously they will have to use

Sanskrit and *we* will have to teach them. So study your Sanskrit well.[3]

Such an anecdote deserves to be considered for what it shows. Serious and intelligent men expected to be able to derive practical scientific principles from *a priori* cosmological teachings. This was the case before 1949. It has been the case since.

Maitreya, the future Buddha waiting in the Tusita heaven for his turn to descend among mortals and redeem an age of mankind, became in China a powerful symbol of hope for better things, adding faith in a personal and approachable messiah to the confidence engendered by an authoritative science of the sacred. He came to be identified with whatever men most ardently desired to quarry from the dark mine of the future. Since men chiefly desired prosperity, contentment and an abundant progeny to continue the family line and make offerings to them when they had passed to the beyond, it is not surprising that Maitreya came to be conflated with a fat, jolly monk popular with children and supposed to have lived in the tenth century. This is the origin of the Laughing Buddha.

Maitreya waits, it was thought, until a world ruler has made the *dharma*, the Buddhist teaching, prevail upon earth. Then he appears. No dogma could be so apt to serve the needs of dissident popular movements seeking legitimacy in the eyes of the population by an appeal to shared myths. The White Lotus tradition, which inspired rebellion against the alien Mongols, explicitly linked Buddhist cosmology with dynastic pretensions: its leader Han Shantong (Han Shan-t'ung) claimed to be a descendant of the Song, and his son Lin Er (Lin-erh) was proclaimed emperor and incarnation of Maitreya. Numerous rebellious movements, of mottled ideological pedigree, exploited the same Buddhist ideas in quest of popular legitimacy. The founder of the Pure Tea sect early in the nineteenth century proclaimed that Maitreya would be born into his family. The leaders of the Boxer uprising in 1900 claimed to receive spirit messages from the eleventh-century Buddhist monk Ji Gong (Chi Kung), a hero of popular stories and another incarnation of Maitreya. In the present century, the Yiguan Dao was founded by another Maitreya, Zhang Guangbi (Chang Kuang-pi) from Shandong, come from heaven to save mankind. There is no need to look beyond the borders of China for the antecedents of Mao's personality cult.

Less politically influential than Maitreya, but perhaps more important in the history of Chinese Buddhism proper, was another bodhisattva (future Buddha), the compassionate Avalokitesvara, the one in whose heavenly sight we stand. What is specially interesting about his career in China is that he changed sex and became Guan Yin (Kuan Yin), the goddess of mercy. There has been some speculation how this came to be. Perhaps the transmogrification was helped along by Avalokitesvara's association in tantric Buddhism with the mandala of the womb element and the goddess Tara. At all events, pious Buddhist laywomen going to pray at temples must always have been specially likely to address to heaven their heartfelt petitions for the birth of sons, passports in the traditional family to respect and fulfilment for mothers. Compassion and motherhood were intimately linked.

Avalokitesvara was the deputy of the Buddha Amitabha, who presided over the Western Paradise, Sukhavati or the Pure Land. Devotion to Amitabha became popular from the Tang dynasty onwards, eventually superseding the cult of Maitreya, but early forms of Pure Land Buddhism can be traced back to the teacher Hui Yuan (fourth to fifth centuries AD), who, at least according to tradition, preached the gospel of the Western Paradise. Pure Land Buddhism was characterized by a pronounced simplicity of practice that endeared it to the unsophisticated believer. Essentially it was a doctrine of grace. The road to salvation that lies through study and meditation is stony and arduous, it said. The ordinary believer cannot hope to make measurable progress in the circumstances of poverty and ignorance which all too commonly stand between him and the religious life. But all is not lost, for whoever with true faith calls upon the name of the Buddha shall surely be saved, to be reborn among the many-splendoured felicities of life in the Pure Land, from which egress to Nirvana is comparatively easy. Notice that this is no mere mechanical magic: ritual chanting of homage to the Buddha is not sufficient to compel grace, for it must be accompanied by true faith, and this is not summoned up by following a manual. The Norwegian missionary K.L. Reichelt discerned in Pure Land Buddhism a religion of faith and compassion which he considered spoke to Christianity. Lay followers of this persuasion would form groups of devotees, practising vegetarianism and meeting at night to call ritually upon the Buddha, *zheng ming* (*cheng ming*), in the hope of attracting the grace of Amitabha.

Here we are taking Buddhism as a paradigm of the sort of popular religion which shaped the Chinese imagination and conditioned its responses to the promptings of history; other systems of belief were of course active too, and they fed each other. Amitabha, the Buddha of infinite light, is, for example, often though perhaps unnecessarily attributed to the influence upon Buddhism of the religion of light specially characteristic of Persia. Certainly, Manichaeism was known in China, and its influence can be detected at several points. The cosmology of Manichaeism distinguishes three phases or moments in the evolution of the cosmos. In the first, the forces of darkness and light are separate. In the second, they are locked in struggle. In the third, the light is apocalyptically victorious. Manichaeism is said to have entered China through the nomadic Uighur peoples of Xinjiang late in the seventh century, and to have pervaded the ideas of Tang Buddhism. Its direct influence declined after the fall of the Uighur kingdom in AD 843, but the lingering ethos of its photolatry may perhaps be detected in later times; for example, in the idea of a King of Light, the messiah sent by Maitreya to save mankind, or in the choice of the name Ming ('clear' or 'bright') as the name of the dynasty founded in 1368 by a former Buddhist novice, Bauer, as we noticed above, detects it in the iconography of Chairman Mao as the Red Sun and 'The East is Red'.

Rather more obviously, the home-grown teaching of Taoism supplied *motifs* for the tapestry of popular belief. We have already seen that in folk religion Taoism was often confounded with Buddhism and other ingredients, native or exotic, each flavouring the others like a rich syncretic curry of inspiration. To explore the Taoist contribution would take us away from our proper concern, but it is interesting to notice what are the three distinctive contributions credited by one scholar to the influence of Taoism upon movements of popular dissidence in early times. According to Y. Murumatsu, Taoist beliefs gave to these movements an ideology directly relating present deeds with future happiness, a discipline of self-control demanded by the unseen spirits believed to be guiding and supervising, and a standard of collective organization turning a rabble into a coherent body capable of military effectiveness.[4] Such traditions, grounded though they are in an antique culture, have a relevance that is modern enough.

Throughout Chinese history, movements of rebellion have drawn upon heterodox systems of belief such as Taoism and Buddhism for a sacred legitimacy. There is no doubt that there is much in Chinese Buddhism that has influenced rebellion, and been influenced in turn by it. To the extent that modern Chinese Communism is an orthodoxy, parallels can be found between it and Confucianism; to the extent that it is a doctrine of revolution, its Chineseness rings with echoes from the Buddhist tradition. But this is not to say that the Buddhism which embedded itself in the collective Chinese mind over so many centuries is no more than an ideology of revolt, or that Buddhist sects are no more than secret societies.

There can be no doubt that Buddhism supplied many of the colourful myths and rituals with which secret societies decked out their programmes of mystery and violence. Modern writings have often encouraged the supposition that in recent centuries there has been little more to Chinese Buddhism than a mishmash of superstitions apt to inspire rebels with a fragile self-confidence. Popular Buddhist sects, often driven to conduct their devotions somewhat furtively by a spasmodic and half-hearted persecution at the hands of a defensive mandarinate, look a little like secret societies to the careless eye of an indifferent posterity. But they were not. Sects and secret societies were two different things. 'Against such preposterous identification,' says de Groot, 'we must earnestly raise our voices.'[5] Overmyer in his study of folk Buddhist religion insists upon the same point. The religious life of the sects was evangelical, not esoteric. Their members, like those of secret societies (or indeed like Buddhist monks), were given cult names to seal their new identity, but there was nothing secret about these names. Their doctrines and practices were inspired by, and accepted the authority of, the established Buddhist monastic order, and in this respect were unlike either secret societies or mystery cults, which were primary associations. Further, unlike rebellious movements, their organization was geared to the prolonged practice of religious exercises in peacetime, not to political crisis.[6]

A line must therefore be carefully drawn between these sects or associations of Buddhist laymen and movements of rebellion. But it is important to see how the confusion could arise in the first place. For it originates in a capital fact about Chinese traditional society that is highly distinctive and essential to an understanding of the social dynamics of Chinese religion.

This fact is that, for whatever reasons, state orthodoxy then claimed (as it does today) total moral and intellectual authority. Therefore it regarded with intense suspicion any form of systematic belief which was not under its own firm institutional control. Therefore, although the Buddhist monasteries and convents were officially sanctioned because they were controlled by the state and conducted rituals on behalf of the state, any form of *spontaneous* religious organization outside the monastery walls was seen as heretical and potentially seditious.

In social colouration, consequently, these sects were skewbald. They lay half in the light and half in shade. Their relationship to political authority was delicate, and it cannot be simply characterized in familiar terms, for Chinese political authority worked in a Chinese way. For most of the time, the sects went peacefully and openly about their business, often enjoying an enviable measure of esteem. Where they were large and influential, benefiting from the patronage of men of substance, a district mandarin would make no waves. The two things most zealously cultivated by him were that no matter of any gravity should be entered in his copy-book and that matter of as much gravity as possible should enter his coffers. Depending for both upon local goodwill, he heeded the prudence of being tolerant in all things. But there were exceptional mandarins, men of egregious ambition or moral austerity, and there were exceptional years, when campaigns against heresy were launched by superiors in a distant capital. Therefore Buddhist popular sects were sometimes persecuted, sometimes driven into one camp with the essentially rebellious secret societies.

So, as Favre says, 'Si elles sont secrètes, c'est uniquement pour échapper aux persécutions.'[7] De Groot explains that the sects were persecuted essentially and legally for corruption of the orthodox ritual order (*li*), but in fact were liable to be treated as rebellious organizations and therefore to have those of their members who were found guilty cut to pieces, with the execution of their relatives.

It all depends upon the light in which the judge thinks it proper and suitable to view the circumstances of their heresy and its collision with the authorities. Suppose they capture a leader or member of a sect, and he is delivered out of the hands of the yamen-runners by the confraternity, or liberated from prison by means of a riot, then this incident is immediately ranked with open rebellion. This is even the case if, in the event of an arrest, there should be a tumult raised, or some passive resistance offered; nay, the slightest outburst of exasperation, a mere utterance of wrath or indignation, may be interpreted and punished as actual mutiny.[8]

Nor was it only the popular sects of Buddhism that were liable to suffer from this official attitude of spasmodic and arbitrary hostility. From time to time throughout the centuries, the religion as a whole suffered imperial persecutions that would have wiped out the faith if they had been effective or prolonged. Several rulers in the period of disunity (AD 221-589) proscribed the faith or sought to decimate the monkhood. In AD 258, under the Wei, Sun Lin destroyed temples and beheaded priests. Thirty thousand were defrocked in 714. The most notorious persecution was that of AD 845 (and of some earlier years which led up to it), by the Tang emperor Wu Zong (Wu-Tsung, 840-6), who was mad. In a series of stages, the youngest first, monks and nuns were returned to lay life, and the lands and possessions of the order escheated to the state. Fortunately for Buddhism, the emperor's Taoist medicines of immortality soon proved curiously, indeed lethally, counter-productive.

This persecution can, if we wish, be readily enough credited to the ruler's whimsicality. An empress dowager who favoured Buddhism he had poisoned. Another stepmother he shot with his bow. On one occasion he shot an inoffensive labourer for pure sport, and on another he suggested that Buddhist monks should be beheaded *en masse*. But, wherever and whenever Buddhism was strong, rulers had rational grounds for distrusting it. Buddhist monks were exempted from civil duties. They paid no tax, were conscripted for no corvée. Many monks were fugitives from the law, or simply professional parasites. Further, many monasteries were extremely wealthy; their broad acres of lush farmland, their well-stocked granaries, their profitable mills and work-shops, and their toiling hordes of workmen were all resources lost to the state. In the eye of the ruler, the order was *imperium in imperio* — a rival for ideological loyalty, a poacher on the government's field of wealth, and a sanctuary for dissidents.

The Chinese state could afford the luxury of intellectual totalism perhaps precisely because, for most of the time from the Tang onwards, the country's administration was (by pre-industrial standards) a stable and centralized bureaucracy. Institutions of power and wealth such as merchant houses, religious foundations and great landed estates were not, as elsewhere in Asia, autonomous agents with which it behoved the ruler to negotiate in order to sustain his pre-eminence at the pivot of a delicate balance, but upstarts that must be controlled. The empire was a formal garden. Gardens need plants that grow and spread, but the plants must be rigorously confined by the dimensions of the gardener's design, not their own.

It is this attitude to heterodoxy that has been inherited by today's governors, though in some respects they may have been better able to enforce it, at least until recent years, than could the emperors of the past. It is an attitude that fixes a gulf between all that is organized, sponsored and expressly permitted by the state and all that is not. All heterodoxy was known as the Left Dao. It was associated with idleness, sedition and the avoidance of taxes. From 1724, an imperial sermon of bracing morality was supposed to be read in public by local officials every fortnight; it showed a frowning visage to Taoism and Buddhism, from which 'a class of idle loafers comes forth'. As in every other case, the authority of Confucius could always be invoked: 'The study of heterodox teachings is injurious indeed' (Analects II.16). The *Book of Rites* (second century BC) said: 'Using licentious music, strange garments, wonderful contrivances and extraordinary implements, thus raising doubts among the multitudes: all who used or formed such things were put to death, as were those who studied what was wrong and persisted in doing so.' (III.4) An official source from the Mongol dynasty (the Yuan) referred opprobriously to 'those who gather large groups of people together at night for religious ceremonies, pounding drums and making a disturbance. It is to be feared that this will produce banditry.'[9] Essentially harmless sects that gathered publicly for rituals at houses known as halls of vegetarianism and worshipped Guan Yin were liable, on these grounds, to be subjected to arbitrary persecution.

Monasteries could at most times be tolerated, but only on imperial terms. As early as the Northern Wei under Taizi (T'ai-tsu, AD 386-409), monks were subject to regulation and had to be officially registered. In the fifth century, decrees declared and limited the numbers of monks that could be ordained at particular times. The famous monk Hui Yuan argued successfully, but against the current of history, that Buddhist monks should be exempted from the requirements of court ritual that they should abase themselves before the emperor, for they had expressly cut themselves off from the social world. In the Tang dynasty, state control of the Buddhist order, large and wealthy though it was, placed it firmly under the authority of the Bureau of National Sacrifice, which alone could issue ordination certificates. Some Tang rulers were enthusiastic Buddhists, but they did not mean to remit what was due to Caesar, and the order bought its conditional favour by functioning in some respects as an instrument of the state itself, for by imperial decree monks were required to conduct ceremonies and memorial services on specified anniversaries, particularly royal birthdays. They could even be required to defend the state with bullets of *dharma*. Kenneth Ch'en, who describes the Chinese evolution of Buddhism in bondage to leviathan, cites a record of certain events in AD 765:

> During the tenth month, the Tibetans crossed the borders and threatened the capital. The emperor ordered two cartloads of the *Jen-wang-ching* (a Buddhist sutra) to be delivered to the Hsi-ming-ssu and other monasteries, and an imperial edict called on Amoghavajra

to install a hundred high seats and to lecture on the sutra. The emperor himself was present to offer incense, pay homage, and listen to the lecture. Within a short while, the invaders were pacified.[10]

Post hoc ergo propter hoc. The government's claim to control the Buddhist order and the associations of lay Buddhists was never remitted. Up to the end, the registration of monks has been a state prerogative, only certain major monasteries being licensed to ordain specified numbers at specified times. The government has not however always been strong enough to enforce its control, and in periods of weakness the system of regulation has been often abused. Often a corrupt trade in monk certificates has flourished. When the Manchu dynasty fell in 1911, the republic inherited the Confucian state's concern to manage and restrict the order; at various times, particularly in the 1920s and 1930s, moves were initiated to bring Buddhist activities under official control, but they led to little – partly because republican governments were almost never strong enough to legislate for the whole country, and partly because many government leaders were themselves good Buddhists highly responsive to the lobbying of monastic interests.

As a heterodox system of beliefs, then, Buddhism was in practice usually able to follow its peaceful way; but in theory it was allowed to enlist the participation of Chinese citizens only on official terms and for official purposes. Sometimes, the theory prevailed. Sometimes, out of insecurity or ideological fervour, the guardians of orthodox theory sought to purge the faith away with medicines of rectitude, succeeding in chivvying and goading it into the cellars where nonconformity and rebellion lurked side by side. It is not surprising then that, along with Taoism, Buddhism contributed myths and rituals to genuinely rebellious movements, and came to be identified, in some minds at least, with the casuistry of treason.

We should therefore look further at those movements, self-proclaimed followers of some at least of the Indian *Muni's* teachings, which went into outright political opposition to the state. Among these, the secret societies were the most conspicuous.

They abounded at many periods of history. Some were tightly organized local groups; some were loose confederations spread over large areas. Some perished, moth-like, in the seasons of upheaval that called them forth; some lingered on for generations or centuries, giving their names and traditions to successive waves of desperate bravoes in times of crisis. Some were out-and-out rebel movements; some hovered near the borders of respectability, functioning in part as village self-defence groups, masonic lodges or religious sects. But, by definition as secret societies, they exposed themselves to persecution by the state wherever they were unmasked. Their names were polychromatic. The Red Eyebrows, the Yellow Turbans, the Red Turbans, the Copper Horse, the Heaven and Earth Society, the White Lotus, the Three Dots, the Triads, the Eight Trigrams, the Small Swords, the Righteous Harmony, the Red Bears, the Black Flags, the Two Dragons and the Tiger, the Elder Brothers, the Mutual Progress, the Green Band and the Red Band, along with many others, spangle the pages of history like a scattering of hundreds and thousands. Writers usually recognize two broad divisions or traditions in modern times: the Triads in the south, the White Lotus in the north. These are not so much unified organizations as clusters of gangs or bands claiming the legitimacy of shared traditions. The White Lotus was particularly heterogeneous. In some of its forms, it was a respectable lay Buddhist persuasion, but, nurtured by blood, it gave its name and rituals to many organizations of violent men.

What sorts of people sought initiation into these often bizarre associations? Their origins are of enormous interest for our understanding of the articulation of Chinese society, a theme to which we shall return later on. Chesneaux lists poor peasants, porters, coolies, itinerant artisans, boatmen, smugglers, patent medicine salesmen, geomancers, bonesetters, itinerant herb doctors and wandering monks.[11] Other scholars variously refer to young people in rebellion against their parents, bandits, deserters, salt smugglers and counterfeiters. These are marginal men. Be it noticed that many of them are itinerants. Farmers, whose work anchored them to one place, remained throughout their lives attached to the graves of their ancestors, and they could easily be found by the tax collector: these characteristics marked them as reliable citizens. Itinerants on the other hand did not quite fit in wherever they were, and it was difficult for authority to tax them regularly or see what business they were about.

Nor were secret society recruits by any means always poor and illiterate. Some organizations (particularly but not invariably religious sects of originally peaceable nature driven underground by persecution) attracted members from among the educated, village heads and government clerks. Families of substance always had their black sheep whose frustrations drove them to identify themselves with the underworld.

Buddhist motifs are woven generously into the mythology of the Triad secret society tradition in southern China. Devotees of the

Chinese cinema are familiar with the name of Shao Lin, the monastery in Fujian (Fukien) province where, in the Qing dynasty, a brotherhood of Buddhist monks became past masters of the martial arts. Through the jealousy of a courtier, the emperor turned against them; their monastery was destroyed in flames after a betrayal by a former monk, and over a hundred perished. According to the legend, those few who survived were miraculously saved by a curtain falling on them. Only five subsequently survived to bequeath the Shao Lin tradition to posterity. These five wandered from place to place. At one point, near to starvation, they were told by spirits in a dream that they would be able to eat the sand on which they lay. Doing so, they then found a tripod censer inscribed with the characters *Fan Qing Fu Ming* – 'Overthrow the Qing, restore the Ming'. Further adventures came their way. At one point they escaped from the pursuing imperial soldiers when a grass sandal magically turned into a boat. At another, they were able to cross a river by stepping on three floating stones. Eventually, and most felicitously for their cause, they found a Ming pretender to the imperial throne. A red glow in the eastern sky was an omen for their success in the quest to restore the old Chinese dynasty, for *hong*, 'red', is a homophone of the Ming reign-name.

Here then is a curious and rarely noticed link between the Chinese ideology of today ('The East is Red') and the romance and magic of the careers of five Buddhist monks in the Manchu dynasty. The sneaking suspicion obtrudes itself that the story as just recounted is apocryphal, but there is no doubt of its historical importance in representing the leading characteristics of the societies whose liturgies it inspired: the accoutrements of magic, the claim to supreme martial skill, the honourable goal of toppling a hated dynasty from the throne, the aura of daring survival amid persecution, the strong religious flavour, the emphasis upon brotherhood – it is all there, and these values are not dead yet.

Generous helpings of myth and magic were stirred into the fervid imaginations of these societies' members by their leaders so that they might all be self-confident, loyal to the cause, and convinced of their invulnerability on the battlefield (this last a notably universal feature of millenarian movements of revolt across the world). The intoxicating brew was eclectic in the extreme, but it was definitely Buddhism that supplied the prevailing flavour. 'The Buddhist element largely predominates in this sectarianism, and for good reasons. Buddhism was the religion *par excellence*, purporting to guide humanity towards the gates of salvation in this earthly life and in the life to come.'[12] The Buddha would not have approved, but his *dharma* was at work in China inspiring revolt from the early centuries of its influence there. In AD 515 the Buddhist monk Fa Qing (Fa Ch'ing) preached a virulent reformism that fired his followers to destroy Buddhist temples, burn texts, and murder officials. 'A new Buddha has appeared. Get rid of the old devils.' In AD 613 Xiang Haiming (Hsiang Hai-ming) in Shaanxi claimed to be Maitreya. In the middle of the Tang, the rebel Wang Huigu (Wang Hui-ku) called himself a new Buddha. In 1047 Wang Ze (Wang Tse) raised an army of Maitreya believers.[13]

Indeed we have already noticed the aptness of the bodhisattva doctrine to the demands of the millenarian imagination. The doctrine of kalpas, too, was eagerly exploited by the secret societies. On the past kalpa, the era of Dipankara Buddha, shone a blue sun; on the era of the Buddha Sakyamuni shines a red sun; on the era of Maitreya will shine a white sun. Awesome cataclysms will attend the transition to the next kalpa, but the mercy of Maitreya will save the true believers. Thus disasters such as the flooding of the Yangzi in 1854 encouraged sectaries to believe that a new kalpa was imminent; and we have noticed above how the nuclear bomb fitted into millenarian calculations.

Buddhism tinctured the initiation ritual of countless societies. The goddess of mercy, Guan Yin, often played an important part in the liturgy, notably, for example, in the pantheon of the Triad societies. The Green Band used Buddhist ritual and gave its members generation names taken from a set of written characters (which, incidentally, included 'Buddha'), on the model of Buddhist dharma names. The Boxers of the 1890s, who, however we classify them, certainly grew from the same soil that nurtured secret societies, had a charm against the effects of drought which said at one point: 'If you do not pass on this message from Buddha you will not be able to escape unnatural death' — typical of the appeal to religious sanctions that solemnized secret society oaths. A Boxer anathema against Christianity declared that 'The heresy has no respect for either gods or Buddha . . . The Buddhist *i-ho-t'uan* can defend the country.'[14]

The Green Band, which rose to grisly eminence in the republican period, used Buddhist rituals. The Elder Brothers, in the 1930s, did honour to the three refuges (the Buddha, the dharma, the Buddhist community) and took the five (Buddhist) vows. But, in the present century, for reasons that have been debated, secret societies have tended to lose their traditional religio-political functions and have become more and more like criminal gangs, their fragments of religious ritual increasingly meaningless shards of forgotten aspirations.

Many associations have at all times been godfather to rebellion without being exactly secret societies, and most of them have had some connection with Buddhism. The case of the White Lotus, for example, is particularly problematic. For many purposes, of course, it is a name and a tradition which have inspired numerous dissident movements in northern China which seem fairly clearly to be secret societies; yet at the same time it is a loosely articulated and often syncretic brand of Buddhist association whose members have often been eminently respectable. The sect is traditionally accorded a fifth-century origin, said to be founded by Hui Yuan (d. 416) according to an early text which gives an account of the lives of the first members of the Lian She, 'Lotus Community'. This derivation gives it a background in Pure Land Buddhism. Muramatsu, though, traces the sect back to 1133, when Mao Ziyuan (Mao Tzu-yüan, 1086-1166) founded it as a branch of the Tiantai school.[15] We saw above how, in Mongol times, a sectarian leader went into rebellion claiming descent from the Song dynasty, and his son was proclaimed to be Maitreya incarnate. In 1351 various rebel forces with Buddhist inspiration and millenarian programmes came together, White Lotus and Maitreya supporters whose common badge of the red turban earned them the name of the Red Army. (Not the last one in Chinese history.) The movement professed a variety of beliefs and practices influenced by Buddhism, Manichaeism, classical Chinese orthodoxy, Taoism and folk magic. An official memorial referred to the White Lotus rebels as having in their magic arsenal a mantra of the five dukes, a diagram for turning one's back on transmigration, a blood basin (for exorcisms) and a book of astrology.[16]

Our knowledge of the popular origins of the twentieth-century Red Army is filtered through sources unlikely to notice the part played by religious ideas and talismanic magic, but we need not suppose that it and its fourteenth-century namesake are so very different, for they grew out of the same soil.

For however many multitudes of its innocent disciples the name of the White Lotus has connoted chiefly a gospel of compassion inimical to the harming of any living creature — many White Lotus groups remained simple vegetarians practising Buddhist piety — the paragraphs of history that the flower wrote are chiefly incarnadined by blood. White Lotus groups late in the Ming helped the Manchus to power. In 1774 and 1775 they were involved in insurrections in Shantong and Henan. The best known of all was the great rebellion of 1794-1803, when rural uprisings set on fire parts of the border areas between Shaanxi, Sichuan and Hubei. Again in the 1860s the White Lotus was linked with the rebellion of the Black Banner in Shandong and Henan. For all that, we should not lose sight of the religious character of many White Lotus groups who followed Buddhism under married clergy, accepted the authority of vernacular Buddhist scriptures, and sought to magnify their good karma and obtain rebirth in the Western Paradise. The White Lotus was not so much an institution as a tradition or a persuasion. To many of its followers it was a way of life. Many more organizationally coherent groups were offshoots from it, sharing many of its characteristics. The White Cloud, for example, stood side by side with the White Lotus in the gallery of heretics according to an official source writing about the fourteenth century: 'Of the community of the Moni worshippers of the fiery heaven (possibly Manichaeism or Islam), that of the White Cloud and that of the White Lotus, these three falsely call themselves Buddhist religions, in order to swindle ignorant people.'[17] The Wugong Dao (Wu-kung Tao) stemmed from the White Lotus tradition, and in turn probably inspired the sect of the Great Way, a sect still active among overseas Chinese and claiming regular Buddhist descent in the Chan tradition. The Yiguan Dao, already mentioned, is related to the Great Way, having a similar cosmology; earlier in the century it was politically active on the side of the Kuomintang against the Japanese, and in the 1950s as Topley reports there was evidence of its leaders hiding in the mountains to direct last-ditch opposition to the Communist Party on behalf of its millenarian programme which predicted the imminent and cataclysmic end of the world.[18]

Buddhism in China, then, had two faces: in origin it was a pacific gospel of piety; *malgré soi*, being intermittently persecuted, it became the archetype of dissidence and heresy. The Buddhologist may see only one face, and the political scientist may see only the other, but it would be improper for the social historian to neglect either.

In both capacities, the faith became so thoroughly Chinese that it inevitably flavoured all popular movements of any scale or impact. Take the Taiping (T'ai-p'ing) rebellion of the 1850s: it professed a barbarous hybrid ideology ostensibly inspired by Christianity, and the question for historians is usually to what extent it was 'modern'. Yet even this pugnaciously untraditional movement could not escape altogether the thought-world in which it was born. As de Groot says: 'Certainly there is a substratum of truth in all the talk about the Christian character of the T'ai-p'ing movement, the writings promulgated by its leader and his adherents having been found tinged with Christian ideas, which, however, on closer examination, can partly be reduced to Buddhism.'[19] And the secret society tradition which looked to the

Buddha for so many of its ideas continued to be active, however indirectly, in the present century. The secret society environment of the early career of Sun Yat-sen and his revolutionary organization the Tong Meng Hui (T'ung Meng Hui), the precursor of the Kuomintang, is too well known to warrant discussion here. In Japan in the 1900s, secret society representatives were active in the merging of various dissident groups in the revolutionary movement. Willy-nilly, the Chinese Communist Party in its turn inherited some characteristics of the secret society tradition. Zhu De, the former army commander-in-chief, had a background in Elder Brothers. Leading Party members such as Wu Yuzhang (Wu Yu-chang) and Liu Zhidan (Liu Chih-tan) had been secret society members. According to Zhu De, the Communist Party inherited from the secret societies the pattern of organization in cells. Further, the infiltration technique, whereby another organization can be taken over by interpenetration of its membership, has a native ancestry where secret societies often extended their power over whole regions by seeding their members in the offices of government, in the imperial army, in all places where influence counted. There was nothing new in this.[20]

Marxism, it has been said, had its roots in anarchism and utopianism.[21] There can be no doubt that much of the popular appeal of Buddhism in China stemmed from its portrayal of a better world. The only difference was that, with greater realism, the Buddhist teaching expected its devotees to wait until the next life before they could enter the happy land. The wide appeal of Pure Land Buddhism attests the yearning of many ordinary people for the assurance of a future state of felicity on whose many-hued delights they can let their imaginations linger fondly. The *Greater Sukhāvati-vyūha Sūtra* supplied all that was desired:

> In this world, there are no signs of sin, misfortune, distress, sadness and morality. No sound of pain, not even the sound of a feeling that is neither pain nor joy, exists there . . . The creatures of this world do not eat coarse food. Whatever they wish to eat is granted them as if it were brought to them, and their bodies and spirits delight in it. They do not even have to put the food into their mouth. And if, having eaten, they should crave various fragrances, the entire Buddha land is filled with them.[22]

Chinese popular Buddhism, Blofeld has emphasized, appeals especially to those who have suffered.[23] If this were not pre-eminently true of Chinese Communism too, there would have been no 1949.

But it was not entirely true that, for the Buddhist, salvation and fulfilment remained necessarily in a distant or posthumous state that had to be taken on trust as a gift that the future held in store. By one route, a specially Chinese route, fulfilment could be obtained in the here and now by a single flash of enlightenment. This doctrine of subitism, the belief that the goal may be achieved in one Great Leap, without laborious study and preparation, belongs peculiarly to the Chan school of meditation practice, which always remained influential in the monastic tradition and of course is well known in the form it took in Japan — Zen. As was written by Xie Lingyun (Hsieh Ling-yün):

> The Chinese . . . have a special gift for direct, intuitive insight into the truth, but find it difficult to acquire something gradually through learning. Therefore they reject the notion of gradual learning, but are receptive to the thought of some single Ultimate.[24]

Mao Zedong, with his cryptic sayings, his calculatedly practical and earthy address, his disdain for the intellectual discipline of prolonged study, and his promises of mountain-moving, mind-convulsing quantum leaps, is a quintessentially Chan figure, at least in these conspicuous if rarely noticed respects.

By a sudden transformation that transcends the particularities of history, a new era can be abruptly materialized on earth.

> Eighteen kalpas have already been completed, and the form of all things is about to change . . . Heaven and earth will be in harmony, among men there will be neither youth nor age, birth, nor death, and there will be no distinction between men and women.[25]

This is not Mao but the vision of an imminent millennium popular in White Lotus movements. It represents the Buddhist (no less than Marxist) ideal of equality among men. The White Lotus regarded inequality, *bu ping*, as one of the evils of today that shall be annihilated in the coming millennium. In Uttarakuru, the northern land of Buddhist cosmography, all people look alike and have interchangeable clothes. Bauer comments on the spurious egalitarianism of the Mao cult:

> The 'equality before god' infuses reality and makes brothers of all those touched by it, monks of a sort, who not only wear the lowliest

but the identical dress so that all individual characteristics disappear.[26]

From the original land distribution campaign until the heyday of the Gang of Four, China submitted to the recurrent dominance of a frenetic and fervid style of politics which, however 'modern' some of the rulers may (or may not) have been, is surely in large measure to be understood as the success, to an unprecedented degree, of a millennial cult.

The Chinese Communist concern, at least officially and among the more educated or urbanised, for the emancipation of women was not totally new in China. Through the centuries, popular religion with its strong tincture of Buddhism had commonly offered to women both opportunities to intermit, however briefly, the narrow domestication of household life and ideals which gave them self-respect.

This was most conspicuous in the heretical movements and secret societies, where as many as possible of the norms of Confucian respectability were deliberately inverted, and indeed the shocking freedom enjoyed in them by women was one of the causes of the horror with which they were regarded by so many. In the 1880s, a local official proclamation against vegetarian heretical sects said:

Vagabonds . . . have induced young women and girls to join their congregations and to acknowledge them as master and themselves as pupils, and other things of the kind. Lascivious indulgence in works of darkness, in places where the sexes associate together, causes corruption of morals and customs . . . As propagandists [certain vagabonds] principally employed poor wives, who introduced widows, feeble folks, women and virgins.[27]

From ancient times, indeed, some sects and societies had had a mystic cult of sexual intercourse. Members of White Cloud and White Lotus groups renounced family ties and constituted themselves an outcaste society with its own *mores*, where women had much more freedom and something more like equal status. In the nineteenth century, a missionary referred to the prominent part played by women in the White Lotus groups: 'It is the harpies of the water-lily who hold sway in the society. It is they who inspire and encourage the fainthearted.'[28] Here, it was said that if a wife joined the society before her husband, she thereby had a seniority which made her mistress of her own house. In the Boxer movement of the end of the century, there were units of girls aged twelve to eighteen called the Red Lanterns and the Blue Lanterns, led by a woman called the Sacred Mother of the Yellow Lotus.[29]

Even in orthodox Buddhism and in the popular sects that were not driven underground, women could find a higher status and greater opportunity for self-expression than secular norms permitted.

Superficially, this may seem to go against the grain of the mainstream tradition of Buddhist other-worldliness, with its emphasis upon celibacy and its higher heavens where people could not be reborn as women (reasonable enough, where femininity was associated with hardship). The Buddha himself is traditionally supposed to have sanctioned the inauguration of an order of nuns only grudgingly, and with misgivings about the consequences. One Buddhist monk in China is reported to have said: 'If there were no women, everyone would be a bodhisattva.'[30] But everything is relative. A little status grudgingly given is better than no status at all, and there is no doubt that Buddhism showed a kinder face to the much put-upon women of China than did the orthodox culture.

To be sure, in practice the majority of farmers' wives could always enjoy a reasonable measure of social freedom and intercourse on their own initiative, and the Confucian theory of male domination was often honoured only in the breach of it; the scolding wife has always been a comic stock figure in the countryside. But what matters is that the theory stood nevertheless, and the higher up the social ladder a family moved, the more restricted was a woman's life. Confucian standards of modesty enjoined a prudish etiquette of segregation. The *Li Qi* even forbids husbands and wives to mingle their personal belongings; they are not to put their clothes on the same rack or stand, and only when they are 70 years old may they put their things in the same box.[31] Let us not forget the regimen of footbinding, *de rigueur* in families of any standing, a form of restriction more virulent in its way than the Muslim purdah. For many women, a visit to a Buddhist temple might be the nearest approach she might freely make to a social outing.

A little feminist spice was stirred into Chinese Buddhism from T'ang times: the Empress Wu, seeking legitimacy for her independent imperial rule, could find no sanction for it in Confucianism, but obliging monks produced an apocryphal sutra, the *Da Yunjing* (*Ta Yün-ching*) in a version according to which the Buddha had prophesied that a girl would one day be born to rule. Confucius could declare an emperor to be Son of Heaven, but the Buddha could go one better and declare an empress to be Maitreya.

Where women were concerned, a less stultifying atmosphere prevailed in the Buddhist sects that nurtured popular religious aspirations. In the White Lotus groups women participated in worship on equal terms with men, and in some groups even the clergy were of either sex. In the Great Way religion in modern times there have been founded entirely female sects, with equal status, running their own Vegetarian Halls.[32] Buddhist monasteries, touched as they were by the fragrance of Guan Yin, goddess of compassion, always carried for the Chinese an atmosphere of the delicacy and mystery which they associated with her sex.

Notes

1. K.L. Reichelt, *Truth and Tradition in Buddhism*, Commercial Press, Shanghai, 1928, p. 259.
2. M. Topley, 'The Great Way of Former Heaven: a Group of Chinese Secret Religious Cults', *Bulletin of the School of Oriental and African Studies*, vol. 26, no. 2 (1963); pp. 363-92 at pp. 371f.
3. H. Welch, *The Buddhist Revival in China*, Harvard University Press, Cambridge, Mass., 1968, p. 308, n. 38.
4. Y. Murumatsu, 'Some Themes in Chinese Rebel Ideologies' in A.F. Wright (ed.), *The Confucian Persuasion*, Stanford University Press, Calif., 1960, p. 245.
5. J.J.M. de Groot, *Sectarianism and Religious Persecution in China* Leiden, (Brill), 1901 2 vols in one, Amsterdam, 1903-4, p. 253.
6. D.L. Overmyer, *Folk Buddhist Religion: Dissenting Sects in Late Traditional China*, Harvard University Press, Cambridge, Mass., 1976, pp. 55-70.
7. Cited by D.L. Overmyer, ibid., p. 58.
8. J.J.M. de Groot, *Sectarianism*, p. 254.
9. Cited by D.L. Overmyer, *Folk Buddhist Religion*, p. 24.
10. Cited by K. Ch'en, *The Chinese Transformation of Buddhism*, Princeton University Press, Princeton, 1973, p. 108.
11. J. Chesneaux (ed.), *Popular Movements and Secret Societies in China, 1840-1950*, Stanford University Press, Calif., 1972, p. 8.
12. J.J.M. de Groot, *Sectarianism*, p. 156.
13. Y. Murumatsu, *Some Themes in Chinese Rebel Ideologies*, p. 246.
14. J. Chesneaux, *Secret Societies in China in the Nineteenth and Twentieth Centuries*, Heinemann, London, 1971, p. 120.
15. Y. Murumatsu, 'Some Themes in Chinese Rebel Ideologies', p. 248.
16. D.L. Overmyer, *Folk Buddhist Religion*, p. 49.
17. Cited by J.J.M. de Groot, *Sectarianism*, p. 150.
18. M. Topley, 'The Great Way of Former Heaven', p. 390.
19. J.J.M. de Groot, *Sectarianism*, p. 554.
20. J. Chesneaux, *Secret Societies in China in the Nineteenth and Twentieth Centuries*, Heinemann, London, p. 144.
21. W. Bauer, *China and the Search for Happiness*, New York, Seabury Press, p. 372
22. Ibid., p. 160.
23. J. Blofeld, *The Jewel in the Lotus*, Sidgwick & Jackson, London, 1948, pp. 68-84.
24. Cited by W. Bauer, pp. 172-3.

25. Cited by D.L. Overmyer, *Folk-Buddhist Religion*, p. 65.
26. W. Bauer, p. 415.
27. J.J.M. de Groot, *Sectarianism*, pp. 170f.
28. Cited by J. Chesneaux, *Secret Societies in China in the Nineteenth and Twentieth Centuries*, p. 60.
29. Ibid., p. 122.
30. See H. Welch, *The Practice of Buddhism*, Harvard University Press, Cambridge, Mass. 1967, p. 117.
31. See J.J. M. de Groot, *Sectarianism*, p. 249.
32. M. Topley, *The Great Way of Former Heaven*, p. 369.

10 BUDDHISM AS A PHILOSOPHY OF LIFE

China's modern 'revolutionaries' grew up in a tradition of rebellion where Buddhism was an integral part of the surroundings, like wallpaper. But the influence of Buddhism upon the intellectual life of the new men, who sought during the last hundred years to bring their country into the modern world, is indeed direct and traceable. A full account has yet to be written of Buddhism's part in helping thinkers to look critically at the old orthodoxy and map out a range of alternatives, but this part was not insignificant. Later generations of self-conscious modernisers angrily rejected the religious enthusiasms of the earlier, as children sometimes will reject their parents' ideas, but Buddhism, as a tradition of heterodoxy with something to offer to intelligent men, was of very considerable interest to the fathers of reform in old China.

Late in the nineteenth century, the confrontation with a menacing western civilization which could not readily be accommodated to the place assigned to it by orthodox thought compelled many Chinese thinkers to distance themselves from their own culture, seeking to assess it critically as one among many, not as the only possible framework for thought. Liang Qichao (Liang Ch'i-ch'ao, 1873-1929), one of the later products of this movement, looked back at the intellectual currency of its protagonists and wrote that 'among the late Ch'ing "Scholars of the New Learning", there were almost none who did not have some connection with Buddhism.'[1] Typical of the ways of thought of the new thinkers was Jiang Fangzhen (Chiang Fang-chen), whom Liang cited:

The dawn of modern European history came from two great waves of [light]; one, the revival of Greek thought, which was the 'Renaissance', and the other, the resurgence of primitive Christianity, which was the 'Reformation'. Our country's new turning point hereafter should also develop from two directions: one, the emotional, which [involves] a new literature and a new art, and the other, the rational which [involves] a new Buddhism.[2]

It is significant that Jiang saw Buddhism as a rational system of beliefs. It appealed to intellectuals to whom Confucianism seemed narrow, and who sought something more complete. Probably the chief instigator of this trend of study was Yang Wenhui (1837-1911), who came from a family that had sons in the mandarinate and himself followed an official career that gave him an unusually cosmopolitan outlook.

He served at one stage under Zeng Guofan (Tseng Kuo-fan), the great proponent of the country's self-strengthening, and later visited England, where he met orientalist scholars such as Max Muller. His interest in Buddhist studies led him to set up a school to train Buddhist missionaries. He vigorously condemned features of popular religion, such as divination, which he saw as superstitious accretions upon the pure faith that could only hinder progress, and he undertook a massive programme to publish Buddhist texts; his press produced about a million copies. His own teachings embodied primarily the doctrine of the Pure Land school.

One of his pupils was the famous Tan Sitong (T'an Ssu-t'ung, 1865-98), who studied the texts of the yogācārin or mind-only' tradition of Buddhist teaching and notably the ancient Avatamsaka. He wrote the *Ren Xue (Jen-hsüeh)*, in which he sought to reconcile his Buddhist inspiration with modern Western science and the ancient Confucian principle of *Ren (Jen,* benevolence or human-heartedness). *Ren* he interpreted as the quasi-scientific concept of ether or as the *élan vital*. He was in his political views a staunch republican and a great iconoclast, teaching that it was necessary to break through the constraining nets or meshes of traditional thinking so that they could be seen for what they were – pure illusion. He was a disciple of the great reformer Kang Yuwei (K'ang Yu-wei) and an associate of his in the Hundred Days of reform when in 1898, very temporarily, Kang had the ear of the young emperor and the emperor tried to assert himself against the Empress Dowager. When she and the conservatives around her counter-attacked, Kang went into exile and Tan was executed, a martyr for republicanism and reform. It is of some significance that he later became a hero to the students of the Normal School in Changsha where Mao Zedong studied.

Another scholar who was to be very influential in the academic world during the republican period was Zhang Pinglin (Chang P'ing-lin, 1868-1936). Like many intellectually inquisitive coevals of his, he spent a period in exile in Japan. He made philological studies of the Taoist classics and reinterpreted them in Buddhist terms.

Then I studied the Buddhist canons, browsing through the various sutras . . . and gradually came to understand their meaning more deeply, although I never really mastered them thoroughly. When I was imprisoned in Shanghai, I devoted myself singlemindedly to the work of Maitreya and Vasubandhu, whose approach is to start to analyze 'psychic phenomena' and who ended by disproving [the existence] of these phenomena. This approach resembled my life-long [pursuit] of sound learning and was therefore easy to accept.[3]

Kang Yuwei (1858-1927), a towering figure in the drama of China's intellectual sea change in the late Qing, was the central figure in the Modern Text Movement, a new thrust in scholarship to reinterpret China's classics in the light of modern textual criticism. Wang's approach to the Confucian texts was a little idiosyncratic. He rejected extant recensions of many scriptures as forgeries from Han times, and claimed to detect a different Confucius behind the orthodox myth, a rather mystical religious figure with an evolutionary doctrine that could be accommodated to the exigencies of different ages. Kang wrote a utopian treatise, the Book of the Great Commonwealth, *Da Tong Shu (Ta T'ung-shu)*, which was influential among his disciples and to a great extent among later generations of reformers.

Kang's importance to his contemporaries, and in particular his association with the hectic programme of innovation in all spheres of government that was attempted, largely only on paper, during the abortive Hundred Days of reform in 1898, merit far more discussion than is appropriate here. What is of immediate concern is simply to notice two important respects in which his thinking was influenced by the Buddhist tradition. One concerns his utopian vision of social reform. In his ideal society, there were to be no abiding family units, and children were to be regarded as the general responsibility of the community. Kang explicitly recognized the value of the Buddhist monastic tradition, whereby the seeker after salvation was supposed to renounce the claims of unique family loyalty and identity; Kang considered that it would be better still to have no family to renounce in the first place. Another characteristically Buddhist idea was the bodhisattva ideal: the highest sort of religious quest is that of the individual who dedicates himself out of compassion for all beings to the enlightenment of sentient creatures as a whole before his own salvation. Kang did not wholeheartedly accept the traditionally Confucian teaching that man's nature is inherently good: for him, it was necessary for government to create the conditions in which the human potential for perfection could begin to be realized, and in these conditions it was the role of the sage or seer to guide men towards enlightenment.

Kang's influence lay in his reputation as a scholar and his dedication to reform rather than in his concrete policies. A number of later scholars, though, succeeded like him in combining revolutionary social doctrines with respect for selected aspects of traditional Chinese thought. Wang Guowei (Wang Kuo-wei, 1877-1927), an intense and introspective philosopher who committed suicide, saw Buddhism as a vital energy forming the Chinese spirit. 'When Buddhism first reached China, the Chinese mind had lost its vigour.' For him, history was now repeating itself: the challenge of Western culture was the second Buddhism.[4] Gu Jiegang (Ku Chieh-kang, b. 1893), who edited many relatively obscure texts to demonstrate the continuity in Chinese culture of a tradition of protest, studied Buddhism in the North-West during the Japanese war and developed a great respect for the lamas, priests of the Tibetan style of Buddhism prevalent among the Mongolians; he considered that there was considerable intellectual vitality in Tibetan religious life. Again, Li Zhi (Li Chih, d. AD 610), an official who gave up his post to dedicate himself to Buddhism, was one of the paradigms of Chinese individualism recommended by the famous scholar Fu Sinian (Fu Ssu-nien), who was successively head of the Academia Sinica Institute of History and Philology, of Peking University, and of the National Taiwan University.

Liang Qichao (Liang Ch'i-ch'ao, 1873-1929) was particularly respected by the reformist thinkers of the present century. With Tan Sitong, he studied the doctrine of the Great Commonwealth under Kang, and he lectured in the new school of literature and political thought at Changsha. His radicalism earned him a spell in exile. He was particularly interested in Buddhism, and wrote among other things *Eighteen Studies in Buddhism*. He saw Buddhism as a good answer to the spiritual hunger of the age and looked for a new uncorrupt faith unlike that of Buddhism in earlier periods of Chinese History.[5] 'Before being able to save myself, I try to save others,' he wrote. 'This is the bodhisattva's motivation.'[6] 'There is no doubt that Buddhism in China . . . will always be an important factor in our thinking.'[7]

In the present century, many intellectuals with some knowledge of Western culture and a desire for modernization were Buddhist activists; some were Buddhist monks. Partiuclarly well-known outside China was Tai Xu (T'ai Hsü, 1890-1947), a monk who, influenced by the revolutionary Qi Yun (Ch'i-yün), wrote a eulogy for the martys of the Canton rising of May 1911 and subsequently involved himself in every form of Buddhist organization that showed promise of wielding political influence. Throughout his career, he busied himself in the propagation of

Buddhist education, in Buddhist propaganda of all sorts, and in the formation of associations with aspirations to supervise the Buddhist life of the country. He constantly sought the approval of successive republican governments for forms of government control over Buddhism in which he might have a dominating political part to play. Holmes Welch, in his study of the fortunes of Buddhism in China in recent times, gives special attention to his sometimes bizarre career, and brings to our notice also the activities of other Buddhist evangelists. Cong Yang (Tsung Yang), for example, ordained at the famous Jin Shan monastery, studied Sanskrit, Japanese and English; with the abundant patronage of Mrs Silas Hardoon, the Chinese wife of a Baghdad millionaire, he spread the Buddhist message, setting up a Buddhist school and eventually founding a Patriotic Girls' School in Shanghai; a confirmed radical, he was a supporter and helper of Sun Yat Sen. Man Shu (1884-1918) was another monk who was active in the modernising movement, teaching English and alternating between his monk's robes and Western dress.[8] There were many such, and they were responsible for a flurry of revivalist activities on a new pattern alien to the traditional rural style of Buddhist piety. Lay organisations, led by educated enthusiasts, mushroomed in some of the big cities, engaging in all sorts of activities: running vegetarian restaurants, setting up study groups, founding orphanages, clinics and schools. The contact with Japan, where many intellectuals encountered the modern world, introduced them to Buddhism in a way that made them take it seriously. A large number of officials, and some warlords, were keen lay Buddhists. A Western observer in the 1920s, L. Hodous, wrote:

> Many officials, disheartened by the present confused political situation, have sought refuge in the monasteries. Some of them are now abbots of monasteries and are using their influence to build them up. All over China there are Confucian scholars who are giving themselves to the study of Buddhism and to meditation. Some of the Chinese students who have studied in Buddhist universities in Japan are propagating Buddhism by lecture.[9]

Many twentieth-century reformers and revolutionaries, of course, have consciously rejected Buddhist traditions *in toto*. Hu Shi (Hu Shih, 1891-1962) by no means a revolutionary but a gradualist reformer, saw Buddhism as a gospel of defeatism and the early period of its prevalence in China as a time of 'humiliating domination'. The attempts of men such as Kang to reinterpret Confucius or the Buddha as teachers with a modern message are now commonly treated as no more than an awkward transition, a necessary but quickly transcended weaning away from the past; and the discursive oratory of a Tai Xu about the aptness of Buddhism to science now seems to many merely jejune, or quaint.

This may be, but it is a mistake to see in the early reformers' interest in Buddhism *no more than* a piece of old-fashioned thinking that had outstayed its time. What we notice about their interest is, especially, that Buddhism seemed to them to be pre-eminently rational — a means whereby the individual could, through the exercise of his intellect, rid himself of the constraints of a conformist society. This aspect is well worth careful thought.

What it shows is the perennial compulsive urge of the revolutionary or reformer to transcend the limitations of his own, socially conditioned, consciousness. This is essentially a bootstraps exercise. Philosophically speaking, it is perhaps ultimately contradictory; therefore it engenders an intense and sometimes obsessive preoccupation with the power of thought. Recognizing the influence upon his own mind of the culture-bound and therefore subjective dominion of history, the thinker seeks to distance himself from himself, to crystallize in the here and now a pure vision and an act of will that can transcend the particularities of his condition and make real a more truly objective perception of reality.

For Buddhism, history is karma, which moulds and shapes the individual's acts. The thinker's goal is to transcend karma by an act of pure vision which leads to enlightenment, but the act of bending energy towards this goal is itself an event in his history and therefore within the dominion of karma and subject to its taint. In a way, this is the old paradox of free will. A great deal of subtle Buddhist metaphysics was addressed to the problem of thought, enlightenment or pure vision and the phenomenal world. The distinctive contribution of Mahāyāna Buddhism, prevalent in China, was to stress the moment of confrontation between mind and the phenomenal world in the given present experience, the immediately conscious event. In this moment, if only we could realize it, the subjective and the objective are fused, identical; the sacred is immanent; the mental is physical. 'Is the Buddha nature in this dog?' asks the Zen teacher. The Vijñānāvada school uncompromisingly pronounced that the world of sense is coterminous with thought. 'The universe is my mind, my mind is the universe,' said Lu Xiangshan (Lu Hsiang-shan).

It is important to recognize that this sort of philosophy is often effectively accepted by those who explicitly reject it. Buddhist idealism has certainly been rejected by modern philosophers of the current Marxist-Leninist orthodoxy. Ren Jiyu (Jen Chi-yü), writing in *Philosophical Studies* in 1961, attacked Buddhist *Hua Yen* idealism as an instrument of the ruling class in past times: 'The Hua-yen school employs all sorts of devious methods to prove that the present world is not real, that it is unknowable, illusory and relative. Its ultimate aim is to lead people away from the human world to the heavenly world.'[10]

This is not subtle. It represents Hua-yen as a sort of dualism which subordinates the material to the mental or immaterial. In fact it is just as much a monism which declares the material and the immaterial to be one and the same. If everything in the universe is material, then there is nothing left for the word 'immaterial' to mean; if everything is immaterial, there is nothing left for the word 'material' to mean, and they come to the same thing. A philosopher may approach this monism either by analysing the material as immaterial, or by analysing the immaterial as material. The two approaches may seem very different, and their proponents may be at odds with each other; but they are climbing up the same tree.

Wang Yangming (1472-1529) produced a philosophy of great interest to modern Chinese thinkers. For him, the moral law is by its nature incapable of being isolated from the action of one's own mind in a given situation. He rejected Buddhist philosophical idealism, but this did not make him a straightforward realist. Truth is found in concrete action. Knowledge is will. The mind must therefore be purified. He made much of the idea of a sort of pure transcendent vision, *liang-zhi* (*liang-chih*) or original good-knowing, which he identified with the Buddhist dharma eye of the bodhisattva.[11]

With the dharma eye, one transcends the paradox of free will. One sees that what is willed, which is unconditioned and absolute, is in fact identical with the willed act itself, which is conditioned by history. It is no long step from here to the Hua-yen mysticism of the identity of everything with everything.

I say: the concept is reality; the finite is the infinite; imagination is thought; I am the universe; life is death; death is life; the present is the past and the future; the past and the future are the present; the small is the great; the yin is the yang; the high is the low; the impure is the pure; the thick is the thin; the substance is the words; that which is multiple is one; that which is changing is eternal.[12]

Funnily enough, this is not a Buddhist philosopher. It is Mao Zedong. As Wakeman says, 'Mao's conceptualization of particular and universal relationships was indiscrete. In some ways it even resembled K'ang Yu-wei's prescientific vision of Taoist or Buddhist universal relativities, which — from a metaphysical point of view — created an identity of indiscernibilities.'[13]

The generation of Chinese intellectuals born in the late dusk of imperial rule felt itself acutely to be a generation of marginal men, torn between a misunderstood Chinese tradition and an undigested modern Western culture. They projected the contradictions that rent their own minds upon the plight of their country, and it is not surprising that in the 1920s and 1930s there was a great deal of debate about the social conditions of knowledge and action. Some thinkers were intrigued by the spurious simplicities of eugenics (recently popular in Europe), the theory that character is conditioned by heredity or racial stock, so that a man's style of thought could be predicted from a sufficient knowledge of his genes. Others, such as Gu Jiegang, preferred class to race as the operative condition. But many thinkers sought to reconcile with their favoured doctrine a belief that by the power of will it is possible to take short cuts, to transcend the laws, whatever they were, which embody history.

Li Dazhao (Li Ta-chao, 1888-1927), for example, was one of the godfathers of revolution in China. From 1913 to 1916 he was in Japan, where so many revolutionaries formed their ideas in an atmosphere of freedom and heady social transformation. In 1918 he became head librarian at Peking University, where he influenced Mao Zedong, his young assistant. He formed the Marxist Study Society; in 1924 he joined the Kuomintang, then still the great vehicle of youth and idealism. His philosophy was consciously influenced by Bergson; he saw time as a stream where the past and future are wholly implicit in the present moment. Thus, the present conscious act is identical with, rather than merely the epiphenomenon of, the course of history. He, like other intellectuals of his period, sought refuge in a somewhat mystical casuistry from the paradoxes of determinism.

Such thinkers, of whom Mao was one, were necessarily exercised a deal by the problem of truth. Is there a real truth that can be known, or is all would-be knowledge simply belief conditioned by historical forces? For Mao, truth lay in the here and now, above all in action.

If you want to know the taste of a pear, you must change the pear by eating it yourself. If you want to know the structure and properties of the atom, you must make physical and chemical experiments to change the state of the atom.[14]

Bauer, quoting this passage, comments:

This thesis, unique in Marxism, is vaguely reminiscent of Heisenberg's indeterminacy principle. But it was not from physics, of course, that Mao derived it, but unquestionably from the conceptual framework of the *Book of Changes* which is also merely half-determinist, as it were. For in contrast to other mantic systems which necessarily imply a rigid fatalism, the *I-ching* oracles only indicate developmental *tendencies* which could be significantly modified and indeed overcome if they and the specific counsel based on them were understood.'[15]

That is, the predisposing but not absolutely determining forces of history are subject to the dharma eye; knowledge creates fact, not vice versa. Without acknowledging it, Mao was treading a path hacked out by the diviners of classical antiquity and the mountain sages of the dharma. As Bauer continues, 'Reality and cognition, object and subject, which are fundamentally inseparable, are thus in a constant process of change which does not approach a distant, fixed pole, but forms part of the nature of being and cognition.'[16]

Of course, it would be gratuitous to suggest that a modern Chinese thinks partly in the same way as an ancient Chinese simply because they are both Chinese. Such a glib inference must be scouted. It is much more likely that they thought in the same way because they were responding to similar stimuli — the dilemmas, perhaps, of the maverick individualist who dreams of perfect self-fulfilment in a period of social change. Marxists in Europe thought in similar ways. Bauer compares Mao closely to Engels, who traded absolute truth for a belief in a sort of relative truth identified with the will and knowledge of the thinker.

Yet [says Bauer] it is also true that precisely because it cannot find a fixed place anywhere in a perpetually changing medium, the ideal society acquires a curious presence. Just as absolute truth is only revealed 'in the *process* of cognition itself,' the ideal society becomes tangible reality only in the revolution, during change, which is the 'only absolute'. But this change is constantly at work in the incessant movement of contradictions in all phenomena (including society) and therefore can be realized at any time in the consciousness of it.[17]

Marxist exegesis, like Taoist philosophy and Buddhist mysticism, deals with paradoxes that sometimes engender a rather arcane scholasticism bewildering to the uninitiated. We cannot follow it into all its refinements, but we may note, with Wakeman, that it resolved the conflict between the belief in the power of human will and historical materialism by redefining the willing self in terms of praxis, confrontation with actual problems.[18]

When the Chinese Communist Party extended its authority over most of the country in 1949, then, it was a party led by a team of unpolished intellectuals, some temperamentally rebellious and some half-educated, frustrated and bitter, who regarded the institutions of government as a laboratory for the alchemy of their philosophical debates, the nation as a blank page on which they could write their formulae. They had no use for religion in their private lives and little inclination to extend it more than grudging tolerance in public. Parallels there may be between Buddhist dialectic and their own, but such parallels they did not have the training to recognize, or the disposition to take to heart if they should be recognized. The Chinese Buddhist Association set up in 1953 was not exactly an instrument for the state persecution of Buddhism, but it was certainly not a vehicle of enthusiastic state patronage either. It was originally no doubt intended as a supervising body which should oversee and control, without being contaminated by, the religious activities of genuine Buddhists throughout the country. This was no exotic totalitarianism generated by fanatical revolutionaries in Europe and imported from motives of ideological provincialism. On the contrary, the government was only doing what all Chinese governments had attempted, though the turmoil of the past century had thwarted most attempts: to establish the exclusive claims of state orthodoxy, limiting and controlling all spontaneous tendencies in any other direction in the interests of the community as defined by its rulers.

Buddhism belies the notion that culturally China has always been completely self-contained and fundamentally disdainful of the world's traffic. The British embassy of the Earl of Macartney in 1793 earned only an edict saying 'our celestial empire possesses all things in prolific abundance' and praising George III for his 'respectful spirit of submission'. The outside world had nothing that China really needed, though perhaps Europeans needed Chinese rhubarb to keep their metabolism in good order. Yet, incredibly, Buddhism, as unlike the family-centred orthodoxy of the Central Kingdom as one could very well imagine, was taken eagerly to heart.

One day historians might be writing the same sort of thing about Marxism, which used to be regarded by old China hands as so totally alien to the Chinese way of thought that it could never take on. Buddhism, like Marxism, had to go through an awkward process of acculturation in which some of its technical terminology, translated into Chinese, found itself clothed in strange new meanings. The early Chinese version of *nirvana*, for example, turned into *wu wei*, which is the Taoist concept of non-activity or intuitive oneness with the spontaneous way of nature.

It is something of a paradox that, however popular Buddhism became — perhaps indeed, for the very reason that it was too popular — the Chinese state never forgot that it was a foreign religion. It had to be treated accordingly in the precise etiquette of Confucian ceremony. Under the Tang, official organization of Buddhist affairs was first the responsibility of the Court of State Ceremonials, which dealt with foreign missions and thus was regarded as the official instrument for dealing with the outside world. The Empress Wu moved the responsibility to the Bureau of National Sacrifice, thus implicitly domesticating the religion; in AD 736 it was shuttled back to the Court, and a year later it was returned to the Bureau. Under the Song, Confucianism re-established its eminence, and prominent scholars jealous of the status of the old orthodoxy were quick to point out the exotic origin, and hence *a fortiori* the barbarousness, of the Buddha's dharma. In a famous memorial to the throne objecting to the ceremony with which the emperor was proposing to receive at the capital a supposed Buddha relic, Han Yu (AD 768-824) wrote:

Your servant begs leave to say that Buddhism is no more than a cult of the barbarian peoples which spread to China in the time of the Latter Han. It did not exist here in ancient times . . . Now Buddha was a man of the Barbarians who did not speak the language of China and wore clothes of a different fashion. His sayings did not concern the ways of our ancient kings, nor did his manner of dress conform to their laws. He understood neither the duties that bind sovereign and subject, nor the affections of father and son. If he were still alive today and came to our court by order of his ruler, Your Majesty might condescend to receive him, but it would amount to no more than one audience in the Hsüan-cheng Hall, a banquet by the Office for Receiving Guests, the presentation of a suit of clothes, and he would then be escorted to the borders of the nation, dismissed, and not allowed to delude the masses. How then, when he has long been dead, could his rotten bones, the foul and unlucky remains of his body, be rightly admitted to the palace? Confucius said: 'Respect ghosts and spirits, but keep them at a distance!'[19]

The cultural insularity was real enough. Many Confucians really did believe, until history finally overtook them, that China possessed all things in prolific abundance and had no need of the exoticisms and prodigies that vulgar foreigners sought to peddle. Yet it is no real paradox that a foreign faith, such as Buddhism or Marxism, should be taken to heart by the multitude. Precisely because it was foreign, it was an alternative creed for those who found the orthodoxy blighting. Precisely because it came from outside, it was most likely to appeal to those who, in times of dynastic crisis, wished to stand forth as proponents of a new order. It may be added that what Buddhism shared in particular with Marxism was the character of a whole cosmology – it did not simply supply a messianic gospel to legitimize political secession, but provided an explanation for everything, a science of the universe into which today's political changes fitted as an essential and predictable episode justified by the principles that governed history. Thus reformist thinkers of the end of the Qing were wont to approve Buddhism as a progressive force, as we saw above: men like Wang Guowei and Gu Jiegang praised the vigour and vitality which they attributed to Buddhism's part in China's development.

It is well worth noticing one conspicuous characteristic that endeared both Buddhism and Marxism to the marginal man, the rebel, the individualist. Each preached that its adherents could not step forth along the path to salvation, national or personal, without cutting themselves off from their old lives, taking on new identities, renouncing their families. Nothing could be more antagonistic to the established tradition of familial loyalty, and, in times of peace under strong central government, this uncompromising doctrine had to be reinterpreted. Kenneth Ch'en has charted the various ways in which Buddhist teaching was glossed, distorted or falsified to accommodate itself to the principle of filial piety.[20] But the gospel of renunciation was always there, implicit in the way of life of the Buddhist monks in all parts of the country. Every monk abandoned his old names upon ordination, acquiring in their place a *mingzi* or Buddhist literary name and a *hao*, a name for daily use. Complex systems of name cycles linked monks in families, exactly modelled on biological families, whereby each master was the father of a family of his pupils, and each successive dharma generation took the next name from a sacred cycle of syllables. Sometimes, monks who were given to the order in childhood would not even know their real family names.

Of course, Buddhism did not go so far as to encourage children to stand forth in public and denounce their parents for supposed breaches of moral principle. It would have been utterly false to itself had it done so. The Chinese Communist leadership, which under Mao sought during some of the more hectic mass campaigns to promote just such revolutionary behaviour, belongs to a different world of culture. Yet the parallel is significant enough in its own way: each movement sought to cut its members off from the cloying bonds of attachment they had formed with the people around them in their old secular life; each sought ruthlessly enough to forge for its members a new identity.

This raises the interesting subject of the education or thought reform imposed by the Communist Party upon those fallible individuals who were to be fashioned into its instruments, and thereby to achieve a new identity. What is rarely remarked, and what is worth a little examination here, is one way in which the political discipline of the new culture patterned itself point for point upon the discipline of the old Buddhist heterodoxy, without anybody ever noticing the fact.

Perhaps nothing contributed quite so pervasively or insidiously to the outside world's perception of life under the Communist Chinese government in its early days as the policy of thought reform or ideological remoulding, *sixiang gaizao* (*ssu-hsiang kai-tsao*), eagerly christened 'brainwashing'. The Chinese term connotes much more than merely a training course in politics. It means the positive re-making of one's cast of thought, deeply bedded in one's personality though that may be. Lurid tales in the 1950s of people, Chinese and foreigners alike, having their spirit broken and turned into pathetic shambling sycophants of the Chinese government and its ideology made it seem that perhaps the Communist governors of China and the USSR had developed a fiendish technology to reach into the mind and reshape it at will.

This perception made 'brainwashing' seem more sinister than it really was. Potentially successful up to a point when applied subtly and in concentration to carefully studied individuals, the methods of thought reform were likely to be counter-productive, in the long run, when applied crudely and without differentiation by bigoted zealots to large groups of people. They could cause endless tension and misery. They could compel outward conformity under the sanction of specific implied threats. But they did not recycle minds on a conveyor belt. The government did not play Pygmalion to a nation. Nowadays, the public in Western countries no longer regards the Chinese educators and governors as an infernal thought police.

But perhaps thought reform is sinister enough. After all, it had its individual successes. Its adoption as a technique of government had profound consequences for the biographies of generations of intellectuals. Its employment embodies the aspirations of an influential persuasion in Chinese politics, a persuasion represented pre-eminently by Mao himself, and many of the most influential people in the country today have been involved in it as subjects or administrators or both. It has frequently been used in re-education and re-training camps and courses since the 1950s when it was notorious; it will be used again.

And, more than anything else, 'brainwashing' seems to belong emphatically to the modern world — the world of the commissar, of Koestler's nightmares and Orwell's fevered imagination, of scientific warfare, of totalism, of materialism. The urbane tolerance which superficially seems to characterize the 'Confucian' past appears profoundly irrelevant to this world. Old China, we might think, can offer no clues to the politics or the mentality.

But, in fact, nothing could be further from the truth.

Probably nearly every society known to history, and most of those that have never achieved entries in the record of history, have lit upon a set of facts about the psychology of stress that can be exploited with advantage by any community interested in modifying the behaviour of its recruits. That these facts are so exploited is usually shuffled off into the darker corners of the collective mind, for a frank avowal of and public debate about the techniques of exploitation would tend to defeat the purposes of the exploiters; therefore they may often be, though not actually concealed, so out of focus in the perceptions of all those involved that they are blurred and forgotten, and later remembered and forgotten again.

What they entail is that an individual may come cheerfully and sincerely to espouse the customs and beliefs of a particular community into which he is recruited if his induction into it is attended by certain conditions calculated to cause in him constant disorientation, confusion and stress of mind. In particular, these conditions can be distinguished:

1. He gets no proper sleep. He is repeatedly woken up after only a few hours; much of the sleep he is able to achieve is taken in irregular dozes through the day;
2. He is compelled under the sanction of certain penalties to learn a large body of obscure and arbitrary rules which apply to what he says and does at every moment of the day, which he is expected to obey constantly, and which he cannot hope to master or fully understand for a very long time;
3. He is surrounded by people who seem constantly to disapprove of him, to find his behaviour obscurely unacceptable, and to be looking for improvements in it which are not impossible to achieve but are difficult in the extreme;
4. He is constantly nagged by a fear of punishment, sometimes in the form of others' anger or disapproval, sometimes in the form of physical chastisement;
5. He is given intellectual problems to solve and given to understand that it is essential for him to solve them, though they appear to be rationally insoluble, so that it is only by some strange sleight of thought that they can be considered overcome;
6. He is given a new identity, and quite explicitly and deliberately cut off from the whole background of his past life.

It needs to be understood that these conditions do not necessarily require to be imposed willy-nilly by an act of despotism upon a passive victim. A recruit may enter the induction process knowing that he can expect to experience stress and disorientation. Some people may derive a thrill of gratification from the self-abasement exacted from them. Many may accept it happily with their minds fixed on the rewards of acceptance in the community, with a new identity, at the end of the process. But, probably, the more obvious it is that these conditions are imposed as a piece of deliberate manipulation rather than as necessary features of community orientation, the less likely it is that the recruit will absorb their effects into his being. Therefore it is natural that, in the course of time, the employment of such techniques comes to be regarded, by recruits and organizers alike, chiefly as traditional and salutary rituals.

The deliberate use of such techniques of stress to induce psychological breakdown and suggestibility to new ideas finds a measure of legitimacy in the line of research inspired by the work of Pavlov. W. Sargant, in his study of 'brainwashing',[21] expressly dissociates himself from the materialist philosophy underlying Pavlov's programme, but argues that his experiments were good ones and genuinely embody principles that apply to human beings as well as dogs. There have been many well-known cases of people experiencing dramatic changes of belief after undergoing severe stress such as illness. Pavlov's work seems to offer scientific techniques to design the stress, tailoring it to the individual temperament and ensuring that the subject reaches a point of crisis after which he is receptive to the implantation of new ideas.[22]

What must be done to precipitate the crisis varies from individual to individual. Generally speaking, the individual must be rendered unable to cope in normal ways with his environment. He may be saturated with an overwhelmingly intense bombardment of stimuli. He may be subjected to agonies of suspense and defeated expectation. He may be disoriented and confused by conflicting stimuli to which he cannot respond. Finally, he may be brought close to collapse by physical debility.[23]

The general pattern of these techniques has time and time again characterized the successes of religious teachers, as Sargant abundantly illustrates. Several stress-inducing principles emerge clearly from an examination of the most successful revivalists and educators. Firstly, and ubiquitously, those subjected to the pressure for religious conversion are made prey to tormenting anxiety, usually about the prospect of eternal suffering in hell. Another recurrent method is to find out in the subject's mind a particular point of tension, a private fear, which is then singled out for unremitted nagging pressure. (This is a little reminiscent of room 101 in George Orwell's *1984*. Room 101 contains the worst thing in the world, whatever that may be for each individual. Incidentally, 101 was the number of the room in Broadcasting House where Orwell produced propaganda during the war.) Again, the subject of religious training may be made to undergo a rigorous programme that robs him of sleep, until he cannot think straight and is in a constant daze, a conspicuous feature of Jesuit priestly education. One other mind-assaulting weapon is the hypnotic impact of persistent rhythmic sound, such as African drumming or Indian chanting.[24] (The psychology of Tibetan Buddhist singing would make a fascinating study in its own right.)

The Chinese Communist Party used a sophisticated array of thought reform techniques from early on, particularly when, during the Japanese War, floods of naive young intellectuals made their way to the Communist-dominated areas and had to be moulded into willing agents of an ideology which at first they did not properly understand. The great educational campaign at the beginning of the 1940s, with which Mao was prominently associated, was a major exercise in ideological remoulding.

Earlier pages here have described an atomised and individualistic society. In 1949, with sudden victory, the Party was faced with the task of organizing such a society in accordance with a socialist programme, inevitably using as instruments officials drawn from that society. The training of officials, at all levels and in every department of social and public life, was the most daunting problem. To the training of these officials the government sought to apply all the most effective thought reform methods used previously in the Party Schools. There was no alternative.

During the first three years, numerous 'Revolutionary Universities' were set up for the purpose. The first was the North China People's Revolutionary University in Peking. The one in Shanghai was called the East China University of Science. There was one in each political-military region. But they were not universities in any real sense. They were residential short-course training colleges, typically offering six-month courses, where potential officials could be isolated from the outside world and exposed without mitigation to the full barrage of thought reform technology. The recruits were miscellaneous – promising school-leavers, returned students, former KMT officials, professional men of all sorts. They all had to be cast in short order in the one mould of reliable and willing agents of the regime. Even by the end of 1949, as many as 500,000 intellectuals were being or had been trained in these or similar institutions.[25]

In the 1950s, as many as possible of the techniques used in these hectic little communities were extended to substantial sections of the population as these were made the targets of successive campaigns. The first of these was the Thought Reform or Reformative Study Campaign of 1951, directed at the nation's intellectuals, traditionally of course a very important group in Chinese society. In schools and universities throughout the land, educated people were formed into study groups, compelled to study political documents, discuss them *ad nauseam*, criticize themselves and each other, and write autobiographical reports or confessions, in the constant knowledge that if their performance was (however arbitrarily and unpredictably) judged unsatisfactory they would be made to suffer. As one writer has put it, 'thus began a campaign which meant for the teachers months of merciless inquisition and sophomoric "study" of Communist ideology with nerve-wracking soul-searching under the direction of half-baked cadres and humiliating confessions.'[26]

The employment of study groups, of criticism and self-criticism, of the writing of reports, and so forth, was extended to subsequent campaigns, such as the famous 'Three-anti' and 'Five-anti' campaigns of the following years which were intended to make good citizens of businessmen and officials.

The rest is history. It is largely a history of diminishing returns. Over the years, the Chinese became increasingly familiar with the campaign style and increasingly cynical. Denunications and confessions became more and more a matter of ritual, sincere conversions to orthodox ideology less and less frequent. The original idea was to reach into the mind and precipitate a real religious conversion; sincerity was essential to it. But what might work successfully with single individuals subjected to expensive special treatment was less and less likely to succeed when it was applied to larger and larger sections of the population, under the management of activists qualified by zeal rather than subtlety. Even at the early stage of the 'Revolutionary Universities', the process was wasteful and inefficient. A single individual who had been through a course reported direct knowledge of one suicide and two commitments to mental hospitals as a result of the nightmare pressures which the students had undergone.[27]

What methods proved more or less effective in Chinese thought reform? Some things are mentioned regularly in the first-hand accounts given by people who experienced it. Participants would be organised in small groups and required to study great masses of material, discuss it endlessly, and seek through the catharsis of self-examination to attain to the 'correct' viewpoint. Activists, originally seeded anonymously in the study groups, would manipulate the discussions, progressively introducing stridency and antagonism. Heresies in political thinking would be bitterly attacked. Anybody could be found guilty of one heresy or another, for these included subjectivism, sentimentalism, deviationism, opportunism, dogmatism, class ideology, technical viewpoints, departmentalism, sectarianism and pro-Americanism.[28] You couldn't win. The tempo was increased; participants would eat, sleep and breathe political study. Finally, they would be required to write reports criticizing their own past errors and showing that they had now seen the light. These reports would be subjected to fierce debate and criticism in competitive group discussions, and would often have to be re-written many times before the organizers would certify an individual as having genuinely experienced thought reform. Confessions commonly had to include denunciations of the subjects' own parents, psychologically perhaps the most difficult hurdle and a potent symbol of rejection of one's past. Mass struggles would often be organized against those judged backward, a terrible object lesson to encourage forwardness.

Richard Walker, in his account of the process, lists as operative factors isolation from friends and family, fatigue, tension, uncertainty about the fate of those who fail, the use of vicious language, and the complete humourlessness of the whole proceedings.[29]

Theodore Hsi-en Chen identifies these features: the participant is subjected to an atmosphere of struggle which may be violent and bitter; the lessons studied are adapted to the needs of the group involved; emphasis is placed on *self*-reform; agitators pulling the strings from behind the scenes set the pace; denunciations, of oneself or others, are of highly specific faults, not just generalities; the pressure on the individual is essentially group pressure, compelling him eventually to speak out; those who fail to perform satisfactorily can expect low-level or menial careers or even hard labour; humiliation is an essential part of the experience; and individualism has to be discarded.[30]

> The Communists leave no doubt that intellectuals must undergo reform, but insist that the reform must be voluntary, that re-education must be self-education. The individual must wage a relentless struggle against his own past and set patterns of thought. He must virtually destroy himself for a new self to be born. The ideological conversion comes after the individual has been brought to see how unworthy his past and how necessary a new life, with a new outlook and a new 'standpoint'.[31]

This clearly all belongs to the psychology of religious conversion. The distinctive features of mass political manipulation in Communist China must obviously be seen in a perspective of religious history. Yet this perspective is rarely adopted, and certain continuities with elements in an earlier tradition are assiduously overlooked. As Sargant says:

> The techniques of political and religious indoctrination are often so similar that in primitive communities, or in more civilized theocratic states such as the ancient Jewish, they are actually identical. Thus a study of the better recorded methods of religious indoctrination will yield results that are, *ceteris paribus*, equally applicable to the political field. Yet some of the most obvious similarities are often ignored because either the religious approach (as in Western Europe or the United States today) or the political (as in Eastern Europe

and China) is accorded official respect at the other's expense.[32]

It is obvious enough that, in most Buddhist monasteries at most times, the typical monk on being ordained does not undergo anything like the full rigour of 'brainwashing'. In a Theravada Buddhist country today, for example, the young man who enters a local village monastery does not lose contact with his family, expects to rejoin it before too long anyway, already knows the other monks as friends and relatives, and is thoroughly familiar with many of the terms and rituals of Buddhist lore. The rigours of monastic life may be tedious at times, but its physical discomfort may be no greater than that of the poor farmhouse which he has just left, and its routine may leave him with a satisfying abundance of agreeable leisure.

It is equally obvious, though, that those few monasteries that have enjoyed the highest esteem, have attracted the largest numbers of lay disciples and weekend tourists, and have been regarded as repositories of the greatest stores of magically communicable merit, have in large measure been those which, by their attachment to a 'pure' tradition of selfless piety, have in fact most closely approximated in their discipline to the conditions described above. Furthermore, there is in the ritual even of the ordinary village monastery rather more evidence of a process directed towards a crisis of identity in the ordinand than is immediately obvious.

In modern China, it is the small number of famous ordination monasteries, those licensed to grant ordination certificates and often seeking to maintain high standards of piety, erudition and meditation under the influence of the *Chan* tradition, to which we should look for paradigms of the *vinaya*, Buddhist discipline.

We find, firstly, that the would-be monk had to learn, in a gruelling pre-ordination course so severe that many simply ran away, the basic set of 250 rules of conduct derived from the *vinaya* of the ancient Hinayana Buddhism and a large body of commandments based on a Tang dynasty text. Further, every monastery had its own special book of rules, called *gui yue*. There were literally thousands of rules that a monk had to learn. One older monk said that the routine of life in the meditation hall, the building where advanced practice was followed, could not be mastered in less than three winters and four summers.[33]

It was considered that the first five years after ordination should be devoted to the study of the discipline if a monk was to master the whole body of rules. Every phase of daily life was bound by the obligations of propriety and etiquette. There were correct and incorrect ways of doing everything, from sitting down for meditation to cleaning the teeth, from feeding the spirits of the dead to visiting the latrines. Necessarily, the postulant or the recently ordained monk felt like a fish out of water.

The routine would be exhausting and painful. In the fortnightly *pratimoksa* ceremonies, monks would be forced to kneel for hours at a stretch while the 250 basic *vinaya* rules were recited and assented to one by one. In the special courses periodically conducted in the meditation hall, the monks were required to squat cross-legged for long periods, forbidden to ease their limbs on pain of disciplinary beating, and the torment of their leg cramps would cause them to sweat profusely and lose sleep at night.[34]

Instruction in the dharma was accompanied by continual scolding and beating. The daily routine would begin at three or four o'clock in the morning, when instructors would come round and belabour those who sought to linger near the arms of Lethe. In some places, observed the Norwegian missionary K.L. Reichelt, it was the rule that everyone must experience discipline: 'I have often seen the blows fall like a shower on diligent and good novices.'[35] In a large monastery, punishments were under the direction of the proctor and the guest prefect. The proctor could summarily give a blow on the cheek; the guest prefect could administer blows with the incense board. Prostration, chanting and fines were common forms of punishment adopted by many monasteries for routine infringements. Any breach of etiquette was liable to attract instant retribution:

> A lay informant recalled that as a boy he had been once permitted to watch the monks of the T'ien-ning Ssu at breakfast. None of them made a sound — something of a feat when eating congee — until a young monk audibly slurped. The proctor, wielding his stick, marched over, paused before him for a moment, and then hit his bare pate a resounding smack.[36]

Typically, the daily routine would leave the monk five hours for sleep at night, with short periods of rest during the day when he could go into a doze. This sort of existence, it is important to recognize, consigns one to a constant state of wool-gathering bemusement in which everything seems unreal, until one gets used to it. It is not conducive to keen lucid thought. During a *Chan* meditation week, 'The objective is to step up the schedule to the point where the mind, exhausted by lack of sleep and frustrated by work on the *hua-t'ou* (a question set for study), will make the jump to enlightenment.'[37] During this special week, monks taking part in the course would have only two hours sleep at night, supplemented by cat-naps. Their life in the meditation hall was strictly regimented, with a great deal of mind-numbing drill — sitting, standing, going around the hall in circles, doing everything by numbers. The routine was accompanied by frequent beating. Many participants would suffer hallucinations as a result of the stress of the exercise, and many fell ill, some even dying.

Ritual branding was part of the ordination ceremony, visible and ineradicable evidence that the monk had taken on a new identity. The practice is evidenced from as early as the second century in India, and is said to have been introduced in China in the eighth century. During the ritual, hollow reeds would be used to mark little circles on the scalp in the places to be branded. There would have to be at least three such circles; it was common to have nine, and some enthusiastic ordinands would choose to have twelve or even eighteen. Kneeling before a table with his arms placed upon it, each ordinand would have his head held by monks behind him. To the accompaniment of chanting, conical pieces of charcoal would be fixed to the branding spots by wax and then allowed to burn down through the wax into the skin. Pieces of turnip would be applied to cool the wounds, and he would then be free to wander about while the pain eased, with oranges to suck.[38]

The institution of meetings for self-criticism is not new in China. Indeed, there is an interesting antecedent in the village covenant system or *xiang yue* (hsiang yueh) fathered by the Ming philosopher Wang Yangming, whereby evil-doers were urged in public village meetings to see the error of their ways and reform themselves by the pressure of community opinion voiced through discussion of their good and bad points. But there is a hoarier ancestry for the public confessional in the fortnightly *uposatha* ceremonies of the Buddhist community, at which each monk must scrutinize his conscience and identify all the transgressions of which he is guilty in public conclave.

Another technique which, whatever its intention, exploits the psychology of stress is the *hua tou* (*hua-t'ou*), the question which a master gives a disciple to meditate upon. Welch reports:

When I have asked Chinese monks about *hua-t'ou*, they have usually mentioned two:
1. Who is this reciting Buddha's name?
2. Before my father and mother gave birth to me, what was my

original face?

Both of these amount to asking 'what am I?' Though monks were at liberty to shift to alternative *hua-t'ou*, it was considered better not to shift often. To keep working on the same question was 'Like a rat gnawing at a coffin — if he keeps gnawing at the same spot, there will come a day when he gnaws his way through.'[39]

Of course there is a considerable difference in purpose between the meditator seeking enlightenment who asks himself 'Who is thinking this thought?' and the cadre who asks himself 'Do I sincerely believe in this orthodoxy?', but there is a psychological similarity. Each is seeking to look *behind* the thought that he is thinking at the present moment and discover what lies there. To give an answer is to formulate a second thought, which demands in turn to be critically assessed. 'Who is thinking the thought: "I am the person thinking this thought"?' 'Am I sincere when I think "I am sincere"?' Each is a tail-chasing exercise which could go on for ever. Each, remorselessly pursued (whether by Party inquisitors or by a monk's own conscience), can be resolved only by a rupture of the normal processes of rational thought. Though in many ways the cadre and the monk are worlds apart, each is submitting himself to the rigours of a discipline which is designed to break up the framework of his routine mental life, to open doors into the parts of his mind that lie beneath the threshold of thought.

This discipline is supposed to make a new man of him. As a new man, he is, ideally, expected to behave in a new way: subject to the demands of a morality that is religious in its foundations. It is worthwhile to glance at the nature of these standards of behaviour for priests, whether of the revolution or of the dharma.

Any faith that acquires a mass following and gains wealth and patronage from the state or from the rich and powerful is liable to be corrupted; this is as true of Chinese Buddhism as it is of Chinese Communism. Yet this should not obscure the strain of puritanism, or moral austerity, that runs through the accepted norms of both. Just as the cadre is in theory supposed to live simply and frugally, forswearing all forms of indulgence out of a high-minded preoccupation with the benefit of others before himself, and just as in practice this prescription is often honoured only in outward and ritual forms or not at all, so too the committed Buddhist gave homage to an exacting code of personal behaviour that permitted him nothing that could be considered a luxury. His clothes had to be of sober and unpretentious tint — according to Pali sources, they could be dark green, mud-coloured or black. Indeed the Buddha's original sewing instructions had required monks to make their robes of rags from corpses.

The life of the monastery has often seemed comfortable enough to outside observers, though it is possible that the austerity of its routine requires a little more stamina than is readily apparent even in the less morally high-flying foundations, but one deprivation endured by all monks who are not flagrantly in breach of their discipline on any interpretation, too easily forgotten by the casual observer, is that of sexual satisfaction with women. Aristophanes has reminded us that the sanction of this deprivation is of no little weight. Many monks in Buddhist countries, in fact, have acknowledged that (at least in the earlier stages of a monastic career) it is the hardest thing to take about the Buddhist life.

Nor can the coenobite sublimate his urges with epicurean gourmandizing. Southern Buddhism allowed monks to eat whatever they were given (subject to certain restrictions) but forbade them to eat after noon. In the Chinese climate, it proved desirable to allow monks to eat in the evening; but one of the most pervasive features of the Buddhist persuasion in China has been a dedication to vegetarianism, which has come to constitute a veritable cult whose magico-religious significance would make an interesting study. Strict monks would forego meat, eggs, fish, dairy products and various vegetables. The 'five strong-smelling plants' — garlic, three types of onions and leeks — were always forbidden. In a Chinese text cited by Ch'en, we read:

> All those sentient beings who practice meditation should refrain from eating the five strong-smelling plants. These five when eaten cooked serve as aphrodisiacs, and when eaten raw will increase anger. Suppose a man should eat these strong-smelling plants, even though he may be able to explain the twelve divisions of the sutras, still the deities of the ten directions would object to his foul odors and would keep a safe distance from him. On the other hand, whenever he eats these items, hungry ghosts will come and lick his lips.[40]

Vegetarianism was always taken seriously, noticeably so by pious lay Buddhists. Particularly significant perhaps is the reason why monasteries were anxious to enforce the rule that no meat should be consumed on the premises, even if smuggled into the guest rooms by an otherwise innocent traveller. It was felt by the population of the area, for whose dead the monks gave services, that the magical effectiveness of these ceremonies would be diminished by any ritual impurity that sullied the monastery. Clearly, we have here to do with a widespread notion of sacred power inhering in the person of the holy man, a power that can be ritually manipulated, increased or decreased like a bank balance. For the lay world, the monk is in a sense a storehouse of magic. It therefore behoves him to follow an ascetic and puritanical code of conduct in order to maintain his store of sacred power at its maximum. There are many respects in which the cadres of today have inherited this archaic legacy of *mana*. However cynical the Chinese may be about the character of the real-life cadres they see around them in daily life, the religiously sanctioned notion of *noblesse oblige* persists still.

Notes

1. Liang Ch'i-ch'ao, *Intellectual Trends in the Ch'ing Period*, Harvard University Press, Cambridge, Mass., 1959, p. 116.
2. Cited, ibid., p. 117.
3. Cited, ibid., p. 112.
4. Cited by L. Schneider, *Ku Chieh-kang and China's New History*, California University Press, Berkeley, Calif., 1971, pp. 265f.
5. Liang Ch'i-ch'ao, *Intellectual Trends*, p. 105.
6. Ibid., p. 105.
7. Ibid., p. 117.
8. H. Welch, *The Buddhist Revival in China*, Harvard University Press, Cambridge, Mass., 1968, pp. 15-18.
9. Cited ibid., p. 74; see also pp. 75f.
10. Cited by K. Ch'en, 'Chinese Communist Attitudes towards Buddhism in Chinese History', in A. Feuerwerker (ed.), *History in Communist China*, MIT Press, Cambridge, Mass., 1968, pp. 158-74 at p. 163.
11. F. Wakeman, *History and Will: Philosophical Perspectives of Mao Tse-Tung's Thought*, California University Press, Berkeley, Calif., 1973, pp. 252f.
12. Ibid., p. 205.
13. Ibid.
14. Cited by W. Bauer, *China and the Search for Happiness: Recurring Themes in Four Thousand Years of Chinese Cultural History*, Seabury Press, New York, 1976, p. 393.
15. Ibid.
16. Ibid.
17. Ibid., p. 397.
18. F. Wakeman, *History and Will*, chap. 5, pp. 60-73.
19. Cited in W.T. de Bary, *et al.* (eds), *Sources of Chinese Tradition*, vol. 1, Columbia University Press, New York, 1960, pp. 372f.
20. K. Ch'en, *The Chinese Transformation of Buddhism*, Princeton University Press, Princeton, 1973, pp. 14-17, 35ff.
21. W. Sargant, *Battle for the Mind: a Physiology of Conversion and Brainwashing*, Heinemann, London, 1957.
22. Ibid., pp. 1-41.
23. Ibid., pp. 9f.

24. Ibid., pp. 135-44.
25. Theodore Hsi-en Chen, *Thought Reform of the Chinese Intellectuals*, Hong Kong University Press, Hong Kong 1960, pp. 17f.
26. Ibid., p. 32.
27. R. Lifton, *Thought Reform and the Psychology of Totalism: a Study of 'Brainwashing' in China*, Gollancz, London, 1961, p. 306.
28. Ibid., p. 300.
29. R. Walker, *China under Communism*, London, 1956 (Yale University Press, New Haven, 1955).
30. Theodore Hsi-en Chen, *Thought Reform*, pp. ' 72-9.
31. Ibid., p. 74.
32. W. Sargant, *Battle for the Mind*, p. 133.
33. H. Welch, *The Practice of Chinese Buddhism*, Harvard University Press, Cambridge, Mass., 1967, p. 88.
34. Ibid., pp. 54-78.
35. K.L. Reichelt, *Truth and Tradition in China*, Commercial Press, Shanghai, 1928, p. 239.
36. H. Welch, *The Practice of Chinese Buddhism*, p. 62.
37. Ibid., p. 75.
38. K.L. Reichelt, *Truth and Tradition*, p. 245.
39. H. Welch, *The Practice of Chinese Buddhism*, p. 69.
40. Cited by K. Ch'en, *The Chinese Transformation of Buddhism*, Princeton University Press, Princeton, p. 98.

PART FOUR

RITUAL AND RATIONAL USES OF EDUCATION

11 EDUCATION AND MODERNIZATION

> Eeyore looked at his sticks and then he looked at Piglet.
> 'What did Rabbit say it was?' he asked.
> 'An A', said Piglet.
> 'Did you tell him?'
> 'No, Eeyore, I didn't. I expect he just knew'.
> 'He *knew*? You mean this A thing is a thing *Rabbit* knew?'
> 'Yes, Eeyore. He's clever, Rabbit is'.
> 'Clever!' said Eeyore scornfully putting a foot heavily on his three sticks. 'Education!' said Eeyore bitterly, jumping on his six sticks.
> 'What *is* learning?' asked Eeyore as he kicked his twelve sticks into the air. 'A thing *Rabbit* knows! Ha!'
> 'I think — ' began Piglet nervously.
> 'Don't', said Eeyore.
>
> A.A. Milne, *The House at Pooh Corner*

Since the so-called Great Proletarian Cultural Revolution, which convulsed China for a decade, it has been obvious that nobody can understand modern China without some attention to the related problems of ideology, culture, education and manpower. In this section the purpose is to show that certain more or less traditional attitudes to education persist even when the vocabulary of debate is modern — whether it is the modernity of Marxist revolution or Western liberalism.

Commentators on modern Chinese education commonly recognize two lines: the 'egalitarian' line professed by Mao Zedong and the 'Gang of Four', which sought to use education as an instrument to change society, and the modernizing line followed by Deng Xiaoping and those around him, which sought to raise standards and emphasize quality education for organizers and professional people. (On ways of designating these two lines, see below, p. 209.) It seems proper to multiply these lines by two by recognizing a further distinction between ritual and rational attitudes to education on both sides. The ritual attitudes are, in an important sense, traditional ones.

The message of the following pages, therefore, is essentially the same as that of the preceding sections: the history of China, even up to the present, is made of whole cloth. There are new colours, but they are part of an old pattern. Chinese education has attracted a great deal of attention from outside commentators, and they, like specialists of other sorts, have tended occasionally, if unconsciously, to be influenced by the 'men from Mars' archetype. The policies and motives of the government, that is, are sometimes seen as new factors operating from outside, as if through men who were not themselves moulded by a prior Chinese cultural environment. The purpose of this survey of problems in education is, then, not to take sides in any debate but to bring out the importance of the distinction between ritual and rational approaches to education; it is just as important, in China, as the distinction between 'liberal' and 'egalitarian' and is not to be confused with it.

Under the 'Confucian' orthodoxy of the past, education was widely regarded by those who did not have it, and by all the less intelligent of those who did, as a ritual, difficult to undergo, by which one could reach a position of power, influence and wealth, and thereby be set far above all those who did not have education. Education was a sort of admission ticket. This attitude is of course familiar enough in all societies. What marks it out as specially important to the understanding of China is that, for one thing, China's civilian bureaucratic style of government put a premium on scholarship as a qualification for office rather than on birth, and, for another, despite the veneration in which scholarship was held, education was in fact not at a very high level among the population at large. (The nature of the Chinese script itself is a serious obstacle to widespread literacy.) Good education was therefore specially rare and specially precious for what it led to.

Another traditional, but not Confucian, attitude was one of contempt for book learning and indifference to the pretensions of officialdom and the vanity of government. This attitude is at its most sophisticated in literary Taoism. Taoists regarded book learning as an empty ritual for which they did not care; they did not care for worldly success either. Others, who could not afford the luxury of disdain for worldly success, nevertheless shared the iconoclastic hostility to conventional 'Confucian' scholarship. They wanted an admission ticket, but wanted it to be of a different sort from the study of the classics. Such people were numerous in the underworld of secret societies and messianic movements; they dreamed of utopias in which the old book learning would count for nothing. A different sort of ritual was to be put in its place: ritual homage to the goals of a millenarian ideology.

These traditional and ritual attitudes infect educational debate within China. The outside observer is prone to see most readily what is rational about the educational policy apparently most like his own philosophy, and what is ritual about the attitudes of those who oppose it. Thus, for some, the 'Gang of Four' democratization plans for education look like bold imaginative proposals on lines approved by (some) research in western countries while the policies of Deng Xiaoping and the modernizers around him look like a return to outworn rigid and stultifying models of Russian and Confucian inspiration. For others, the 'Gang of Four' line was an absurd caricature of education leading straight to anarchy, while the later policy was a return to genuine concern with the content and quality of education.

Perhaps one side is more right than the other; but we will do well to recognize that the battle over education and 'culture' has not been fought out entirely on the ground of rational debate between scholarly theorists. There are rationally debatable grounds both for concentrating scarce educational resources on a minority of privileged schools and for spreading education as widely as possible, redefining it in the process; but we must not overlook the fact that the contenders in the battle were actuated by social concerns that, in great measure, treated education, however defined, as a ritual; and these ritual attitudes are traditional. To whatever extent ritual wins, whatever the ritual may be, reason loses, and so does China.

Here we shall be looking particularly at the factors of frustration among educated people, the reasons why at certain periods the discontented and the displaced were so numerous. There were turbulent students on and off through imperial history. There are examples, from various dynasties, of students and officials incurring execution after controversy involving governments and eunuchs, of Imperial College students petitioning the Emperor to execute certain high officials, of violent conflicts between students and imperial employees inducing a change of policy towards invading barbarians, and so forth.[1] In the nineteenth century, as is well known, the prospects facing candidates for the official examinations worsened. The Taiping (T'ai-p'ing) movement, however various the factors which actuated the groups which composed it, was led by a frustrated intellectual — an often-failed examinee who, in his disappointment, lapsed into frenzied fits and periods of illness in which he had delirious visions.

Under the imperial examination system there were three degrees for which candidates sat: the *xiucai* (*hsiu-ts'ai*), the *juren* (*chü-jen*) and the highly esteemed *jinshi* (*chin-shih*). Towards the end of the nineteenth century, about two million candidates were examined each year, and it has been variously estimated that some 20,000 to 60,000 passed.[2] The discrepancy between candidature and conferment is not as bad as it seems: many of those who failed each year would make other attempts, and eventually pass; some could buy themselves into office; and others could find contentment in teaching, though this was always *faute de mieux*; but it was still bad.

Meanwhile, the contact with Western culture was fostering a type of social drama that has in the present century been played out in numerous unindustrialized countries: the propagation of modern education as an end in|itself, leading to the creation of an ultimately large class of 'marginal' men alienated from the traditional world and unable to gain employment in the modern world.

In a period of change from classical to modern education, the government could scarcely win, for, whichever sort it favoured, graduates of the other would be deprived. In 1903-4 a new uniform school system was organized. Up to 1911, on the Japanese model, the design was for government five-year lower primary schools leading to four-year higher primary schools, five-year secondary schools, three-year higher or matriculation colleges, and three-year or four-year university courses.[3] The abolition of the examination system in 1905-6 did not, of itself, discredit the entire paraphernalia of Confucian-style education, for in many quarters Confucian education was already discredited, but it infallibly demonstrated the futility of aspiring high from a foundation of purely classical education. The revolution of 1911 supervened before any new system could become entrenched, and amid the uncertain politics of the republic no regular form of recruitment to office was established.

One important consequence of Western influence, belatedly responded to by the empire, was the spread of Western schools. The full cultural effect of the values imbibed at these institutions was to be long delayed, for their Old Boys were insignificant in numbers compared with the total school system. But, in the long run, they infected their generation as a whole. One attitude promoted by education at Western schools was veneration of science — even pseudo-science, for it seemed to offer panaceas of modernity. Another was an ambivalent attitude to the West — thoroughly imbued with its cultural assumptions, but for that very reason nationalistic. Another was the absorption, perhaps unconscious, of the Christian values which saw Confucianism as a heresy and also offered a 'transcendalist' view of the world which allowed for the possibility of changing the world by will-power. This last influence perhaps converged with the legacy of Buddhism discussed above.

These attitudes were important to the nurturing of the revolutionary

Table 11.1: Educational Enrolment (National totals in thousands)

	Primary	Secondary	Tertiary
1912	2,750[a]	52[a] 100[m]	0.481[b] 40[m]
1915-16	4,123[h]		
1918-19	3,800[m]	100[m]	20[m]
1919-20	4,816[e]		
1920-1	6,000[e]		
1921-2	6,456[e]		
1922-3	6,602[h,m]	200[m] 103[e]	35[e] 34[m]
1927-8	8,000+[e]		
1928-9			25[d]
1929-30	8,800[m,h] 11,000[e]	300[m]	50[e] 29[d] 30[m]
1930-1	11,500[e]	440[g]	38[d]
1931-2	11,600[j]		44[d,i] 34[h]
1932-3			42[d]
1933-4			43[d]
1934-5			39[d]
1935-6	15,100[m]	583[f]	41[d] 40[m]
1936-7	11,500[a]	546[a]	42[d] 43[a]
1937-8	12,800[k]	390[k]	40[d] 42[k]
1938-9			36[d]
1939-40		623	44[d]
1940-1	13,546[l]		52[d]
1941-2	15,059[l]	800[m]	59[d]
1942-3	17,721[c]		64[c,d]
1943-4	18,602[l] 17,800[k]	1,103[k] 1,002[c,f]	74[d]
1944-5	17,222[l]		79[d] 70[k]
1945-6	21,832[l]		83[d]
1946-7	23,800[m] 24,000[c]	1,876[c]	129[c,d] 78[k] 130[m]
1947-8			155[d]

Notes: a. F.L.H. Pott, 'Modern Education' in H.F. MacNair, China (Berkeley and Los Angeles, 1946), pp. 427-40. .
b. Ibid., figure for government institutions only.
c. J. Chester Cheng, 'The Education System in Modern and Contemporary China', in E. Stuart Kirby (ed.), Contemporary China (Hong Kong, 1960), pp. 181-99.
d. I.C.Y. Hsu, 'The Reorganization of Higher Education in Communist China, 1949-1961', China Quarterly, vol. 19 (1964) pp. 128-60.
e. V. Purcell, Problems of Chinese Education (London, 1936).
f. China Handbook (Chinese Ministry of Information, Chungking, 1944).
g. J. Israel, Student Nationalism in China, 1927-1957 (Stanford, 1966).
h. C.H. Becker, et al., The Reorganization of Education in China (Paris, 1932).
i. The China Year Book (Shanghai, 1938), p. 316.
j. Wang Shih-chieh, Education in China (Shanghai, 1935), p. 24.
k. China Handbook 1937-1945 (New York, 1947), pp. 323, 327, 329.
l. Chang Jen-chi, Pre-Communist China's Rural School and Community (Boston, 1960), p. 29.
m. Wang, Y. Chu, 'Intellectuals and Society in China, 1860-1949', Comparative Studies in Society and History, vols. 3-4 (1961), pp. 395-426, p. 420.
Source: Reproduced from I.W. Mabbett, Displaced Intellectuals in Twentieth Century China, Institute of Southeast Asian Studies, Singapore, Occasional Paper No. 26, Singapore, 1975.

gcncration. But wc must not forget how very few were the people with modern education, of any sort.

Table 11.1 presents a number of figures from various sources representing enrolment in primary, secondary and higher education. Like other figures derived from Chinese statistics, including those from the last 30 years, they are not particularly reliable, and there is some conflict between the calculations of different students. But for the present purpose it is enough to let them express the general trend.

Any graph which curves more and more steeply upwards will serve to present the general trend from 1911 to 1949. The numbers of people receiving education doubled or more in each decade.

This is a rate which of course the resources of war-torn governments to provide employment could not match. But it is not necessarily a recipe for revolution. A doubling or a quadrupling of disgruntled graduates and fearful students need have no social consequence when the number multiplied is only a handful. Modern education started almost from scratch; the running was long made by mission institutions in a few port cities, and in 1912 there were fewer than 500 students in government institutions of higher education.[4] By 1923, even if we use some optimistic official enrolment figures, the primary school population constituted abut 1½ per cent of the population or something like a twentieth of the age group. Of every thousand people, a quarter of a person was going to secondary school and a twelfth of a person was receiving higher education.

Here, then, we have noticed some very approximate figures for enrolment in educational courses in the earlier part of the century. They represent numbers of people who expected, at some stage in their lives, to rise above the level of manual toil. How many of them were disappointed?

In 1929, L.K. Tao made an attempt to calculate the number of unemployed intellectuals, and estimated that there were then about 140,000 classically educated men between 40 and 60 years old, many of them not in intellectual employment. To this number he added 780,000 people with modern secondary or tertiary education, and, after including returned students from Japan and the West and allowing for privately tutored people and other categories, calculated that there were about a million and a half intellectuals. Of these he considered that only 400,000 were absorbed by government employment, and a similar number by teaching. The professions seemed between them quite unable to account for the remaining 700,000.[5]

If these estimates for 1929 are correct, there must have been a very considerable advance in the numbers employed in government, education and the liberal professions during the next few years, for in 1933, according to an American government-sponsored survey of employment statistics, the figures for these categories were 2,579,000 in government and education and 272,000 in liberal professions, with a further 134,000 in finance, banking and insurance.[6] These, indeed, were the years when the Kuomintang was at the height of its power and best able to assure the conditions in which intellectual employment could grow.

However, the inference that the government began to soak up the swelling pool of graduates and assuage discontent would be quite fallacious. Government employment grew, but not by selecting graduates on merit. True, in 1928 was passed the organic law creating the examination *yuan* which in the following years was under the direction of Dao Qitai (Tao Ch'i-T'ai, who was hardly a radical reformer). Its programme was to institute examinations for all officials, but this programme was never fulfilled. In 1930-4 an 'evaluation' of incumbent officials was conducted, of whom, by 1934, 47,163 out of 59,625 were confirmed in office.[7] Examinations were never allowed in more than a minority of the civil service − about 2,000 by 1938, whereas between 1933 and 1937, 25,447 people entered without taking examinations. Pass rates were low (only 5 per cent in the 1931 examination). Recruitment was constantly surrounded by scandals and complaints of corruption. As the government handbook later put it: 'As the number of persons selected through examinations is still small, many public functionaries receive employment through their qualifications of having graduated from schools, served in public organs for a certain number of years, or won merit in the course of the revolution.'[8] Thus, among students it was common knowledge that government employment was still not based primarily upon educational qualifications; further, there was a pronounced tendency to employ returned students from Western countries, while those from Japan, traditionally prone to the circulation of seditious philosophies, increasingly felt themselves to be a disfavoured second stream.

It is difficult to assemble any reliable information about the employment situation during the war. Certainly, under the pressure of the times, the government attempted to maximise its revenues and to fasten its grip on the country through an oft-multiplied corps of officials, teachers, and agents of ambiguous status; but, according to official figures; from 1931-44 only 97,000 people passed examinations for elective posts and 38,000 for government appointment.[9] The government officials were not contented and self-fulfilled men enjoying high status and the fruits of scholarly endeavour. The real income of government servants fell by 90 per cent between 1937 and 1943, and 21,000 were laid off in 1945 for reasons of economy.[10]

So far, we have considered quantitative measures as a guide to intellectual frustration – figures for enrolment and employment. These by themselves give little sense of the plight of the individuals who were victims of the squeeze, the marginal men, in limbo between two worlds. There were various qualitative factors not revealed by statistics. Of these the chief is, quite simply, poor teaching. Ill-educated school leavers are prime material for unemployment. As for the early period of modern education around the beginning of the century, the quality of what passed as modern education in poor villages may be imagined from the state of China's resources at the time of the 1911 revolution and is attested by many studies.

In many cases the only 'modern' thing about the primary school is the sign-board over the front gate, while within the school an old-time unscientific pedagogue is teaching the old-time classics in the old-time unscientific way. In other schools, half-baked boys from nearby Grammar Schools have essayed the role of village pedagogue, to the disgust of the patrons, who have been seeking to restore the old system, under which a gentleman |with whom everyone in the village was acquainted, and who was universally respected, dealt out the time-honoured platitudes and at least did no harm even if he didn't do much good.[11]

This was Shanxi in 1914. Here, the 'model governor', Yan Xishan (Yen Hsi-shan), set earnestly to work to build an educated citizenry. Partly as a result, there was by the 1920s a generation of tertiary lecturers who were scarcely qualified to dispense the learning that their charges sought. We are told in the same source of university geologists who could not recognize quartz, of civil engineers without sufficient mathematics to survey a small lake in less than a semester, of an engineer who used a catalyst containing sulphur in a costly furnace and fused ore, catalyst and furnace into a solid mass, and of ironmongers and cobblers lecturing in the language school under a demented principal. For various reasons, 'by 1930 Shansi [Shanxi] University was little more than a vast resort, presided over by professors who supplemented their inadequate wages by gambling with their pupils and attended by students so indifferent to learning that the library closed its doors for want of patronage'.[12]

This was outback Shanxi. Even in centres of relative cosmopolitanism, universities suffered from ramshackle organization. Professors sought to keep themselves afloat by multiplying their appointments. Chen Duxiu (Ch'en Tu-hsiu) had ten chairs.

In 1932, the Japanese launched a surprise attack on Shanghai, using bombers. Apart from the destruction suffered by ten colleges, there were indirect repercussions affecting education in northern China. Many thousands of refugees sought education in other cities; many were unable even to seek education because their parents could not afford it, businessmen whose trade suffered from the occupation of Manchuria and smuggling of cheap goods. Thousands dropped out of school and college. When the occupation was carried to China proper, 77 higher education institutions moved inland, there to carry on their work in circumstances of desperate shortage. In the Japanese zones, it has been estimated that a third of the secondary schools ceased functioning, and about six million primary school pupils were affected.[13] L.W. Pye remarks that, after the war, many who had remained and completed their education under Japanese occupation were apprehensive about their fate, fearing discrimination against them by those who returned from the interior.[14]

The problem was therefore not simply that more and more people were being poured into the intellectual job market, seeking appointments from governments that were less and less able to pay them. The frustrations of the educated were compounded by the fact that their education was usually hopelessly inadequate and frequently disrupted.

Such people were especially likely to cut their attachmens to old values and drift into dissident movements. In 1919 a suggestion seriously entertained by the Peking regime was that examinations for office should be re-instituted as a way of appeasing student dissidence. In the 1920s it was recorded that, in Shanxi, the warlord governer Yan Xishan (Yen Hsi-shan) feared that his government would topple if jobs could not be found for his graduates. When the national capital was later moved by the Kuomintang to Nanking, thousands of petty functionaries with a precarious hold on the lower rungs of official employment were unable to find fresh employment, and a private charity had to step in to transport them to their homes. In the 1930s, vast numbers of inadequately employed intellectuals flocked to Yanan (Yenan), the Communist stronghold in the north-west. Of course, want of employment was not the only motive impelling them, and many came from prosperous and cultured homes; but there were many who must have been influenced in their political thought by the bitterness of frustrated aspirations.

All these considerations point in a single direction. The history of China's frustrated intellectuals through the first half of the century shows the special appropriateness of Marxism as a gospel for them. Let us remember that, by virtue of their background, frustrated intellectuals once in power needed an orthodoxy that would replace and discredit the old one (that had rejected them), enshrine civilian values and political centralization, legitimize their own rise to power, and make sense of the world as a whole. They wanted more than piecemeal policies for reform, which was all that Western liberalism could offer; they wanted an entire cosmology, which Confucianism had been. Marxism gave them all this so soon as they cast themselves (overlooking the absurdity of doing so) as the embodiment of the proletariat. Marxism further confirmed their ambivalent attitude to the West: it came from the West, but it offered a superior criticism of the West and claimed to show how the West should be surpassed. Finally, it offered easy answers to the intellectually insecure.

This does not mean that the professional Marxists necessarily welcomed the students with unqualified enthusiasm, or vice versa. Mao Zedong, for example, regarded students in general as 'subjective and individualistic, impractical in their thinking and irresolute in action'.[15] But the conditions for a marriage were present.

Studies of the student movements during the years before the final Communist takeover are rare, but Suzanne Pepper's investigation of some student campaigns during the civil war is revealing.[16] She examines the December 1st Movement in Kunming (the wartime capital) in 1945, the 1945-6 demonstrations against the USA, the Anti-Hunger Anti-Civil-War movement of May to June, 1947, and the May 1948 movement protesting against perceived American support of Japan. These all involved the vigorous activity of good students in good institutions, a measure of support for them by their lecturers, government repression, great publicity and public sympathy. There was nothing overtly or essentially revolutionary about such movements. But circumstances made rebellion more and more attractive; in government thinking, everybody had to be either a Kuomintang supporter or a rebel. Evidence of student attitudes to the Communist party is ambiguous; it appears that few were prepared to declare outright for the Party, but most distrusted the Kuomintang and favoured a coalition between the KMT and the Communist Party. By its all-or-nothing attitude, the government polarized the country and drove students into the arms of the Yanan outlaws.

In 1949, the new regime had the good will of many or most educated people. In later years, the good will evaporated. What went wrong?

In another valuable study, Suzanne Pepper identifies some of the problems common to poor countries seeking to expand and modernize their educational programmes: the costs and social problems involved in creating mass education are prohibitive; educational expansion, while it it is partial, sharpens social discrimination rather than blurring it; education creates unemployment; and a generation gap opens up, exacerbating discontent and dissidence.[17] As she shows, China shared these problems. As we trace discrepant attitudes to education in the period of Mao Zedong, all these problems will be conspicuous.

Notes

1. Chow Tse-tung, *The May Fourth Movement*, Harvard University Press, Cambridge, Mass, 1960, p. 11.
2. V. Purcell, *Problems of Chinese Education*, Kegan Paul, Trench, Trubner, London, 1936, p. 36; L.K. Tao, 'Unemployment among Intellectual Workers in China', *Chinese Political and Social Science Review*, vol. 13 (1929), pp. 251-61.
3. See W. Franke, 'Education in pre-1949 China (1905-1949)' in Centre d'Etude du sud-est Asiatique et de l'Extrême-Orient, *Education in Communist China*, Brussels, 1969, vol., 1, pp. 16-33.
4. See F.L.H. Pott, 'Modern Education' in H.F. MacNair (ed.), *China*, California University Press, Berkeley and Los Angeles, 1946, pp. 427-40.
5. L.K. Tao, 'Unemployment among Intellectual Workers in China', *Chinese Political and Social Science Review*, vol. XIII, no. 3 (1929), pp. 251-61.
6. J.P. Emerson, *Non-agricultural Employment in Mainland China, 1949-1958*, US Dept. of Commerce, Bureau of the Census, Washington, 1965, p. 71, Table IVB.
7. H.W. Mast, 'A Heavy Hand in the Examination Hall: the Earliest Attempts of the Kuomingtang to Staff a Modern Civil Service, 1928-1937', *Studies on Asia*, vol. 8 (1967), pp. 87-117.
8. *China Handbook 1937-1944*, Chungking, 1944, p. 56 (reprint China Publishing Co. Taipei).
9. Ibid., p. 57.
10. Chang Kia-ngau, *The Inflationary Spiral: the Experience of China 1939-1950*, John Wiley, New York, 1958, pp. 63f. 131.
11. Cited from a letter in D. Gillin, *Warlord: Yen Hsi-shan in Shansi Province, 1911-1949*, Princeton University Press, Princeton, 1967, p. 67.
12. Ibid., pp. 76f.
13. F.L.H. Pott, 'Modern Education', p. 438.
14. L.W. Pye, 'Mass Participation in Communist China: its Limitations and Continuity of Culture' in J.M.H. Lindbeck (ed.), *China: Management of a Revolutionary Society*, University of Washington Press, Seattle, 1971, pp. 3-33; see p. 16.
15. S. Pepper, 'The Student Movement and the Chinese Civil War, 1945-

1949', *China Quarterly*, 1971, pp. 698-735 at p. 726.
  16. Ibid.
  17. S. Pepper, 'Education and Revolution: the "Chinese Model" Revised', in *Asian Survey*, vol. 18, no. 9 (Sept. 1978), pp. 847-90 at pp. 848-50.

12 EDUCATION AND MANPOWER BEFORE THE CULTURAL REVOLUTION

When a rich man becomes poor he becomes a teacher

Chinese Proverb

In 1949, the new regime began with bright hopes of satisfying the ambitions of the meritorious. For the first time in the century, there was a fairly stable government with considerable control over taxation and an earnest commitment to advance public education. In the 1950s many education statistics were published and these have been closely analysed by students, some of whose calculations are represented in Table 12.1.

This table shows that, even if Kuomintang and Communist Party figures are wrong by a substantial margin, in whichever direction and for whatever reasons, the dramatic increase in enrolment in the first half of the century was sustained or surpassed under the new regime in the 1950s. The rise was not entirely smooth, but it was inexorable.

It did not continue thereafter, however. 1958 saw the introduction of many new part-time schools in the countryside; it was said that by 1959-60 three million had been enrolled in part-work part-study schools in the communes, and a renewed effort was made, after the lean period around 1960, in 1964-5. Illiteracy campaigns, 'red and expert universities' and spare-time courses at various levels were instituted in communes and factories, but in most cases they offered emergency education not leading to qualifications clearly comparable with those of pupils from regular schools. The statistics from this period are therefore confused and confusing, and they represent a big effort to swell the educated population which, particularly following the crisis years 1959-61, probably could not be surpassed for some time. The revolution in education had to wait. Thus in the early 1960s there was a more cautious policy, which can perhaps be seen in the central teaching material writing programme of 1961 and Chen Yi's (Ch'en Yi's) speech of that year restoring specialists to favour and speaking of a proper balance between work and politics.

Writing in 1960, L.A. Orleans was interested not so much in intellectual unemployment as in the shortage of educated manpower for the tasks of development. He calculated that there were very roughly 700,000 people who had completed secondary education by 1949 and 2.6 million from 1949-59.[1] These figures could be more than doubled

Table 12.1: Educational Entry, Enrolment and Graduation 1948-9 to 1964-5 (National totals in thousands)

Year	1 Primary Enrolment	2 Junior Middle Enrolment	3 Junior Middle Leavers	4 Senior Middle Enrolment	5a Senior Middle Leavers	5b Senior Middle Leavers	6a Total Secondary Enrolment	6b Total Secondary Enrolment	7a Higher Education Entrants	7b Higher Education Entrants	8a Higher Education Enrolment	8b Higher Education Enrolment	9 Higher Education Graduates
1948-9	24,000	832		207									21
1949-50	29,000	1,067	250	238	46		1,039	1,270			117		18
1950-1	43,000	1,384	240	184	44		1,305	1,567	35		139		19
1951-2	51,000	2,231	186	260	35	36	1,568	1,964	35	66	156		32
1952-3	52,000	2,572	396	360	58	55	2,491	3,145	65	72	191	194	48
1953-4	51,000	3,109	572	478	72	70	2,932	3,629	71	90	212	216	47
1954-5	60,000	3,320	863	582	106	(86)	3,587	4,245	94	90	253	258	55
1955-6	61,000	3,830	783	366	156	156	3,902	4,707	96	164	288	400	63
1956-7	64,000	4,340	1,096	780	203	180	4,196	5,900	165	107	408	401	56
1957-8	84,000	7,340	1,091	1,180	222	(220)	5,120	6,280	107	148	435	442	72
1958-9	92,000				242	(350)	8,520	9,880	152	250	660	717	70
1959-60								15,000	270	280	810	790	135
1960-1	90,000	12,900									955	810	162
1961-2											819		178
1962-3											820	810	200
1963-4													200
1964-5													170

Notes: This table is reproduced, with permission, from I.W. Mabbett *Displaced Intellectuals in Twentieth Century China*, Singapore, Institute of Southeast Asian Studies, Occasional Paper No. 26, 1975, pp. 48f.

Column 1: J. Chester Cheng, 'The Educational System in Modern and Contemporary China', in E. Stuart Kirby, ed., *Contemporary China* (Hong Kong, 1960), pp. 181-199. For 1960-61: Theorore Hsi-en Chen, *Teacher Training in Communist China* (Washington, 1960), pp. 5f.

Column 2: L.A. Orleans, *Professional Manpower and Education in Communist China* (Washington, 1961), pp. 35, table 3. For 1960-61: Theodore Hsi-en, *loc. cit.*

Column 3: Calculation from L.A. Orleans, *Professional Manpower, op. cit.*, pp. 38, 38, tables 3, 4.

Column 4: L.A. Orleans, *Professional Manpower, op. cit.*, p. 35. table 3. He questions the plausibility of the 1956-7 figure (from an N.C.N.A. source). 1958-9: U.N.E.S.C.O. *World Survey*, Vol. 4, p. 339, table 2.

Column 5a: L.A. Orleans, *Professional Manpower, op. cit.*, p. 38, table 4 and n. 3.

Column 5b: J.C. Kun, 'Higher Education: Some Problems of Selection and Enrolment', *China Quarterly*, No. 8 (1961) pp. 135-148.

Column 6a: Addition of columns 2 and 4.

Column 6b: J. Chester Cheng, *op. cit.*, table E.

Column 7a: L.A. Orleans, *Professional Manpower, op. cit.*, p. 61, table 1.

Column 7b: J.C. Kun, *op. cit.*

Column 8a: L.A. Orleans, *Professional Manpower, op. cit.*, pp. 68 f. table 3; U.N.E.S.C.O. *World Survey*, Vol. 4, p. 340, table 3; D.J. Munro, 'Egalitarian Ideal and Education Fact in Communist China', in J.M.H. Lindbeck, ed., *China: Management of a Revolutionary Society* (Seattle, 1971), pp. 25-301. For 1960-61 and 1961-62: Cheng Chu-yuan,' *Scientific and Engineering Manpower in Communist China 1949-1963* (Washington, 1965) table 6, p. 74.

Column 8b: J. Chester Cheng, *op. cit.*, table E. For 1960-61: Theodore Hsi-en Chen, *op. cit.*, pp. 5f; for 1962-63 R.D. Barendsen, 'Education in China:A Survey', *Problems of Communism*, Vol. 13, No. 4, (1964), pp. 19-27 at p. 26.

Column 9: L.A. Orleans, 'Communist China's Education: Policies, Problems and Prospects', in J.P.R.S., *Economic Profile of Mainland China* (U.S. Printing Office, 1967), p.508.

if we included those who had completed junior but not senior secondary education. The government was successfully able to provide employment for most of these. According to one survey, the numbers of government officials did not rise dramatically during the decade, but in a state where nearly all of business, manufacturing and the professions were absorbed by the government, a wide variety of people had some sort of official status, however low, and such people are usually known as cadres, *ganbu* (*kan pu*), functionaries in party or government. State cadres have been defined as people on a salary in a range of posts from the clerical grade upwards, including technicians in industry, agriculture, public health, education, mass media and so forth. Official figures for these have been given as 720,000 in 1949 and 2,750,000 in 1952, the 1952 figure later being given as 3,310,000, 5,270,000 in 1955, and 7,920,000 in 1958.[2] This represents a tenfold increase in the numbers of officials in a decade.

But, with educational enrolments increasing frantically through the 1950s, as we have seen they were, the revolution could not continue indefinitely to look after its children. Blind to the lessons of history, it trained up a generation of recruits to limbo, a generation which it expected to learn revolution, but which remained imbued instead with the traditional and human desire to use education as a ritual initiation into prosperity and influence, or at least to elevation above the masses who worked with their hands.

Expectations were greatly raised, for many, by the fact that it was a Communist movement that won in 1949. More and more children entered schools with bright hopes that they would be equipped in them to enter the elite; more and more found that what they received instead was a miserable apology for an education which was just enough to make them dissatisfied with the lot of their parents who stooped in ricefields, not enough to fit them for anything else.

Progressively through the 1950s, greater strain was placed upon the ability of the country to supply teachers of all sorts. Towards the end of the decade, this strain was increased as the government sought to multiply the avenues of education. Unable to finance schooling for everybody, it sought from 1956 onwards to foster what have often been called 'private' schools, low-budget local community schools offering a rudimentary education. In 1958 it was said that 30.5 per cent of Guizhou's primary pupils were in community schools; Hebei (Hopei) and Liaoning claimed over 19 per cent of their secondary pupils to be in such schools. Agricultural secondary schools, in which pupils spent a great part of their time in organized manual work, seemed to offer a gratifying combination of advantages: they cost much less than regular schools, they contributed to agricultural and workshop production, and they fostered the manual toil ethic. About three million pupils entered them (and other vocational middle schools) in 1959, about three-sevenths of the secondary school intake and three-thirteenths of the children aged thirteen. Spare-time education was vigorously promoted in the same period; communes and factories instituted special courses for their inmates while schools were assigning their pupils to part-time work in factories and communes. 'Red and expert universities' sprang up, where lecturers who were often farmers with incomplete primary education but who were said to possess superior political consciousness taught practical subjects like advanced farming methods. Such methods of education, difficult to conduct with success even in periods of plenty, lost vigour in the exhaustion of 1960-1, but there was renewed drive behind half-time commune schools in 1964-5.

In circumstances of hectic expansion, when quantity was, perhaps often quite properly, pursued with vigour while quality languished, the competence of teachers was bound to suffer. Numerous are the evidences of primary school pupils being taught by youths whose junior secondary education was incomplete, junior secondary pupils under the mentorship of teachers without even a soupçon of tertiary teacher training and perhaps with little at the senior secondary level, and so on up the ladder. The teacher training education stream received below-average students and was not highly regarded, for students preferred to set their sights on less uninspiring professions, and understandably teachers' morale was very low. In universities, more and more courses were compressed into less and less time; political discussions claimed much of the time otherwise available for private study; tutors were youths with little idea how to do their jobs or men with a precarious grasp, if any, upon the subject matter they were supposed to teach, which they frequently did by reading out notes at high speed in order to cover the syllabus.

In the 1950s, Russian influence on education was very strong, a fact which, because of the inappropriateness of Russian models, can be reckoned as an impediment and frustration to the aspirations of the less lucky or gifted. In the first Five Year Plan period (1953-7), between 700 and 800 Soviet advisers taught in tertiary institutions, training graduates, supervising Chinese staff, setting up new courses, organizing new facilities, compiling teaching materials and conducting short training courses. A hectic programme of translation was launched to make Russian textbooks available in Chinese. By 1956, about 1,680 titles had been translated.[3] Notoriously, mediocre translations of material originally written in a completely different educational environment proved a major handicap for ill-equipped and struggling Chinese students. Russian models affected course structure, teaching methods and the whole philosophy of education during the first Five Year Plan, which sought to place emphasis on the expansion of secondary and tertiary education, concentrating on technological and scientific training, particularly of engineers. Russian-style training was narrowly specialized, designed to enable each individual to carry out one sort of task rather than to give a broad grounding in a discipline. This approach presupposed that more detailed forward planning of manpower needs could be undertaken than was in fact possible, and distanced students from the real content of the education they were supposed to be receiving.

Where education was of low standard and success went only to the most capable and persistent students, it is proper to consider the social background of students as another factor of frustration. The reason is that students from worker or peasant households were much less likely than others to have the personal resources, derived from home background, upon which incompetent teaching was bound to throw them. Therefore an increase in the proportion of worker and peasant students was likely to be matched by an increase in failure and dropping out.

Before 1949, the simple need to pay school fees had dictated that very nearly all who got as far as universities had a background of moderate prosperity and, to whatever extent that entailed, of culture; but in the following years, although school fees could not be abolished and economic selection continued to operate, strenuous efforts were made to increase the proportion of students from worker and peasant families. According to the *Peking Review* it was 29 per cent in 1955-6, 34 per cent in 1956-7, and 36 per cent in 1957-8.[4] In the autumn of 1965, claims varied from about 50 per cent to 67 per cent. In the Cultural Revolution, many of the grievances voiced were by students of poor background against those with prosperous background, and by those who couldn't cope against those who could. (One slogan was: 'What need do we have of intelligence? Our heads are full of the thoughts of Chairman Mao'.)

These considerations make it clear how important it is to recognise premature withdrawal from school or university as an important factor of frustration in its own right. Impressive enrolment statistics may be misleading; we do not know how many of the wide-eyed children going into class with their slates will be weeding paddies or tending vegetables in a year's time. Large withdrawal rates have long been common: even if (*per impossibile*) the teaching is good and the fees are trifling, the poverty of the Chinese village, where every bit of practical help in the home or fields releases more lucrative adult labour, and perhaps the peculiar arduousness attending the learning of Chinese, load the dice heavily against the child's prospects.

Further, the increasing encroachment of politics on the educational curriculum came, in the Great Leap Forward period, to interfere with learning. Pupils could not win – in the early 1950s they were baffled by obscure textbooks translated from Russian, and in the later they were assailed by the purgative medicine of an opposite philosophy – Mao's doctrine that education involved political enlightenment, 'redness', first and foremost; actual education, 'expertness', was only grudgingly accorded an ambiguous parity, if that; more and more time was taken up by meetings, rallies, political lectures and stints of community service out of doors in the great classroom of life. Later, when around 1980 the new leadership sought legitimacy for policies which in fact emphasized study at the expense of politicization, much was made of instructions given by Mao in 1953 calling for the training of technicians and scientific workers; but there is no doubt about Mao's real views. In 1957 he said: 'Politics and professions form a unity of opposites, in which politics is predominant and primary . . . It is wrong to talk about becoming expert before becoming red, which is tantamount to being white before being red.'[5]

Mao believed fervently in political education through contact with practical problems and ordinary people (the very opposite of the old 'Confucian' approach). This idea, along with the very practical reasons, was at play in the policy of sending educated people to work in the countryside. Frustrated intellectuals included not only those who dropped out early, but also those who found themselves abruptly translated from school, university and office to the fields in the 'sending down' or rustication of students and officials to spells of manual work in the countryside. The schooling of hundreds of thousands of urban youths was cut short; in 1966 it was said that, since 1962, more than a million educated young people had been sent to the country – many from middle schools, some from higher education institutions in subjects that were regarded as inessential. All in all, there were from time to time many reasons why a pupil's or student's education might end prematurely: slow progress, high fees, agricultural need, poor teaching, lack of sufficient cultural background, war and civil commotion, and rustication. Those who cleared all hurdles to the first year of university often found that, in the face of incomprehensible lectures, it was impossible to prepare for the examinations.

Of course it was not only an over-supply of the half-educated and ill-qualified that blighted the prospects of successive generations of would-be officials and cadres: it was also an under-demand for the services even of the well-qualified. In part, low demand for recruits must be seen as a product of generational rhythm, an idea of vital importance to the understanding of trends in Chinese intellectual employment. If a government and all its servants are removed, there is instantly a great demand for the services of young people untainted by association with the old order; further, if the new goverment commands a more general loyalty, it is likely to have a more efficient control over the administration of revenue and hence to deploy greater resources for employment of servants. A young generation is enlisted in the service of politics; but, since turnover through death and retirement instantly dwindles to almost nothing, quite speedily those school-leavers and graduates who come behind find that the avenues of advancement are so clogged with jostling throngs that their own progress is slow. Over the years, the clogging becomes more extreme. It may turn out in the end that another government and its servants are expelled by another young generation deprived of opportunity. The cycle can become a vicious circle. In fact, after the 1950s, promotion at all levels slowed down dramatically.

This can be seen in the Communist Party itself, which constituted a route to responsibility and authority more important in a way than official employment. Everywhere, in government offices as in factories, business of all sorts, schools and collectives or communes, it was the local Party members who occupied the most important official positions, and, even when they did not, got things done. Full-time, paid Party officials, certainly, were a small proportion; but Party membership could help an individual to better his lot in other ways.

Membership of the Party grew from 3 million in 1948 to 5 in 1950, 8 in 1954, 9 in 1955, 13 in 1957, 14 in 1959 and 17 in 1961.[6] These 17 million were not all occupying positions of responsibility. The majority were peasants and workers with little hope of being anything else or of wielding more than petty authority.

Eighty per cent of them had joined since 1949, were largely employed in the communes, and were available to bear much of the blame for what went wrong after the Great Leap. A *Red Flag* editorial in 1964 spoke of the average age of many leadership groups throughout the organization being over 40, and raised the question what would happen when these people retired; it suggested that adding new blood was an important priority. These men in their forties were not the old guard; they were the whole generation of young recruits from the early 1950s, now squatting in all the higher offices and thwarting the advancement of those who came after. Here, surely, we can see the makings of a generational conflict, with certain of the 'old guard' allied like fond grandparents with frustrated youth in opposition to the intermediate generation of bureaucrats.

Nor need we think that being a commune cadre was especially gratifying to intellectual ambitions. Intellectuals did not necessarily become cadres, of course; if they did, they found themselves credited with some work points for their administrative duties but obliged to work much or most of the time in the fields to keep body and soul together, especially when there was pressure from above to decentralize commune government; they were urged to learn from old peasants, to promote production, to supervise brigades and teams personally, to avoid all manner of contrary heresies; and they were always liable (as in 1960-1) to be purged as dead wood, probably to the glee of those previously under their authority, and replaced by peasants of more suitably destitute background. In the end, there could be no way of annulling the hunger of the educated for respectability, responsibility and authority short of a measure of social engineering or 'indoctrination' which rustication, despite its intentions, was in fact unlikely to achieve and which even the Great Proletarian Cultural Revolution and the endeavours that have since been put forth are most unlikely to bring about. All that has gone before, then, shows how the policies of the 1950s, adequate though they may have been for the needs of the time, combined to pile up a mountain of discontent which was all too likely to become a volcano.

One cause of frustration in the early 1960s, a cause that was never to be finally removed, was the knowledge that many officials were getting their children into good schools and into universities through influence. This was the infamous 'back door', by which, both before and after the Cultural Revolution, parents in official positions were able quietly to circumvent whatever regulations there might be. As a red guard publication claimed during the Cultural Revolution, writing about the former minister for higher education,

The shady element Jiang Nanxiang managed to shove his 'distinguished' son into the Peking University's Attached Middle School by means of a telephone call and a note. This boy had been rejected by his original school after repeating several times. The teachers were instructed quite shamelessly to teach this boy as an 'honourable political assignment'.[7]

That the category of frustrated intellectuals was expanding rapidly is a point that can to some extent be corroborated by quantitative measures as well as by these indirect indications. Of course, the apparent precision of statistics is spurious, but from them we can get some idea of the numbers of unhappy people whose expectations, derived from an education better than their parents', were cruelly dashed.

It is at intermediate levels that we may find the important degrees of unhappiness — among youngsters keeping co-operative accounts who completed junior secondary schooling but were denied the chance to go on to senior and qualify for a city job, or their juniors still at school who knew that the same fate waited for them, and among clerks in factories with secondary education who were denied the chance to become engineers, for example. Naturally, these unhappy people cannot be identified and enumerated simply by calculating the numbers who reached one level of education and failed to proceed to the next. This would be a fatuous supposition. What the figures yielded by such calculations do suggest, though, is that when they rise, the *quantum* of unhappiness (whatever it may be) rises, and when they fall, it falls.

J.C. Kun drew up a table comparing the numbers leaving senior secondary school with those entering higher education from 1952 to 1959.[8] It is reproduced here as columns (a) and (b) of Table 12.2, which may be compared. Interestingly, until 1955 there were more entrants than leavers. This is because the government was anxious to promote higher education as a high priority for economic development, and many entrants were school-leavers from years before who had not had a chance of a tertiary education under the old regime.

It is possible to deduce from certain calculations of L.A. Orleans[9] some figures for junior secondary school-leavers, and from these to subtract the numbers of senior secondary school-leavers three years later. Columns (c) and (d) in Table 12.2 embody the results of this subtraction, the figure for each year representing those who left junior secondary school three years before and failed to leave senior this year. (The two columns are based on two disparate series of figures for senior middle school-leavers.) Each figure represents two sorts of people: those whose education ended at the junior secondary level, and those who entered senior but dropped out. Both might well include frus-

Table 12.2: Numbers Withdrawing from Different Levels of Education (Thousands)

Year	Section 1 (a)	Section 1 (b)	Year	Section 2 (c)	Section 2 (d)
1952	36	66	1950-3	192	195
1953	55	72	1951-4	168	170
1954	70	90	1952-5	80	100
1955	(86)	90	1953-6	240	240
1956	150	164	1954-7	369	392
1957	180	107	1955-8	641	643
1958	(220)	148	1956-9	541	433
1959	(350)	250			
1960		280			

Year	Section 3 (e)	Section 3 (f)
1954	-1	
1955	-11	
1956	-28	3
1957	2	16
1958	0	18
1959	36	20
1960	21	29
1961	41	-55
1962	43	-30
1963	42	50
1964		80

Notes: Section 1:
Column (a) reproduces column 5b in Table 12.1 and numbers senior middle school leavers.
Column (b) reproduces column 7b in Table 12.1 and numbers higher education entrants.
Section 2:
Columns (c) and (d) represent the subtraction of senior middle school leavers in the later year trom junior middle school leavers in the earlier year, three years before. Column (c) is based on columns 3 and 5a in Table 12.1; column (d) is based on columns 3 and 5b.
Section 3:
Column (e) represents the subtraction of higher education graduates each year from senior middle school leavers four years before (columns 9 and 5a, Table 12.1).

This table is reproduced, with permission, from I.W. Mabbett, *Displaced Intellectuals in Twentieth Century China*, Singapore, Institute of Southeast Asian Studies, Occasional Paper No. 26, 1975, pp. 48f.
Column 1: J. Chester Cheng, 'The Educational System in Modern and Contemporary Cina' in E. Stuart Kirby (ed.), *Contemporary China* (Hong Kong, 1960), pp. 181-99. For 1960-1: Theodore Hsi-en Chen, *Teacher Training in Communist China* (Washington, 1960), pp. 5f.
Column 2: L.A. Orleans, *Professional Manpower and Education in Communist China* (Washington, 1961) p. 35, Table 3. For 1960-1: Theodore Hsi-en Chen, *Teacher Training* pp. 5f.
Column 3: Calculation from L.A. Orleans, *Professional Manpower*, pp. 35, 38, Tables 3.4.

Table 12.2: (continued)

Column (f) represents the subtraction of higher education graduates each year from higher education entrants four years before (columns 9 and 7b, Table 12.1).

Column 4: L.A. Orleans, *Professional Manpower*, p. 35, Table 3. He questions the plausibility of the 1956-7 figure (from an NCNA source). 1958-9: UNESCO *World Survey*, vol. 4, p. 339, Table 2.

Column 5a: L.A. Orleans, *Professional Manpower*, p. 38. Table 4 and n. 3.

Column 5b: J.C. Kun, 'Higher Education: Some Problems of Selection and Enrolment', *China Quarterly*, no. 8 (1961), pp. 135-48.

Column 6a: Addition of columns 2 and 4.

Column 6b: J. Chester Cheng, 'The Educational System', Table E.

Column 7a: L.A. Orleans, *Professional Manpower*, p. 61, Table 1.

Column 7b: J.C. Kun, 'Higher Education'.

Column 8a: L.A. Orleans, *Professional Manpower*, pp. 68f., Table 3; UNESCO *World Survey*, vol. 4, p. 340, Table 3; D.J. Munro, 'Egalitarian Ideal and Educational Fact in Communist China' in J.M.H. Lindbeck (ed.), *China: Management of a Revolutionary Society* (Seattle, 1971), pp. 256-301. For 1960-1 and 1961-2: Cheng Chu-yuan, *Scientific and Engineering Manpower in Communist China 1949-1963* (Washington, 1965), Table 6, p. 74.

Column 8b: J. Chester Cheng, 'The Educational System', Table E. For 1960-1: Theodore Hsi-en Chen, *Teacher Training*, pp. 5f; for 1962-3 R.D. Barendsen, 'Education in China: A Survey', *Problems of Communism*, vol. 13, no. 4 (1964), pp. 19-27 at p. 26.

Column 9: L.A. Orleans, 'Communist China's Education: Policies, Problems and Prospects' in Joint Publications Research Service, *Economic Profile of Mainland China* (US Printing Office, 1967), p. 508.

trated youths. Of course each figure should be larger to compensate for an unknown number of senior entrants who had left junior more than three years before — there were many over-aged pupils in the 1950s — but, whatever the number may be, it is the same as that by which the total number of frustrated intellectuals is reduced by the absorption of over-aged pupils into senior schools. One number cancels the other.

We can expect a lag of a year or two before the truncation of a generation's education has an impact. However, the figure for each year incorporates a suitable lag, since it refers to people who failed to enter senior middle school three years ago or dropped out one or two years ago. Obligingly, though perhaps fortuitously, our figures, drawn as a graph, would show a sharp peak in 1958, a year of turbulence.

A slightly longer series can be obtained by subtracting from the number of senior secondary school-leavers in a given year the number of graduates four years later. Four is a very rough average for the varying lengths of higher education courses. Column (e) in Table 12.2 embodies this calculation, and column (f) embodies the subtraction of graduates for each year from the numbers who entered higher education institutions four years before. The negative figures in column (e) reflect the matriculation of over-aged students in years when secondary schools could not supply the required intake. The negative figures in column (f) reflect the statistical confusion and the shortening of courses attending the turmoil of the Great Leap period; the high figures following them, though, whatever the quality of the education which the people involved received or failed to receive, are in line with the general trend, and fortify us in the belief that, in the run-up to the Great Proletarian Cultural Revolution, in stark contrast to the earlier 1950s, more and more young people were being deposited upon the professional market with inadequate or unusable education, little prospect of advancement, and little emotional resource for adjustment to a life of manual toil.

Notes

1. L.A. Orleans, *Professional Manpower and Education in Communist China*, US Govt. Printing Office, Washington, 1961, pp. v-vi.
2. V.C. Funnell, 'Bureaucracy and the Chinese Communist Party', *Current Scene*, vol. 9, no. 5 (7 May 1971), pp. 1-14.
3. Jan-Ingvar Löfstedt, *Chinese Educational Policy*, Almquist/Humanities Press, Stockholm, 1980, p. 62; cf. pp. 78f.

4. *Peking Review*, 12 (May 1958), p. 16.
5. Mao Zedong, *Selected Works*, Foreign Languages Press, Peking, vol. 5, p. 488.
6. H.F. Schurmann, *Ideology and Organization in Communist China*, California University Press, Berkeley, 1966/8, p. 129.
7. T.P. Bernstein, *Up to the Mountains and Down to the Villages*, Yale University Press, New Haven and London, 1977, pp. 53f.
8. J.C. Kun, 'Higher Education: Some Problems of Selection and Enrolment', *China Quarterly*, no. 8 (1961), pp. 135-48 at p. 138. Cf. Jan-Ingvar Löfstedt, *Chinese Educational Policy*, p. 92.
9. L.A. Orleans, *Professional Manpower*, tables 3, 4, pp. 35, 38.

13 THE CULTURAL REVOLUTION AND ITS AFTER-MATH

'Present the diplomas!'

The Chancellor moved some thin stone slabs from the base of the wall and arranged them in front of his feet; I couldn't see too clearly, but they must have been engraved. 'Everyone at this graduation is first in his class. What a grand and glorious accomplishment! The diplomas are all here and, since everyone of you is first in his class, you can simply come up and get them in any old order you please. Assembly dismissed!'

The Chancellor and the other teacher helped the pessimist, who was sitting on the ground, to his feet. With slow steps all three left. None of the students bothered to come forward for his diploma. They simply resumed climbing the walls, rolling on the ground, and raising hell in general.

Lao She, *Cat Country*

Clearly, then, the Great Proletarian Cultural Revolution can be understood in part as a response to a dramatically increasing number of frustrated intellectuals. Equally clearly, this is not the whole picture. But here our concern is with attitudes to education as a career ticket, and certain aspects need to be selected.[1]

These five aspects deserve attention:

(a) Before the Cultural Revolution, there was emerging in the country's educational system, in despite of all decrees to the contrary, a division into two streams, the first including those more favoured by background and intellect, the second including those who, led by the whole temper of their upbringing to expect advancement along a great highway of promotion, found themselves turned aside into shabby culs-de-sac.

(b) At the time of the Cultural Revolution there was a large number of young people with some education who had been 'sent down' to the countryside without any early prospect of obtaining urban office employment, and whose fate many or most of the red guards could expect to share.

(c) In the course of the Cultural Revolution there operated gradually and partially upon the chaos of random faction a broad principle of alignment that set a majority of under-privileged and ill-favoured against a fortunate minority.

(d) Large numbers of youths from poor homes and with feeble educational foundations had been failing to complete their secondary or tertiary schooling once it was begun, and the demands for educational reform voiced in the Cultural Revolution were precisely such as could be expected to remove the disadvantages of such people in their struggle to carry the burden.

(e) Educational reform in the years following the Cultural Revolution was directed to the accommodation of their wants.

In the early 1960s, as was remarked above, the revolutionary zest of the Great Leap Forward was temporarily spent, its advocates demoralized by three years of economic reverse. Chen Yi's speech in the autumn of 1961 to Peking's graduating students, emphasizing expertness even at the expense of political activism, marked a trend towards educational orthodoxy. Lu Dingyi (Lu Ting-yi; in charge of the party's propaganda department, and hence responsible for education), Zhang Nanxiang (Chang Nan-hsiang, minister of higher education), Deng Tuo (Teng T'o, another prominent victim of the Cultural Revolution) and others were later identified with this trend. Basic training subjects and foreign languages were accorded longer hours in schools and colleges; productive labour and political activity were accorded shorter. In 1967, at a national conference on science and technology, many attacks were made on China's educational standards by speakers who wished to see them rise. As quality was emphasized at the expense of quantity, enrolment in many schools and universities fell, perhaps to the level of the mid-1950s.

Lu Dingyi was particularly associated with the policy of concentrating resources upon favoured schools. In huge disproportion, construction, equipment and books were lavished upon a small number of urban schools that were in a position to attract the capable and the fortunately born, the latter being chiefly the children of well-placed officials. To some extent these two groups coincided, for the children of officials had enjoyed security, an assured standard of living, an urban environment, and quite often a good cultural background besides, circumstances which gave them every advantage from the kindergarten upwards. To some extent, the two groups did not coincide, for the children of officials were sometimes spoilt brats; while those of 'bourgeois' parents had the best cultural backgrounds. Such children found themselves welcome at the well-endowed schools — called 'little pagodas' − all the same, and if their parents were important enough, and their mentors sycophantic enough, they received a fawning attention which could only embitter their gifted but less illustrious peers. The attitudes of those who ran these schools were, no doubt necessarily, governed by political pressures. We should recognize this. A ritual concern with pass rates rather than with the real content of education determined the behaviour of headmasters. Stanley Rosen tells of the headmaster of a Canton 'little pagoda' whose goal was to get 60 per cent of his school-leavers into university in 1963, 70 per cent in 1964, and 80 per cent in 1965. His values were obsessively competitive; at one point he 'folded his arms across his chest and took an oath: "If we don't catch up to Guangya [another Canton prestige school], I won't be at rest even if I die." '[2] Competition can be healthy; but what is significant here is the way in which goals were achieved: headmasters could achieve their goals not by improving the teaching but by juggling the school intake and by high-pressure cramming methods that had little to do with real learning.

'Little pagodas' largely excluded children of ordinary farm people or town workers; the majority of these, if through their parents' self-sacrifice and the mercy of fate they won through to secondary schooling, found themselves to be second-rate students in second-rate institutions with a second-rate future. Those few who went to good schools sat side by side, day in, day out, with the young people who were going to beat them to good jobs in a few years.

It is easy, perhaps too easy, to dwell on the bitterness that such circumstances must have engendered. As far as the educational policy went, it had its logic, for if resources were spread with rigorous equality, in practice as well as doctrine, no school could provide a really good environment for the early education of those from whom would be required the exercise of the most advanced skill for the next half-century. It was not necessarily wanton injustice, by its nature; but in its operation there were sufficient numbers of sycophants, hypocrites and self-seekers to make it often become so. In a country that could afford desks and swivel-chairs for all those who learned to aspire after them, the social harm need not have been great; in China, it was inestimable.

In 1963 and 1964 came a new trend; the weather vane began to turn; the thoughts of Mao were at work again in political counsels, abetted by the influence of the frustration that was now infecting a generation. The drive for revolutionary purity was first embodied in the socialist education campaign in the countryside, a movement to divest

the lower levels of officialdom of their besetting corruption. It began
in 1962 and was directed, under Liu Shaoqi's (Liu Shao-ch'i's) supervision, against junior officials guilty of fraud and laxness in commune
administration; in 1963 and 1964, more threateningly, it was turned
against more and more senior people and began to converge with other
revolutionary campaigns in a new tempo of urgency. There was a campaign to rid intellectuals of bourgeois ideas, a revival of the half-study,
half-labour, school movement, a programme of propaganda to emulate
the army, and renewed emphasis on 'sending down' to the countryside.

Yet, though disgruntled youths shared with the keepers of the
government's conscience a spirit of hostility towards those who found
too easy the ways of power and office, there was not total consonance.
Underprivileged youths wanted to compete on better terms with the
more happily favoured for official positions because they valued official
positions; Mao Zedong, as he frequently made unequivocally evident,
wished to change the attitudes to official positions of the privileged,
and, by the same logic, the attitudes of the under-privileged as well.
The second stream in the educational system found itself tossed from
Scylla to Charybdis: first humiliated by the spectacle of little pagodas
dotting the landscape, then, in compensation, sent in great numbers to
learn the honour that attaches to honest toil. Many school and university heads, out of harassment or snobbishness, found it suited them
very well to consign their second streams, full of turbulent and second-
rate students as they were, to productive work in the country. One of
the very first sites of Red Guard activism was a rural camp for half-
study, half-labour, to which in 1965 Nanking University sent many of
its weaker students to reduce overcrowding and get rid of nuisances.
In March 1966, the *People's Daily* commented on the numbers of
idle urban youth without skill or schoolroom, who, it said, should be
sent to the countryside. Perhaps a spell of army life was considered to
be the best sedative for the restless spirits of rusticated students and ex-
students; at all events, the army appears to have played a significant
role in the prologue to the Cultural Revolution. In some places, the
army (now, purified by the ostensibly loyal Lin Biao (Lin Piao), an
elect instrument of revolutionary grand policy) was organizing Red
Guard training camps in the spring of 1966; though it was not new for
the army to run such camps, it has been said that the military Political
Department assumed new functions then, taking over numbers of
camps from the (by then disfavoured) Young Communist League.[3]

That sending-down to the countryside was widely regarded, and commonly employed, as a device to get rid of malcontents seems clear enough. Thomas Bernstein, in his important study of the whole movement to settle urban youths in the villages cites evidence that surfaced during the Cultural Revolution:

> Red Guards protesting against revisionism in the program charged that policy makers and administrators had defined its purpose as ridding the cities of delinquents, failures, and bad-class elements, that is, those unable to qualify for higher school or factory work . . . These definitions, so the charges went, communicated themselves to rural cadres and peasants, who resented treatment of the countryside as a dumping ground for urban rejects, and who consequently looked down on the urban youths and mistreated them.

It requires an effort of imagnation to picture the gall and rancour endured by once-hopeful youths sentenced to rustication. In the 1960s it was not for them, as it had been for their seniors a few years before, a country holiday which, even if it went on too long and brought discomforts in its train, was an acceptable price for security and promotion. For them it was a black curtain that fell across their future. If they were country born, they could in time wean themselves from their illusory hopes of advancement and readjust their temperaments to a way of life which was familiar enough; but if, as so many secondary school pupils had, they had known only town life before, they went through purgatory, unused to unrelenting toil, primitive housing, strange tasks, dirt, ill-lit nights, poor diet, scant recreation, and the malevolent discrimination of rustic taskmasters who despised them as immature, unhandy, burdensome and unwanted guests, and whom they in turn despised as surly oafs.

This was the fate waiting for a large proportion of school and university students when, abruptly in June 1966, the Cultural Revolution jumped like a spreading fire from the corridors of power to the school yard and the lecture hall, and the red guard movement sprang up. Some red guards, perhaps many, had already tasted 'sending-down' and wished for violent action to rinse its bitterness away. There were many factors of alignment, often local and contingent. 'Little pagodas' had their own opposed factions, where red guards on either side had little to fear for their future careers. It is only necessary to recognize that there was a spirit of boiling frustration abroad; given that enough people felt it because of their objective circumstances, it could spread by contagion and become a part of the cultural atmosphere.

The latter part of 1966 was a period of confusion. On 13 June the Central Committee of the Party and the State Council announced that entrance examinations for tertiary education were to be reformed, and that meanwhile enrolment was to be postponed for six months. On 18 June the *People's Daily* carried an article asserting that examinations had bourgeois characteristics, and would need to be thrown into the melting pot along with many 'incorrect' books and teaching materials. In schools and universities throughout the country, schoolmasters and lecturers found themselves with no work to do; but for many of them it was no holiday. Some, who had been victims of political struggle in the earlier stages that were managed from above, fought back against their colleagues and superiors and busied themselves in meetings and propaganda with their students. Some endured periods of imprisonment with constant political struggle and sometimes physical assault in class-room gaols with young warders. Others went home, hoping that they would not be missed and fearing from day to day that they would be 'pulled out' and plunged back into the whirlpool.

In August, students and pupils were caught up in the 'four olds' campaign against whatever might be regarded as decadent, reactionary or superstitious ideology, thoughts, customs and habits: in cities every-where, houses were raided by enthusiastic and diligent youths seeking tokens of wealth and moral corruption such as gold bars or classical Chinese texts. In the autumn, attention turned to other things. One was the spreading of revolution to the factories; this was not to be a major theme of the Cultural Revolution until the end of the year, for there was anxiety among Mao Zedong's colleagues, or at least in the mind of Zhou Enlai (Chou En-lai), that production should not suffer, but in many places red guards summoned meetings on factory floors to formulate grievances and raise enthusiasm.

Another enterprise, for most red guards perhaps the major form of involvement, was the 'exchange of revolutionary experiences' − rail travel was free for red guards, and up and down the country went battered and insanitary railway carriages stuffed with excited boys and girls on their way to broaden their experience. Peking was the major destination of these revolutionary exchanges, *chuan lian* (*ch'uan lien*), for it was in Peking, the capital, that cues might be found pointing to the future trend to policy; it was important to red guard leaders all over the country to know what the promoters of the cultural revolution had in mind, in order to judge which actions woud have the blessing of supreme authority and which would risk later condemnation. For this reason red guard groups gave considerable attention to their foreign relations. Red guards who came from Peking were treated with reverence as bearers of the word. Every city had its liaison stations where visitors were received and activities were co-ordinated.

A third form of activity was power seizure. In many cities, whole government departments handed over keys and seals to swarms of youngsters, whether voluntarily, sensing that their usurpers had the highest authority in the land behind them, or after a fight. In the background, the army was allegedly neutral. But this neutrality was widely seen to favour 'revolution'.

Through all this, political confusion remained prevalent. There was organization, but the red guard movement was not a homogeneous and disciplined organism. The cry of Mao for rebellion had struck a chord, there is no doubt of that, and 'little generals' everywhere were, for the most part, prepared sincerely enough to regard him as a champion. It was not until 1967 that cynicism became really widespread. But, however ready the provincial rank and file might be to show its loyalty to Peking, Peking could not directly control its chosen instruments with such long and tangled strings, and most of the energy of the red guards was taken up in conflict with each other, each organization proclaiming itself a protagonist of the pure faith, and all its rivals infidels. Each organization waged jihad. Politically, the urban scene was a kaleidoscope of different shades of red, a kaleidoscope that was shaken into a new pattern with every convulsion.

These facts about the Cultural Revolution are commonly enough known. What deserves attention here is that the political turmoil was not totally without consistency or principle. There were ephemeral organizations and factions grouped around active individuals, all declaring themselves loyal to Mao; but it is questionable whether all were Maoists in any real sense. Mao was at once a consensus builder and a consensus shatterer. Through the confusion, however dimly, there emerged a real pattern, a line of division between the first and second streams of students. If the Canton school we noticed above is at all typical, it is clear that within a prestige school there would commonly be a favoured stream of pupils specially selected for saturating attention so as to boost matriculation figures. A former red guard from a well-favoured secondary school in Canton — a school whose pupils could all apparently expect to obtain good posts afterwards — discerned a recognizable body of 'conservatives' who were consistent in first being reluctant to attack their school authorities and, later, being reluctant to attack the work team sent in by the party to organize the Cultural Revolution in the school.[5] These conservatives were those who had a 'revolutionary background' — that is, their parents had party or official positions. These, naturally enough, stood to gain most from the existing situation. When the work team came it proceeded by first restricting red guard membership to those, including these fortunate children, whose revolutionary credentials were impeccable. When word came to the militant red guards that elsewhere less favoured pupils were taking matters into their own hands, the work team identified with the minority first stream and with the losing side.

This was not a typical school, but it was a typical pattern. Everywhere, resentment was voiced against authorities regarded as bourgeois revisionists conspiring to keep the ordinary masses down. One red guard publication, for example, condemned a junior secondary school as a feather bed for children of high cadres, engaged in elitist collusion with the army and concentrating on examinations for higher secondary school to the detriment of Mao's line.[6] Everywhere, school and university education was roundly condemned: examinations were treated as gods, glibness and 'book-learning' were praised, political education was neglected, teaching was done by rote — 'stuffed duck' methods were commonly castigated — courses were too long, students were overworked. Many such criticisms strike a familiar chord, or a familiar dischord, in the minds of those involved in education in the West, but it is not legitimate to apply automatically to China a judgement that has been formed in totally different surroundings. In the first place, it is inappropriate to regard Chinese teachers and lecturers as a uniformly enlightened and professional body, capable of doing a good job if allowed to do so without interference. On the contrary, it is clear from the 1950s situation reviewed above that many of them were quite incompetent, largely inexperienced, placed in the wrong positions, overworked, and incapable of teaching except by the mechanical recitation of inappropriate and hastily edited material obscure to them, incomprehensible to the students, and deadly dull to both parties. Further, ritual 'bookishness', mere rote learning, is indeed something in the Chinese cultural tradition that can legitimately be seen as an obstacle to free enquiry. Deng Xiaoping (Teng Hsiao-p'ing) later tried to turn the issue to his advantage by the slogan: Get the truth from the *facts*.

On the other hand, it is inappropriate to regard the teachers as a vindictive, snobbish and arrogant body of tin gods, for it must be acknowledged that they still included many who were competent, professional in their attitudes, and thoroughly dismayed by the effect on their classes of a substantial proportion of ill-prepared youngsters incapable of making much progress except in a special primary school and more interested in extra-curricular activities than in attempting such progress. Thus, the criticisms had much substance, but the trouble had its root at least as much in past policy and in the poverty of the country as in the turpitude of the mentors.

From the end of 1966 on there were many calls to return to normality, but the turmoil was slow to die down, for a whole generation of frustrated youths had been given the hope that they could after all grasp the country's destiny in their hands: they were reluctant to forsake that hope. In province after province, town after town, revolutionary committees were formed to unite the revolutionary capabilities of soldiers, reformed officials and party men, and organizers of mass movements, many of the last being red guard leaders who were unwilling to acknowledge the revolutionary legitimacy of former enemies with whom they were now expected to co-operate, or to share the glory of their brief power with older and staider men. Months, years, passed, and still schools stayed closed while students had no stomach for classes, and teachers were still morally convalescing. In the New Year of 1969, 87 out of 280 tertiary institutions reopened. It was not until 1970 that regular education got under way again throughout the country. A quarter of the human race had gone without education for its young for up to four years.

Special teams of workers, peasants and soldiers, regarded by the more revolutionary of China's statesmen as politically the most reliable classes, were entrusted with the task of supervising the inauguration of the new, proletarian, education, and it was said in 1971 that they were to stay in the schools 'for a long time'. Teachers were to be reformed by manual labour and unite with cadres and with the supervisory teams. All receiving education were to learn military methods. This is a reminder of the importance of the part played by the army, which for some years after the Cultural Revolution indeed was clearly dominant in nearly all the counsels of the land. The 'revolutionary great criticism' was to continue, initially under the guidance of these propaganda teams. There is evidence that the teams were not welcomed, for teachers and lecturers did not take kindly to being told how to do their jobs by people who knew nothing of education, or to the frequent meetings on how to run affairs. Teacher morale did not rise. One cadre assigned to be trained as a teacher said 'This is like jumping from a basket of rice into a basket of husks.'[7]

As Marianne Bastid wrote in 1970:

The teachers' ranks have been so well 'purified' that some schools are very short staffed. The remaining teachers are so much afraid of being accused by the students that they dare not enforce any kind of discipline; in order to keep safe, they mumble some excerpt from Mao Tse-tung's works all day long. They beg to be given another job. They think that if they are to be paid with work points, they would earn more by doing manual work full-time. Nobody wants to become a teacher.[8]

Difficulty was found in recruiting sufficient numbers to staff the education system at its former levels, and much use was made of rusticated youths, ex-soldiers and officials who could do a little part-time teaching. Enrolment was slow to rise at first; an analysis of provincial figures by *China News Analysis*, a periodical report that does not baulk at mentioning bad news, suggested that large numbers of children even of primary school age, particularly perhaps girls, were still not at school.[9]

The debate about curricula and organization in schools after the Cultural Revolution began some time before things were working normally again. Early in 1969 the *People's Daily* and *Red Flag* gave space to letters and articles on education, giving evidence of a trend of thought less radical than might have been expected. A *New China News Agency* release listed these goals: ending the educational regime of bourgeois revisionists, propagating love of Mao, training dedicated communists, waging class struggle, emphasizing politics in education, attending to practice rather than theory, combining study with labour, adapting education to the needs of farmers and workers, raising the educational standard of peasants and workers, controlling the upbringing of children, shortening the period of education, and cutting government expenses. In 1971 a national educational work conference was held, and campaigns to further educational objectives were prosecuted: to extend rural education to the point where every production team should have a primary school, every brigade a lower middle school and every commune a higher; to recruit workers, peasants and soldiers into universities, selecting them on the basis of recommendations from their communities; and to raise academic standards.

This last represents a trend back towards orthodoxy that was temporarily apparent. At the end of 1972 there were signs that established scholars were being rehabilitated. In 1973 it appears that entrance examinations for universities were in fact playing an important part, helping to weed out two-thirds of the applicants for places. But in the middle of the year attacks on examinations were published — fairly enough, candidates (who had to be workers, peasants or soldiers) could complain that after years since their schooling spent in muddy fields and ill-lit huts they were scarcely equipped to sit examinations – and politics were back in command. In 1974 enrolment was based mainly on recommendations, examinations, if any, occupying only a minor place.

Courses at all levels were shortened. Five years of primary school were to be followed by two or three years at junior secondary, two or three at senior secondary, and three or four years at tertiary levels (although many shorter tertiary courses were also offered). Productive as opposed to 'book' work was emphasized; schoolchildren were to do up to two months a year in workshops or communes, and participate in various ways in the life of the wider community (in anti-illiteracy teams, commune libraries, physical education programmes, and so forth). Efforts were made at all levels to encourage a sense of participation on equal terms by the pupils, teachers and community associated with every school.

Rustication, 'sending down', came back to strength, and the young men who for a brief space had been able to fancy themselves lords as they cowed policemen and intimidated officials in the cities now learned that there was no room for them on the dais of power after all. In 1968-9 four or five times as many people were rusticated as in earlier campaigns. In 1972-3 the rustication programme seems to have been slowing down as it ran into opposition. An investigation in 1973 revealed that evacuees, unwelcome as ever in the communes, were worse than ever fed, housed and treated, and steps had to be taken to improve their conditions.[10] But the programme was thereafter promoted as vigorously as ever, and by December 1975 there were twelve million young people 'sent down' to the countryside.

The plight of these twelve million people is an important chapter in Chinese social history. It was fraught with consequences, not only for the careers of the 'sent-down' youths themselves but for the attitudes to education of youngsters still in school (who all too often could see little point in studying if their future was to be only as peasants) and for the society of the rural areas to which they were sent (where they were all too often unwelcome guests, keenly resented as an unwanted burden).

Theoretically, the programme was now no longer to be a sort of rural national service, but was rather to be a life sentence. In practice, there was always hope of reassignment to a town job after a while: one might earn merit through political activism and be rewarded by retransfer, or one might bribe one's way back, or political policy might change. Recently, indeed, 'sent-down' youths have been returning to the towns.

It required every resource of indoctrination and propaganda, blackmail (threats to the job security of the parents of youths refusing to leave town) and administrative coercion to give effect to this massive programme, a more ambitious measure than has proved possible in any other country in a similar position. Once they were in the villages, youths had to adapt to their new conditions as best they could. Publicity about the attempts made between 1973 and 1975 to improve the administration of the programme reveals that serious shortcomings were widespread. Rusticated youths were not becoming fulfilled and satisfied farmers. They frequently were quite unable, or unwilling, to adapt to their surroundings; and they were often vulnerable to the active discrimination and malevolence of resentful locals. Physical abuse was by no means unknown. As Thomas Bernstein writes, 'Materials circulated within China that have reached the outside world indicate that severe punishment of rapists of female urban youths was an important component of the remedial campaign.'[11]

Thus, if the second stream that formed among China's youth early in the 1960s won its victory in the cultural revolution, it was a hollow victory indeed. In its brief glory, in the political vindication of Mao Zedong that followed, and in the reassertion of politics in education, lay the outward form of its victory; but the substance was bound to elude them in any outcome short of full-scale civil war and revolution making a clean sweep of the country's officials and organizers. At bottom, though few realized it, and then too late, frustrated educated youths were at odds with Mao's prescriptions. What they wanted was that they should first become qualified and then become cadres. This was a traditional attitude. On the other hand, what Mao wanted was that they should first become qualified and then become willing and versatile workers and peasants, placing their practical skills at the service of the revolution. What both parties shared was an attitude of suspicion and resentment towards the first stream and the philosophy of the little pagodas; but, with the first stream discredited, the incompatibility of their desires was necessarily laid bare.

It is therefore not surprising that in the 1970s there should have been evidence of simmering discontent among young people in the workforce who could be presumed to be dissatisfied with their employment. After 1968, about twenty million people were reaching working age each year, and the competition for advancement — from rural to urban employment, or from manual to professional — was intense, when barely half a million jobs became available in the towns. Several years in the 1970s were marked by unrest in the labour force, fomented by young malcontents; there was 'anarchism' in the railway yards and factories, and officials were afraid to act firmly. In the classrooms, teachers were demoralized. In 1972, one said: 'Manual labour is easy; there is no need to use one's brain.'

Figures for enrolment in schools since the Cultural Revolution are fragmentary and difficult to fit together into a complete pattern. In 1971 it was said that primary and secondary enrolment had increased by 30 per cent since 1965. At the end of the 1960s, tertiary enrolment may have been about 70 per 100,000 of population; about 41 per cent of children of school age were in school; the literacy rate was 47.5 per cent. In big cities, by 1971, 80 per cent of children of school age were said to be attending school, a clear reflection of the large and socially important gap remaining between town and country life.

In 1973, new enrolments in tertiary institutions were said to number 153,000. In 1976, education ministry officials were saying that there were 150 million children in primary schools, 44.6 million in secondary schools, and 900,000 in technical schools, and that tertiary institutions enrolled 500,000 students. It is difficult to know how authoritative such figures are. The same officials were saying that these figures represented a 5.4 times increase in primary school enrolments since 1949, a 28.9 times increase in secondary school enrolments, and a 2.2 times increase in tertiary enrolments since 1949. Reference to Table 12.1 will show that these calculations tally approximately but not very well with information about the earlier period available outside China.

The Cultural Revolution was intended to renew the revolutionary spirit of the young, and to overhaul thoroughly the whole educational experience, so that its effects on the mind would be deep, politically correct, and lasting. It may be doubted whether education became (at least after the influence of the 'Gang of Four' was removed) so very much more revolutionary in content than it was in the 1950s. A new system was introduced involving five years in primary and two or three in junior secondary school for as nearly everybody as possible; this was to be followed by two years of senior secondary school for about one-third of rural pupils and two-thirds of urban; then three years' manual work; then, for those selected, two or three years of tertiary. Different sources specified four or five years for secondary schooling.

Perhaps, for a while, students were getting some of the bad from both worlds. Along with the legacy of the Cultural Revolution, teaching methods actually employed in classrooms were often the old mechanical rituals in which teachers themselves had been trained. They knew no other. Like the French king, they had learned nothing and forgotten nothing after the revolution. A foreign observer, S.L. Shirk, reported:

When I visited Chinese schools in 1971 I was struck by the degree to which traditional teaching methods were still in use. I saw only one or two instances of group discussion, and rote learning was still the rule. Given the widespread publicity about Mao's pedagogical ideas during the Cultural Revolution, teachers and principals seemed remarkably unaware of any challenge to their traditional educational philosophy. When I asked one Nanking primary school teacher why the children sat up so straight (in ramrod fashion), she replied, 'It's good for their posture, and it's good for discipline.'[12]

Curricula were geared to perceived national needs, as in the past, with tertiary education heavily weighted towards engineering and medicine. A showplace secondary school (the example is Nanning Third Middle School) might offer three years of instruction in junior school, and two in senior, and offer courses in literature and language, politics, mathematics, physics, chemistry, biology, microbiology, history, geography, physical education, painting and music.

By the end of the 1970s, political education, struggle meetings, rallies, study of Mao's thought and so forth were by no means as hectic and intense as during the Great Leap, or under the influence of the 'Gang of Four'. But the distinctive Chinese cultural context was still of course very pervasive. Language textbooks illustrate lessons with such sentences as these:

Who is that P.L.A. man?
Let's go and settle down in the countryside after we finish school.
The P.L.A. men love the people.
Though the superpowers of the world talk about détente, the revolutionary peoples should not be deceived.

In the mid-1970s, it is now apparent, there was a very strong movement in schools everywhere — not just in a few test cases — to 'revolutionize' education, to overthrow conservative authorities, to discount examinations and book learning, to put politics in command. All this is now labelled the work of the 'Gang of Four', but clearly there is more to it than the politicking of a handful of individuals — it was a movement that throve on the disgruntlement of frustrated intellectuals, of students who felt discriminated against and sensed that unless they did something about it they were headed for limbo. There were idealists too. And they were often able to get their way because they had friends in high places; some of those friends were out of action, but that does not mean that there were not still quiet sympathisers constituting a sizeable minority in every department of officialdom.

Visitors to China were told that the 'Gang of Four' victimized teachers, branding them as authoritarian figures out of touch with real people (some of them doubtless were), claiming that teachers put 'intellectualism' wrongly ahead of the proper revolutionary approach, fomenting insubordination, training students to fight authority, and calling on them to hand in blank answer papers in examinations. Indiscipline was rife.

The full extent of this was not clear at the time, but it was apparent that the politicians later dubbed the 'Gang of Four', Mao's wife Jiang Qing (Chiang Ch'ing) and her friends, were using their positions to influence education. One of their targets was the examination system, later reinstated despite the declared ideals of the cultural revolution, and the epitome of conservative institutions that rated 'expertness' above 'redness'. Mao himself had said: 'Our present method of conducting examinations is a method for dealing with the enemy, not a method for dealing with the people. It is a method of surprise attack, asking oblique or strange questions.'[13]

Publicity was given to the cases of probably previously briefed students who handed in blank papers in university examinations. Instructive is the case of Liu Lihua, who went from Heilongjiang to university in Shanghai and protested against the 'work in command' philosophy of the examinations. The account of this case very interestingly shows that the de facto two-stream or 'little pagoda' structure of education was quietly readopted: evidently many second-rank (and perhaps some turbulent) students were given a certificate after two years while others stayed to complete more worthwile courses. Apparently some students were given certificates of graduation after six months. An important case, later notorious, was that of the candidate Zhang Tiesheng, who wrote a letter complaining about the examination system instead of answering the questions.

Then came 1976, a year of shocks. After it, nothing could be the same.

In January, Zhou Enlai died. Deng Xiaoping gave the funeral speech, and thereafter disappeared from view. Hua Guofeng (Hua Kuo-feng) became acting Premier. In April occurred the famous riots and demonstrations on Tiananmen Square, mourning Zhou and supporting Deng. On July 6th, Zhu De died, aged 90. On September 9th, Mao died, aged 82, of Parkinson's disease or cerebral arteriosclerosis. On the night of October 6th, the 'Gang of Four', said to have been plotting a coup after Mao's death, was arrested; Jiang Qing (Mao's widow, who had been for some time acting as his spokesman and patronizing the Cultural Revolution left-wing), Zhang Chunqiao (a Shanghai Party official with political office in the army), Wang Hongwen (a 'workers' representative', actually a Party man with a power base in Shanghai), and Yao Wenyuan, whose writings had inaugurated the Cultural Revolution's cultural phase and who was head of propaganda in the 1970s. All of these were in the Politbureau; the first three were on its Standing Committee. On October 7th Hua was declared head of the Party. (In later years he was to be eclipsed and discarded as Deng, reinstated in July 1977, consolidated his position.)

The 'Gang of Four' had gone, and in the following years those who thought like them were weeded out. A new period of educational history began, the period of education for modernization.

Notes

1. There is of course a substantial literature on the Great Proletarian Cultural Revolution. For a wider coverage than can be attempted here, see: M. Bastid, 'Economic Necessity and Political Ideal in Educational Reform during the Cultural Revolution', *China Quarterly*, no. 42 (1970), pp. 16-45; W. Hinton, *Hundred Day War: the Cultural Revolution at Tsing Hua University*, New York Monthly Review Press, New York, 1977; Ken Ling, *Red Guard: from Schoolboy to 'Little General' in Mao's China*, ed. M. London and Lee Ta-ling, London, 1972; R.N. Montaperto, 'From Revolutionary Successors to Revolutionaries: Chinese Students in the Early Stages of the Cultural Revolution' in R.A.S. Scalapino (ed.), *Elites in the People's Republic of China*, University of Washington Press, Seattle, 1972, pp. 575-605; V. Nee, *The Cultural Revolution at Peking University*, New York Monthly Review Press, New York, 1969; M. Singer, *Educated Youth and the Cultural Revolution in China*, Centre for Chinese Studies, University of Michigan, 1971.

2. S. Rosen, 'Obstacles to Educational Reform in China', *Modern China*, vol. 8, no. 1 (1982), pp. 3-40 at pp. 7f.

3. J. Fass, 'Attempts at Reform of University Studies during the Cultural Revolution in China' in Centre d'Etudes du Sud-est Asiqatique et de l'Extrême-Orient, *Education in Communist China*. Proceedings, 2 vols, Brussels, 1969, vol. 1, pp. 54-70.

4. T.P. Bernstein, *Up to the Mountains and Down to the Villages*, Yale University Press, New Haven and London, 1977, pp. 77f.

5. G. Bennett and R.N. Montaperto, *Red Guard: the Political Biography of Dai Hsiao-Ai*, New York, 1971 (Allen & Unwin, London, 1971).

6. 'The August 1st School System for Children of High-Ranking Cadres', *Chinese Sociology and Anthropology*, vol. 1 (1969), pp. 3-24.

7. *China News Analysis*, No. 868 (21 January 1972).

8. M. Bastid, 'Economic Necessity and Political Ideal in Educational Reform during the Cultural Revolution', p. 43.

9. *China News Analysis*, No. 868 (21 January 1972).

10. *Current Scene*, vol. XII, no. 10 (October 1974), pp. 15-19,

11. T.P. Bernstein, *Up to the Mountains*, p. 156.

12. S.L. Shirk, 'Educational Reform and Political Backlash: Recent Changes in Chinese Educational Policy', *Comparative Education Review*, vol. 23 (June, 1979), pp. 183-217 at p. 187, n. 7. These observations tally with those of another visiting educationist at around the same time, John Fyfield (J. Fyfield, *personal communication*).

13. S. Schram (ed.), *Mao Tse-tung Unrehearsed*, Penguin, Harmondsworth, 1974, p. 204.

14 EDUCATION AND SOCIETY

But education is not a strictly economic proposition. It is imbedded in too complex a web of interacting social and political variables for the economic goals to be able to dominate as the new strategy seems to assume they can.

Suzanne Pepper

The early 1970s were a period of confusion in educational policy; administration was decentralized, and it was easy to find evidence of different policies at different times or in different places at the same time. Since the fall of the 'Gang of Four' in 1976 it has become possible to see the picture more clearly in retrospect, and it is generally agreed that one can usefully identify two styles or philosophies of education that have been influential in the counsels of the governors; sometimes one or the other has been dominant, and sometimes they have been in more or less even conflict.

One commentator, Jan-Ingvar Löfstedt, has sought to periodize Communist China's history of education, identifying the two lines of thought and practice that alternated in dominance. The first, the one which has recently been favoured by the leadership of Deng Xiaoping, prevailed, by and large, in the mid-1950s, in the early 1960s, and after 1976. The second, the one with which the 'Gang of Four' is associated, and which to a great extent represents the policies of Mao Zedong, prevailed in the period of the Great Leap Forward (1958-9) and in the period 1966-76.[1]

There is no unanimity on the question how these lines should be designated. Unger describes them as the 'developmental' and the 'redistributive'.[2] Pepper describes them as the 'hierarchical' and the 'egalitarian'.[3] Take the first, the one that was vigorously pursued from the late 1970s as part of the modernization programme. Jackson and Hayhoe, reviewing various theories, see it as 'pragmatic'.[4] Such terms as 'pragmatic' and 'moderate' are often used of the policies of Deng and his group; yet they fail to take account of the feverishness, bordering on frenzy, of the modernization policy that was inaugurated not long after the death of Mao. To many, it has seemed that in his concern to remedy the ills consequent upon the Gang's regime Deng went too far in the opposite direction. Good or bad, the policy is one that emphasizes competition. At every level of education, the rewards go to those who show themselves better, and they are systematically set apart from their fellows for the purpose. In 1976, a *Hongqi* article hostile to this philosophy sardonically described it as the capitalist law of competition: 'Whoever is strongest in competition can climb to the pinnacle of the pagoda.'[5]

Of course, words are but labels, and as we have seen the periods of 'egalitarian' education philosophy have been characterized by competition too, but the criteria for distributing rewards have not been educational. Another way of expressing the dichotomy, often used in China, is to contrast equality of opportunity with equality of results. The latter represents an ideal that is difficult indeed to achieve. But the 'egalitarians', or revolutionaries, sought consistently to make education serve the purposes of social engineering, and this is a cardinal fact about their policies which clearly sets them apart from the (often equally violent) 'moderates'. One aspect of the revolutionary philosophy, not perhaps very egalitarian, was the rigorous denial of any sort of educational opportunity to all those arbitrarily listed as landlords and rich peasants, and their children, and their children's children. Other features of this philosophy are well summarized by Suzanne Pepper: the incorporation of manual labour in the curriculum, resolute opposition to separate tracks of education in inferior and superior schools, or specially favoured priority schools and ordinary ones, or separate streamed classes within schools, hostility to the principle of unified examinations at secondary and tertiary levels and to the 'marks in command' classroom ethos, approval of incorporating a period of labour between secondary and tertiary education, decentralized educational administration, the use of 'revolutionary committees' to run institutions, the fostering of red guard activity, resistance to authoritarianism, and the operation of spare-time and alternative institutions such as the 'July 21st universities' for workers and 'May 7th' colleges in the countryside.[6]

These are the features of the programme espoused by the so-called 'Gang of Four' and those who thought in the same way, or who didn't think much but recognized the same political interests. The early 1970s were their heyday, but their dominance was never unchallenged and criticism began early. In his own oblique and subtle way, Zhou Enlai probably opposed their educational policies, concerned as he was for a stable environment for modernization policies. As early as 1972 a long article was caused to be published by Zhou Beiyuan (Chou Pei-yüan) arguing for the fostering of higher standards in education.

But it was only after the fall of the Gang that criticism of their line in education became orthodox, detailed and voluble. Zhou

Rongxin, the Minister of Education in 1975-6, was just too early to benefit from the turning of the tide, and suffered for his views. He inspired articles emphasizing the need for discipline in schools and criticizing the excess of labour and practical activities at the expense of study. He sought quality in education, and criticized the effect on standards of the come-and-go 'open door' schooling then favoured. He said such things as 'No-one actually studies' and 'When one speaks of education, one could say that it isn't worth a cigarette butt.' As a result of such sentiments, he became the target of a campaign in January 1976, with Chi Qun (later cast as villain) put in as hatchet man. Zhou died in April 1976, under a cloud. With the second resurrection of Deng Xiaoping, he was rehabilitated, and in August 1977 was the post-humous beneficiary of a big tribute meeting.[7]

Zhou was the first Minister of Education to be appointed for some time. The Cultural Revolution had done away with the ministry in 1966, and it was left to the Fourth National People's Congress to re-establish it in 1975. Its revival symbolized the big push towards centralization that characterized the policies of the modernizers around Deng.

The Eleventh National Congress of the Chinese Communist Party in August 1977 began to put nails in the coffin of the Gang. Hua Guofeng's report blamed on it the decline in the quality of education. Decisions were taken to establish new programmes for science and technology, to set up a new university enrolment system, to compile new textbooks, to keep free for professional work five-sixths of the working time of scientific and technical personnel, and to expand the budget for science and education. The Ministry of Education produced a plan to improve quality in education, and proposals were made to make eight years of schooling compulsory in the countryside and ten in towns by 1985.

The turning-point was perhaps in 1978, when a series of decisions and public announcements closed the door on the Gang of Four and its policies. The National Conference on Educational Work opened on April 22nd with a forthright speech by Deng; 6,000 people attended the opening ceremony. As was to become a leitmotif of educational discourse, Deng emphasized that quality must be the watchword. This was the first of four directives which he offered to guide the work of educators. The others were the fostering of good discipline in schools, with attendant improvement in the morale and enthusiasm of teachers; the pursuit of the goal of modernization; and the raising of the political and social status of teachers. Liu Xiyao, the Minister of Education, outlined the draft 1978-85 programme, urging the speeding up of training, attention to the needs of modernization, and the raising of standards.

In March and April, 1979, the Ministry of Education sponsored a National Planning Conference on Education and Science which urged improvements in teaching methods and produced an 'Outline Plan'. In May, a forum on ideological education examined the problems attributed to disruption by the 'Gang of Four' in previous years.

All shortcomings were blamed on the Gang, and piece by piece the apparatus of its hegemony, or of the revolutionaries whom the Gang symbolized, was systematically dismantled. The Workers' Propaganda Teams were withdrawn in 1977-8. The Revolutionary Committees were discarded in 1978. Liu Xiyao in his 1978 speech confirmed that the educated were now supposed to be expert and not just red.

Quality, higher standards, improved teaching methods, and morale were catchwords of the new policies. Well they might be: the confusion of the previous years, however we assign blame for it, had robbed many or most educational institutions of the standards which they ought to have maintained on any rational philosophy. One commentator cites a medical college, heavily responsible for the standard of medicine in its province, where much of the content of its education had been abandoned, standards of recruitment had fallen dramatically, and the estimated average competence of its graduates was roughly comparable with what one might expect of a good 'barefoot doctor' or rural medical auxiliary.[8] The whole point of the philosophy of simple low-level medicine represented by the 'barefoot doctors' was that they should be able to handle straightforward medical cases and hand on the rest to the higher levels; but now there were almost no higher levels.

The improvement of methods and morale began with attitudes to teachers, shattered as they were by the appalling persecutions of the Cultural Revolution. In early 1977 there was a 'Respect the Teacher' (*zun shi*) campaign. To encourage individual excellence among pupils, numerous contests were organized, such as the National Mathematical Contest in May 1978. Liu in his 1978 speech emphasized morale and standards especially, demanding better school discipline, better techniques, and the publication of journals for educators. Self-respect was to be restored to the teaching profession by a system of awards and citations for excellence. A relaxed atmosphere was to be fostered in which people should feel free to speak their minds, a hundred flowers should bloom.

Easier said than done. Free speech has always been an exotic plant in China, and it was to be long before the slogan could sound anything but hollow. But the policy was there. A forum in Wuhan agreed that a variety of views was to be encouraged, and its agreement was publicized. The *People's Daily* expressed itself in favour of historical and literary criticism which would look at different sides of every question, ready to criticize heroes and see the good in conventional villains. There is no doubt that the leadership wanted a different atmosphere, for if the country was to modernize efficiently, ideas must be tried on their merits. One Western observer has accused Deng and his men of fostering mere 'book knowledge', and seen signs in China of 'uncritical acceptance of value-free science and the renewed "worship of things foreign" '.[9] There is a note of reproach here. Clearly the issue is complex. A desire for genuine improvement was doubtless there; so was the danger that the fervid 'moderates' would oppose to the Gang's educational ritualism a scarcely less stultifying ritualism of their own, as represented by the over-centralization and over-standardization of the new policies.

An important feature of the quest for improved quality was the revival of the priority schools, the specially favoured institutions, usually in towns, which attracted the label 'little treasure pagodas'. Early in 1978, the *Peking Review* referred to the 'Key Schools' which the Ministry of Education was running in the interests of educational quality. A number of these, directly under the national Ministry, were set up in Peking, Tianjin, Shanghai and other big cities, both as repositories of the high standards considered necessary for the training of an elite and as models for other schools to follow.[10] They were generously endowed with library and laboratory facilities; systematic discrimination ensured that good teachers and materials were concentrated in them.

This was one of the more sensitive of the traditional policies, vulnerable to charges of elitism. In 1978, lip service was still being paid to Mao, and Liu in his important speech sought to justify the discriminatory educational policy by reference to Mao's authority; he mentioned a vaguely specified instruction by Mao in 1953 to enrol better students, an 'instruction' that was several times called in by different spokesmen as a justification for what was being done. In March 1978 the *People's Daily* published a list of 88 tertiary institutions designated as priority schools; another was added later, so that by 1979 there were 89 little pagodas out of 598 tertiary institutions in the country.[11] Priority schools were established at all levels, by local government in all the districts as well as by the Ministry, and the policy was that schools could be added to the list, or removed, as a result of actual educational performance. Here was a powerful incentive indeed for teachers to concentrate on academic work.

These priority schools are a response to a real problem. However much a government in China may want to spread education widely, it may be dangerous to neglect the needs of economic betterment for a concentration of resources at some points so that competent men may be trained for a great variety of essential tasks. As Pepper says: 'In China today, the argument is that running all kinds of schools, including keypoints, is essential for an economically underdeveloped country that must modernize but cannot yet afford on a universal basis the quality education necessary to achieve that goal'.[12]

Length of schooling was another policy area important for the new programme. The old system, based on American principles and introduced to China in 1922, involved six years of primary schooling, three each of junior and senior secondary schooling, and up to five of tertiary education. In the Cultural Revolution, and indeed since the Great Leap Forward, this had repeatedly been condemned as excessive and unsuited to the conditions of the country. Cultural Revolutionaries had worked on revised schemes substantially contracting the period of schooling. After the demise of the Gang of Four, the move was back to the traditional system wherever it could be instituted, chiefly in the towns, and universities returned to tertiary programmes lasting four or five years, medical schools offering five years with an additional five years' residence.

Curricula in schools were now again standardized, with approved new textbooks being brought into use in the school year beginning in 1978 and the Ministry in Peking exercising control over the planning of teaching throughout the country. R. Price has compared the revived centralized style of administration with the 1950s system based on Russian models, and found little difference.[13]

At a time when every effort was being made to improve the qualifications of teachers, it was difficult to supply teachers in the numbers ideally required. Class sizes in primary schools around the end of the decade were still about 50.

One of the most important ingredients of the now discredited 'revolutionary' educational philosophy, underpinned by Mao's dictum that one should take as one's classroom the whole of society and not just the stuffy confines of the school, was the requirement for pupils to spend a substantial amount of time each year engaged in productive toil. So deeply bedded in the Maoist gospel of revolution was this principle that it could not be lightly discarded, but it came soon to be substantially abridged.

Guidelines laid down in 1978 declared that the period of each year to be given to labour should be one month from grade four in primary school, six weeks in junior secondary, eight in senior secondary, and four in tertiary. It was not clear to what extent these periods were either required or merely recommended, or how they were to be related to the content of the schoolroom curriculum. As some observers have pointed out, they did not of themselves entail a substantial reduction of the labour incorporated in the curriculum during the 'Gang of Four' period, but there is no doubt that they have been interpreted so as to allow much less distraction from school study. Liu's speech in 1978 favoured relating labour to study, and all sorts of more or less practical activities genuinely conducive to learning could now be counted as labour.

The new educational policies sought to establish and control a mainstream of regular full-time education in government schools with accredited standards, and to operate various programmes of part-time, spare-time and semi-formal education to help those who could not for one reason or another be incorporated in the mainstream. In doing so, of course, they tended to open up the gap between two streams of people being educated, a gap which in the eyes of the revolutionaries should never be allowed to exist. But it was in the interests of the modernizers to do something at least for the second stream. In 1980 there were functioning numerous courses of full-time study with pay for workers on study leave, spare-time courses, and in the bigger cities radio and television courses. Many were studying by correspondence. The Shanghai Television University reopened in May 1978; the Central Television College opened in 1979. In remote country areas, peripatetic teachers went from place to place imparting rudimentary primary education. The ideal of universal education had still not been reached, even officially; in 1978 a proportion of 30 per cent adult illiteracy was officially announced.

Two sorts of institutions that had lately been much favoured were the July 21st Colleges and the May 7th Colleges. The former were designed to train technical staff recruited from among urban workers, and the latter were rural training institutes offering agriculture-oriented courses to potential organizers on the communes, some full-time but mostly spare-time. Liu Xiyao asserted that such colleges should be run well. The revived stress on standards and qualifications, however, appears to have had the effect of causing some of them to be dismantled for want of competent staff.

The protection of excellence entailed that a line should be drawn between the good and the not-so-good. This meant, for example, streaming within schools, which was official policy from 1978. It also meant that those who aspired to a college education would have to go through the regular established ten-year school course first; but many localities, especially in the countryside, could not offer the full ten years. In these circumstances, a need was partly filled by the special or technical senior secondary schools, institutions which despite their secondary status could provide a useful training leading to jobs with a little more status than farm labour; they offered vocational courses in teacher training, public health, agricultural science, commerce, fine arts, handicrafts, and so forth.

The new policies had the effect, in various ways, of discriminating against the countryside; it followed naturally, however regrettably, from the concern with protecting standards. The effects were apparent at all levels. In 1977 and 1978 about 95 per cent of the school age population were supposed to be in primary schools; in 1979 the proportion had dropped. Why should this be? In fact many country primary schools were not regular government schools at all but self-help schools run by the communes with whatever staff could be scratched together and subsidies from the state. During and after the Cultural Revolution, decentralization and self-help were encouraged, and many communes eagerly sought to run their own school systems whether they could afford to do it properly or not; it was a way for officials to distribute patronage and for the half-educated to rise to the status of teachers. Now such activities came under a chilly scrutiny; from the government's point of view many of the community (*minban*) schools were substandard and used resources inefficiently; therefore many were closed down, and their pupils disappeared from the enrolment statistics.

Secondary schools in the countryside could not compete with the resources of the towns. Influential people did not live in the country; those who did were so preoccupied with economic survival that they could rarely provide their children with the background and facilities to study hard and well. The officially sanctioned tracking system established a superior track of regular full-time government schools leading through ten years to the possibility of college entrance and an inferior track of part-time schools where pupils had to spend a great deal of time engaged in productive work to help the school budget; the chances of tertiary education were slim for them. The effects of this sort of discrimination were masked in the late 1970s by the way in which college matriculants were classified, for, though the great majority of them were designated as workers and peasants, the category 'peasant' included young people born and bred in the towns but rusticated in the wake of the Cultural Revolution; they were not genuine products of rural education. S.L. Shirk gave a graphic example: the chances of college admission for an urban 'little pagoda' school-leaver were ten times the chances of a pupil in an ordinary rural school which she visited.[14]

This was geographical discrimination. Another sort is direct social dicrimination. Arguably, the reintroduction of a centralized system of examinations for tertiary entry in and after 1977 could work against such discrimination in some ways.

It needs to be remembered that unstructured experimental forms of education which throw pupils heavily upon their own resources tend to favour those from advantaged families. In the long run, the Cultural Revolution did just this, for it was a sort of radical educational experiment in which education practically disappeared. The well-off, principally the families of officials, could help their children most, particularly when they could engage tutors. Their children were much better placed to win places in universities when normality returned.

In 1973 Zhang Tiesheng, a protégé of the 'Gang of Four', had written a letter to the examiners on his answer paper instead of answering the questions set in an examination for which he was a candidate. His protest against the examination system became a *cause célèbre* after his letter was published in the *People's Daily*. Entrance examinations did not in fact stop, but they were to some extent discredited while the Gang was politically on top. Now Zhang, the hero of the revolutionaries, was reviled and denounced as a fraud.

An immediate and thoroughgoing reinstitution of examinations did not take place, however. Central examinations for entry to universities were set, but candidates had to pass through a sieve of assessments by colleagues at their workplace and local government organs to gain approval for matriculation; the examination was just one ingredient in the process. It is easy to see how, with so large a discretionary function, officials could continue to wangle their friends, relatives and suitors into colleges by the infamous 'back door' for as long as it was possible to use private influence.

In December 1977, 278,000 candidates out of a total of 5.7 million, or 4.9 per cent, were admitted to colleges. Most of them were Party or Youth League members, a fact doubtless reflecting the importance of connections. Between 20 per cent and 30 per cent were young people direct from secondary schools, while many were former pupils since rusticated.

In 1978 a conference on enrolment prepared for a second round of centralized examinations in July, when there were six million candidates, the age limit was 30, and about half the entrants came straight from school.

In 1979 the age limit was lowered to 28, though not many were let in over 25. A squeeze was being put on the over-age rustication victims who were now no longer allowed, and about 67 per cent of the entry came straight from school. Meanwhile, the year before, a programme of graduate training had got under way with 9,000 graduates (out of 57,000 candidates) passing examinations qualifying them for advanced courses.

A totally impartial examination can at least ensure that entrants are selected on merit, but in China the examination system was qualified by other criteria, and many people were still getting into colleges by the back door. This indeed has been one of the major scandals besetting Chinese public life. Any system of college admission which places any weight on recommendations by individuals is open, in a society such as China's, to widespread abuse, and it is clear that the system often worked especially to the advantage of the children of officials.[15]

The somewhat anti-intellectual trend apparent in 1981 could only tend to benefit the manipulators and the wheeler-dealers, paradoxically it may be, for the 1981 university entrance requirements were changed to combine with examination performance certain other criteria such as conduct, extra-curricular activities, and sport.[16] Such subjective criteria would necessarily open the door wider to the machinations of influence.

Background doubtless gave the children of officials and Communist Party members educational advantages, but their success in dominating the matriculation lists seems to require further explanation. Being a member of the Youth League or the Party helped a great deal: in 1977, 74 per cent of college admissions were of people so qualified. S.L. Shirk, interviewing an academic, asked if many university students were children of cadres, and the answer was: 'Oh yes, almost all.'[17] Yet in 1979 the Party membership was 38 million, about 4 per cent of the population. The cadre corps, with which the Party overlapped in part, numbered 18 million, about 2 per cent of the population.

One factor which might, in a small way, have served to intensify even further the competition for scarce college places was the inclusion in the ranks of those eligible the children of so-called 'landlords' and 'rich peasants', which we noticed before. In 1979 there were said to be about four million people in these categories; an examination conducted by the Central Committee of the Party determined that most of them had mended their ways and deserved to be counted officially as people; the label was removed from all but about 50,000 of them. A *People's Daily* article declared that there was now to be no discrimination against these families, previously denied any sort of political activity or even enrolment in senior secondary or tertiary education.

Figures for educational enrolment in the years following Mao's death are, as for earlier periods, contradictory and confusing. Observers outside China have not succeeded in reconciling the various official claims and producing an accepted standard set of results. Sometimes there are discrepancies within one source.[18] Problems affect the interpretation of figures at all levels.

At the primary level, figures for enrolment in the late 1970s vary between 140 and 150 million. Some authorities, notably Price and Löfstedt, regard this as a clear exaggeration, as the population of primary school age children would not have been more than about 120 million.[19] Since the 1982 census, it appears plausible that the disparity may not have been so very great, but it remains true that official claims are unlikely to represent the true situation. As Löfstedt says about the 1979 figures, 'These figures are, of course, highly unreliable, and probably inflated due to statistical inaccuracy, over-aged children, drop-outs, etc.'[20]

Another problem is that some figures appear to show an actual drop in school enrolments at the end of the decade. Pepper, for example, cites figures for primary enrolment of 150 million in 1977, 146 million or 150 million in 1978, and only 140 million in 1979.[21] Further, on some figures the general secondary school enrolment dropped between 1978 and 1979 from 65.48 million to 59 million. The figures are doubtless so unreliable that little can be confidently inferred from them about trends, but it is quite likely that there was indeed a decline, for the reasons that Pepper suggests: the beginning of effectiveness of the birth-control campaign, the recentralization of education which caused some substandard community schools to be weeded out, the shift back to production of non-productive workers (including some community school teachers), and general retrenchment.[22]

One thing that is clear is that prospects for advancement up the educational ladder were not bright. Opportunities for rustication victims to enter colleges were phased out after a couple of years. In 1979, whereas more than 80 per cent of primary school-leavers were at

Table 14.1: Educational Enrolment, 1965-82 (National totals in thousands

	Primary Schools			General Secondary Schools		Tertiary Institutions		
1965		116,000			14,418		674	
1966		115,000			14,600		700	
1967								
1968								
1969								
1970							200	
1971		127,000					200	
1972		127,000			36,000		200	
1973		145,000			36,500		350	
1974		145,000		36,500	44,600	325	400	
1975		150,000			—		400	
1976		146,000			58,300		500	
1977		146,160	150,000	64,600	58,280	620	584	
1978	146,240	146,000	150,000	65,000	68,900	800	850	880
1979		140,000	146,630		59,050	1,020		
1980		146,270			55,081	1,144		
1981		139,720			47,028	1,154		
1982								

Sources: Various estimates cited by Jan-Ingvar Löfstedt, *Chinese Educational Policy, Changes and Contradictions 1949-1979*, Stockholm, 1980, Table 3, p. 192, and S. Pepper, 'Chinese Education After Mao', *China Quarterly*, no. 81 (March, 1980), pp. 1-65; *Beijing Review* 1981 (no. 1), p. 8; 1983 vol. 26 (No. 40) p. 26; *Guangming Ribao,* 1 October 1981; *China Aktuell,* October 1981; sources cited by J. Fyfield, *personal communication.*

least entering junior secondary school, only 40-50 per cent of junior secondary leavers were entering senior, and only about 4 per cent of senior secondary leavers were entering tertiary colleges,[23] where enrolment was said to be about 1.02 million. Stanley Rosen has assembled, in convincing detail, the evidence of this dramatic foreclosure of opportunity besetting the prospects of educated youth in the 1980s.[24] He contrasts the pathetic rate of success of senior secondary school-leavers in entering higher education in 1979 with earlier years; in 1965 over 45 per cent of school-leavers had been getting through, as against less than 4 per cent in 1979.[25] The desperate obsessiveness of the race to reach college should not seem neurotic or misdirected to us, for we should not judge it by the standards of modern Western countries; what gives Chinese attitudes to education their distinctive *animus*, now as at many times in the past, is the sheer absence of alternatives to the civil service career. The massiveness of the 1970s 'sending down' programme, attempting to turn educated hopefuls into grubby peasants for the rest of their lives, attests this vividly.

As Rosen says, 'Jobs as state cadres or workers in state-owned enterprises — regarded as 'iron rice bowls' — have become virtually fully staffed. There will be very few openings of this type for the next ten years. The only available jobs will be those considered 'earthen rice bowls' — those in collectively owned enterprises.'[26]

A well-articulated educational system catering for everybody's needs simply could not be created all at once, if ever. Inevitably, for a long time to come, there would be many whose brief educational careers would be cut disappointingly short. The previous regime had coped with the problem of educated and unemployed urban youth by sending them to the countryside indefinitely, there to learn the dignity of honest toil; the idealistic (if not fanciful) rationale of this programme was now tacitly discarded, and so in turn was the programme itself.

Before the Cultural Revolution, it was said that 1.2 million people had been 'sent down' to the country. For the Cultural Revolution period and up to the beginning of 1976, the number of educated youths sent down was twelve million. Some of these were able to sit college entrance examinations in 1977 and 1978, but not many got through. Liu's speech in 1978 referred to rusticated students, and asserted that 'we should show them our deep concern'.[27] That year it was reported that 17 million urban youth had been 'sent down' since 1968, of whom ten million remained in agriculture at the end of the period (the rest having been reassigned).[28] From 1978, attempts were made to reduce the programme, now seen more candidly as a last resort to avoid urban unemployment; in these circumstances it was asking a lot to expect its victims to reconcile themselves cheerfully to their fate. In the 1978-9 holiday season, when many rusticated young people were visiting their families in the towns, discontent surfaced in vigorous agitation. Shanghai was the scene of disruption and demonstrations by seething crowds of youths protesting against their rural working conditions. Many people were trickling back into the towns illicitly and staying there, and the authorities had the utmost difficulty in persuading school-leavers to accept rural assignments. In Spring 1979 about five million had migrated back to the towns. By August 1980 there were said to be only about a million and a half 'sent-down' youths left in the countryside. Attempts were made to cope with urban unemployment by new labour-intensive schemes. Every encouragement was given to the formation of co-operatives in the service sector of the economy, which might provide work for school-leavers without great expense to the government. For the longer term, the new gospel was to expand the country's smaller towns to provide employment.

It was never to be expected that the new post-Gang leadership could easily get things all its own way; whatever course of action it chose there was bound to be opposition. The question was whether this opposition could be ridden out in the long term. Perhaps the most important question concerns social expectations: until a generation or two ago, any Chinese who obtained more than just a few years of education *expected* to rise above the level of manual toil, but now this situation has dramatically changed. People must learn new expectancies. Perhaps the policies of tracking and streaming in the schools may (for better or worse) help people to learn their place and quench the springs of hopeless aspiration; in the meantime it is a bitter medicine. Reports came from Jilin about local proposals to abolish the 'slow' streams in the schools and the entrance requirements for primary priority schools. Such proposals, points out Suzanne Pepper, do not necessarily emanate only from people directly linked with the 'Gang of Four' and its supporters.[29] They represent an 'egalitarian' trend of thought that cannot be ignored after the Cultural Revolution; too much has changed. In her view, compromise with the Cultural Revolution educational programme may be the most genuinely pragmatic.[30]

S.L. Shirk offers an analysis of the social impact of educational policy by group interest. The new policies, she says, are clearly likely to attract support from scientists, teachers and many educational officials, but are likely to run into trouble with peasants, youth (especially former red guards) and many cadres in the system as a whole. These last are not necessarily those who espoused the Cultural Revolution wholeheartedly but those who oppose rapid change which threatens the stability essential to bureaucratic survival, object to the tendency of examination-based selection on merit to deprive them of strings to pull and patronage to distribute, feel threatened by the new technocrats (their own education having been unspecialized) and see danger in the reinstatement of Cultural Revolution victims anxious to pay off old scores.[31]

China's leaders can be expected to choose educational policies, and deal with the opposition to them, in ways perceived to be most conducive to their political survival, not in ways which 'ought' to be adopted in an ideal world. Outside advice is gratuitous. In order to survive politically, they need to gratify as many as possible of the people in, or actively hoping to reach, positions of influence at all levels of society. By and large, such people have one or the other of two attitudes to education. For some, it is a ritual, difficult to undergo, which effectively sorts out the successful from the unsuccessful, to the benefit of the former. This is a traditional attitude, enshrined in the values of pre-Communist society. For others, it is a ritual of a different sort (ritual slogans, ritual memorization of clichés) which makes it possible for almost anybody to succeed if he has the 'right' ideas (whatever these may be). This attitude is one that may appear rational in a period of rapidly expanding opportunities; in the nature of the case not all periods are of this sort. It is an equally traditional attitude, but it is the tradition of folk culture and underworld organization rather than 'Confucian' orthodoxy.

Those who are successful and relatively contented can be expected to gravitate towards the first attitude, with which indeed the modernizers clearly identified themselves. Those who are not successful and are discontented can be expected to gravitate towards the second attitude. Those who do not occupy positions of influence will feel discontented if they believe they deserve such positions. They will hold this belief if they have previously expected the qualifications they possess to lead naturally to positions of influence. It is in part a question of cultural lag. The modernizing leadership could expect to survive the threat from the 'have-nots' to the extent that social expectations lowered. Educational policy has accordingly been calculated to lower expectations in the long run.

There is though a further question. The success of the modernization policy does not depend only on the government's ability to make one ritual definition of education prevail over another. It depends in substantial measure on the extent to which ritual definitions can be transcended and rational ones learned, so that critical enquiry may take its proper dominant place in the content of education. Many of the statements made in China nowadays sound enlightened to sympathetic outsiders, but the danger is clear enough that the victors in the contest with the notorious Gang should tend towards the rigid centraliation, standardization and empty memorization characteristic of a difficult ritual that sorts out the mandarins rather than of good education.

Notes

1. Jan-Ingvar Löfstedt, *Chinese Education Policy. Changes and Contradictions 1949-1979*, Almquist/Humanities Press, Stockholm/Atlantic

Highlands, NJ, 1980, p. 183.
2. J. Unger, 'The Chinese Controversy over Higher Education', *Pacific Affairs*, vol. 53, no. 1 (1980), pp. 29-47.
3. S. Pepper, 'Chinese Education After Mao: Two Steps Forward, One Step Back and Begin Again?', *China Quarterly*, no. 81 (March 1980), pp. 1-65.
4. R. Jackson and R. Hayhoe, 'The Changing Role of Teachers in Post-Mao Perspectives', *British Journal of Teacher Education*, vol. 5, no. 3 (1979), pp. 219-30.
5. Cited by S. Shirk, 'Educational Reform and Political Backlash: Recent Changes in Chinese Educational Policy', *Comparative Education Review*, vol. 23 (June 1979), pp. 183-217.
6. S. Pepper, 'Chinese Education After Mao', p. 9.
7. J. Gardner, 'Chou Yung-hsin and Chinese Education', *Current Scene*, Vol. XV, nos. 11-12 (1977), pp. 1-14.
8. S. Pepper, Education and Revolution: the "Chinese Model" Revised', *Asian Survey*, vol. 18, no. 9 (September, 1978), pp. 847-90.
9. R.F. Price, 'Schooling for Modernization', *Australian Journal of Chinese Affairs*, no. 2 (July, 1979), pp. 57-76.
10. 'Running Key Schools Well', *Peking Review*, vol. 21, no. 8 (1978), pp. 14f.
11. S. Pepper, 'Chinese Education After Mao', p. 23; cf. S. Rosen, 'Obstacles to Educational Reform in China', *Modern China*, vol. 8, no. 1 (1982), pp. 3-40.
12. S. Pepper, 'Education and Revolution', p. 888.
13. R.F. Price, 'Schooling for Modernization', pp. 66f
14. S. Shirk, 'Educational Reform and Political Backlash', p. 199.
15. S. Rosen, 'Obstacles to Educational Reform in China', *Modern China*, vol. 8, no. 1 (1982), p. 13.
16. Ibid., p. 31.
17. S. Shirk, 'Educational Reform and Political Backlash', p. 191.
18. See Jan-Ingvar Löfstedt, *Chinese Education Policy*, Table 3, p. 192 and pp. 76, 79, 81, 85, etc.
19. Ibid., p. 161; R.F. Price, 'Schooling for Modernization', p. 59.
20. Jan-Ingvar Löfstedt, *Chinese Education Policy*, p. 161.
21. S. Pepper, 'Chinese Education After Mao', p. 6.
22. Ibid., pp. 6f.
23. Jan-Ingvar Löfstedt, *Chinese Education Policy*, pp. 154ff.
24. S. Rosen, 'Obstacles to Educational Reform in China', pp. 23-5.
25. Ibid., Table 1, p. 32.
26. Ibid., p. 33.
27. Liu Xiyao, *Report at the National Educational Work Conference*, 22 April 1978 (Ministry of Education, PRC).
28. S. Pepper, 'Chinese Education After Mao', p. 48.
29. Ibid., p. 63.
30. Ibid., p. 65.
31. S. Shirk, 'Educational Reform and Political Backlash', p. 212.

INDEX

Agricultural Producer Co-operatives
(A.P.C.) 61
agriculture
  mechanisation 59, 79
  methods 51-60
  organization 51, 59
  regional variations 22, 23, 24,
    29, 50-1
  traditional 43, 59
  see also farming
Amitabha, Buddha 121
Analects of Confucius 126
Anhui (Anhwei), province 51
Anti-Confucius campaign 10
Avalokitesvara, future Buddha
  120-1

bamboo 18, 19, 23
Bastid, Marianne 200
Bauer, Wolfgang 116, 134, 147
Beidaihe (Peitaiho) 61
Bergson, Henri 146
Bernstein, Thomas 196, 203
bian wen (pien wen), Buddhist stories
  114
bilharzia 90
Blofeld, J. 133
Bodhidharma, Chan patriarch, 52,
  108
bodhisattvas, future Buddhas 119-22,
  130, 136, 141, 145
Book of Changes 114, 147
Book of Rites 126
Boxer movement 120, 130, 135-6
'brainwashing' see thought reform
Buck, J.L. 50, 55, 59, 74, 93
Buddha 110, 113, 130, 162
Buddhism
  and Chinese culture 148-51
  and rebellion 103, 118-37 passim
  and reform 139-48, 150
  and science 140, 144
  control by state 126-7, 149
  importance in Chinese culture
    101, 104-5
  in society 107-17
  monasteries 106, 125

monastic discipline 158-63
ordination 126, 160
persecutions 124-5
revivalism 105-6
sects 108-11, 120-36
thought reform 158-63
Buddhist New Youth Society 105
Buddhist ordination 126, 160
bureaucracy 125, 179, 181, 186
  see also mandarins

cadres see bureaucracy
canals 44
Canton 198
Canton Rising of 1911 142
Cathay, name for China 8, 39
celibacy 162
Central Television College 215
Chan (Ch'an), Buddhist sect 108-9,
  134, 158-9
Chang, K.C. 40, 41
Changan (Ch'ang-an) 22
Changchun, industrial city 17
Changsha (Ch'ang-sha) 142
chemical fertilizer 58-9
Chen Duxiu (Ch'en Tu-hsiu) 175
Ch'en, Kenneth 126, 150, 162
Chen, Theodore Hsi-en 157
Chen Yi 179
Chesneaux, Jean 128
Chi Ch'ao-ting 34
Chiang Kai-shek 22
China
  name 8, 9, 10
  periodization of history 3
  society 3
  unity 34, 35
Chinese Buddhist Association 148
Chinese character 102, 104
Chinese Communist Party 4, 7, 78,
  133, 148, 175-6, 185, 211,
  217-18
Chou Li, Confucian text 41
Christianity 132-3, 170
civilian tradition 36-8, 47-8, 72, 101
clans 86, 88
clothing 15, 16